Llewellyn's

Herbal Almanac

2002

Editing/design: Michael Fallon
Interior Art: Mary Azarian
Cover Design: Lisa Novak
Cover photos © Digital Vision,
© Digital Stock.

You can order Llewellyn annuals
and books from New Worlds,
Llewellyn's magazine catalog, or
online at www.llewellyn.com. Call
toll-free: 1-877-NEW WRLD to
request a free copy of the catalog, or
click on "Catalog Request" under the New Worlds
heading on our web site.

ISBN 0-7387-0034-7
Llewellyn Worldwide
PO Box 64383, Dept. 0-7387-0034-7
St. Paul, MN 55164

Table of Contents

Growing and Gathering Herbs

Culinary Herbs

Herbs for Health

Herbs for Beauty

Herb Crafts

Herb History, Myth, and Magic

*Growing
and
Gathering
Herbs*

A Guide to Composting in the Herb Garden

≈ By Chandra Moira Beal ≈

T here are many reasons to try composting—not least of which is that compost is nature's way of recycling, and therefore is a natural way to protect the planet.

Compost is the end product of a biological process that turns organic matter into a nutrient-rich soil conditioner. In your own life, composting is a practical and convenient way to handle organic kitchen waste and to return organic matter to the soil. Composting saves landfill space and reduces the cost of collecting and recycling wastes. It also helps to neutralize the acidity and alkalinity of soil, improves its texture, and protects land from erosion and temperature extremes.

How Compost Works

Organic matter contains carbon and nitrogen as basic building blocks. Plants need these building blocks in the soil to grow. And when organic matter decomposes, carbon and nitrogen are released. That is, a team of microbes and bacteria break down organic matter, and release the two elements from plant cells.

Composting begins when you toss a bucket of kitchen scraps into a heap. A mass of good compost will break down naturally into a mass of the basic elements carbon and nitrogen. Later, other life forms such as fungi, protozoans, worms, and beetles take a turn in breaking down organic matter into compost. When the compost is added to the soil, its nitrogen and carbon feed the plant cells, and thus a natural circle is completed.

Where to Begin

There are many different methods for composting. Creating a good compost can be as simple as building a pile of scraps on the ground in a corner of the yard or an elaborate system of bins.

A particularly easy and inexpensive method that I recommends begins by collecting five wooden pallets of equal size. These can often be found behind grocery stores and restaurants, discarded. Most folks will be glad to see you take them off their hands, but just to be sure always ask permission before hauling them away.

Next, pick a shady and well-drained spot, and place one of the pallets on the ground. Arrange the other four around to make four walls, then tie the pallets together with wire, rope, or clothesline. Leave the ties on one wall loose so you can fold it down for easy access.

In time, the bottom pallet will decay and should be replaced. This type of compost bin can be built in less than an hour and is portable if you need to move it to another spot in the yard. Cinderblocks can be substituted for pallets and stacked to create a custom bin. Another simple method is to position hardware cloth or chicken wire in a circle and secure the ends together. The key in a good compost bin is to make sure there is a good amount of air circulating through the pile.

Maintaining the Compost

Good compost is dark and has a sweet smell like freshly turned earth. It can take six months to two years for material to decompose fully and be ready to use on gardens and house plants, so be patient. Try to maintain a balance of nitrogen-rich materials (fresh green plant material), and carbon-rich materials (dried cuttings from your lawn, leaves, wood, ashes, shredded paper), or your compost will be smelly and unhealthy.

Compost needs air to break down, so turn the pile often to expose the layers. The more surface area there is, the faster your scraps will decompose. Picture an ice cube melting in the Sun, and you'll get the idea.

Chop materials into short pieces with a shovel or machete; long branches and twigs will take too long to break down, so leave them out. The compost should be as moist as a wrung-out sponge. The inside of the pile will generate heat and therefore kill weed seeds, insect eggs, and disease-carrying organisms.

Although some composting systems can get quite elaborate, the process itself is very simple. If you keep the pile moist and turn it often, nature will do all the work for you. And you get to enjoy the results!

Useful Materials for Composting

Kitchen waste (fruit and vegetable peelings, egg shells, coffee grounds, tea bags, corn cobs)

Human and pet hair

Vacuum bag contents (dust, hair, lint)

Lawn clippings, leaves, miscellaneous plant waste, bark, wood shavings, hay

Newspaper, shredded office paper (whole pieces will take too long to break down)

Feathers

Ashes

Fingernail clippings

Felt

Rabbit manure, urine

Materials Not Good for Composting

Human, cat, or dog feces

Meats

Cheese and other dairy products

Fats and oils (salad dressing, cooking oil)

For Further Study

Let It Rot!: The gardener's guide to composting. Stu Campbell. Storey Publications, 1998.

Mother Nature's Herbal. Judy Griffin, Ph.D. Llewellyn Publications, 1997.

The Rodale Book of Composting. Deborah L. Martin and Grace Gershuny, editors. Rodale Press, 1992.

Worms Eat My Garbage. Mary Applehof. Flower Press, 1982.

An English Country Walk

By Carolyn Moss

A s I live in England, I would like to take you down the lanes, across the meadows and fields, and through the woods and various groves around my home. Here, we will be able to gather herbs, fruit, and flowers to cook up some lovely reminders of a summer's walk. I will have to warn you in advance—be sure when picking things for consumption that they are away from car fumes and animal mess!

As we start out, in midsummer, the hedgerows are full and green. The verges look cloudily romantic with a lacy dressing of greenery. The fields are wild and overgrown, and the forests are darkly verdant.

There are many edible food ready for the picking on a country forage in the moderate climates of most countries in North America, Europe, and Asia. If we included medicinal plants and herbs in our search, then our baskets might overflow with the bounty! After reading my descriptions below, you may decide to keep your eyes open next time you go for a stroll. All you have to do is keep your eyes open and enjoy all that nature can offer you.

Foods in the Fields and Meadows

Meadowsweet

Among the many plants that grow in open fields and meadows of England are meadowsweet *(Filipendula ulmaria)*. In its natural state meadowsweet, also known as queen of the meadow, is a lovely sight. It has hazy cream-colored flower heads and is heavily scented. It grows where there is much dampness around ponds and by ditches.

A tea brewed from its leaves is said to soothe headaches and, indeed, traditional country herbalists used willow bark *(Salix* spp.) and meadowsweet for minor aches and pains. Later, early doctors tapped into the healing effects of these plants to extract an active pain-relieving ingredient, salicylic acid. This was made into aspirin, although synthetic versions are now used. Along with its medicinal use, willow also makes a good cordial when boiled with sugar; it also makes a nice wine.

Dandelion

Also to be found in quantity on the verges—or pretty much any-where—are dandelions *(Taraxacum officinale)*. This plant's leaves are wonderful as salad greens so long as they are picked early in the year before they have become overgrown, and therefore tough and bitter. In French markets, dandelion greens are sold in bunches. In England and the United States, we can have them for free just by picking.

Take care, however; in excess dandelions act as a diuretic, (hence its French name is *pis en lit*, or "wet the bed"). A few leaves in a salad should not be a problem. They are, like most deep green leaves, full of vitamins and minerals.

Garlic Mustard and Nettle

Next, we might come upon garlic mustard *(Sisymbrium allaria)* in the English fields. This is slightly less common than dandelion, although if you come across a patch it is likely to be a large patch. Garlic mustard, also called jack-by-the-hedge, has a strong garlicky scent, but it is not related in any way to the onion and garlic family. The young leaves of this plant can be used in salads, while the older leaves may be lightly steamed or boiled as with spinach.

In a similar vein, common nettle *(Urtica dioica)* is a nice addition to your diet. Found in the fields, nettle, when picked young, can be cooked alone as with spinach, or it may be added to other greens. Nettle may also be chopped and put into soups or rice dishes, therefore adding a valuable boost of vitamins and minerals in the spring.

As with dandelions, only the fresh young nettles should be used. Later in the year the plant gets so tough and unpalatable it would put you off picking wild greens for life.

Sorrel

In the fields, you might find a delicious and gourmet delight in sorrel *(Rumex acetosa)*. In a grassy meadow, the sorrel stands out with its reddish tint. A herb that is common to temperate climates, sorrel adds a lemony bite to salads when leaves are young and small. The older leaves can be lightly cooked or made into the sorts of sauces and soups beloved of fancy French restaurants. A simple sorrel sauce can be made by lightly cooking sorrel leaves in butter, adding half a cup each of heavy cream and chicken stock. When thoroughly blended and heated through, put the leaves in a food processor to puree. Serve the puree with chicken or fish for an elegant dinner.

Fungi

Various fungi will be apparent on our excursion. So among the field greens, we can expect to garner a number of basic field mushrooms. Although you should pick fungi should only when you are absolutely sure you can identify what you are harvesting, there is nothing like the flavor of a mushroom picked with the dew still on it, fried minutes later in butter. The nutritional value is also, of course, many times higher than something that has been sitting in a shop for days.

Food from Hedgerow and Forest

Wild Rose and Elder

The hedgerows of England are replete with many treats. Wild rose *(Rosa eglanteria)*, known to Shakespeare as eglantine, has simple delicate blooms which fade to leave lovely deep red rosehips. Full of vitamin C, these rosehips have traditionally been made into a syrup for children to take in the winter months when fresh fruit and vegetables are sparse.

Nearly as common as the wild rose is the elder *(Sambucus* spp.). For a short season in midsummer the elder is full of sprays of heavily scented cream flowers. These can be made into a non-alcoholic "champagne" by soaking ten or so flower heads in eight pints of water. Add a sliced orange or a sliced lemon (or both), and leave for two days. Strain the liquid through muslin, and add three cups sugar and two tablespoons cider vinegar. Stir well, making sure the sugar is dissolved, then bottle it in beer bottles (not fully sealed to avoid explosive gasses) for a week. Drink the brew down within four to six weeks.

Even simpler is an elderflower cordial made by soaking twenty-five flower heads, four cups of sugar, two sliced oranges, a sliced lemon, and three pints of water for twenty-four hours until the sugar is fully dissolved. Bottle and store in the refrigerator. This can be diluted with sparkling mineral water for a cooling drink or used to flavor puddings and ice cream. In the fall the elder is laden with purple-black berries which can be made into a nice cordial (two cups of berries to two cups of brown sugar, simmered until the sugar is melted then strained and bottled). Or they can be used to make fabulous country wines. Elder is an excellent source of vitamin C.

Wild Plum, or Sloe

Far less common than rosehips and elder is the fruit of the black-thorn *(Prunus spinosa)*—the sloe, or wild plum. Small and hard, and almost black, in a raw state this fruit is unpalatable. Do not be alarmed, however, sloe does make a wonderful drink that many people enjoy at Christmastime in front of a roaring fire—that is, sloe gin.

Sloe gin is made by picking three cups of sloes, preferably after the first few frosts. Prick them each with a pin and place in a glass jar with a lid. Pour in one cup white sugar and four cups of gin. You may choose to throw in a drop of almond essence or a few cracked plum stones to add a bit of flavoring, but this is optional. Cover the jar tightly and leave in a dark cupboard, shaking it daily for a week. Then leave the jar for three months, giving it the odd shake when you think of it. Afterwards, strain the contents into pretty bottles and enjoy. Sloe gin can be enjoyed after three months, but it is even better the following year.

Rowan

The rowan, or mountain ash *(Sorbus aucuparia)*, is a tall tree in the hedge with bright and vibrant orange-red berries. The berries of this tree cannot be eaten raw, except by the birds, but may be made into a jewel-red jelly to be enjoyed with cold meats and cheese; this dish is a particular favorite in Scotland. To make the jelly, simply boil up equal quantities of berries and sugar with a quarter of the quantity of water. When a set is achieved (check in a preserving book if you're not sure about this), strain through muslin without squeezing (or it will go cloudy). Store this beautifully colored preserve in jelly jars.

Sweet Woodruff

Over the stile and into the woods, there are fewer flowers to be found as the trees give permanent shade to the soil. Here, however, we can find a rare gem—sweet woodruff *(Galium odoratum)*. Wild in parts of Europe, this little herb is cultivated in the United States. Sweet woodruff will only grow in shade, and it is found wild only in densely wooded areas. In the Sun the leaves lose their green color and fail to thrive.

Growing only to six inches or so, woodruff leaves have no scent as they grow. However, due to the presence of the chemical coumarin, when wilted or dried, woodruff exudes a marvellous fragrance similar to new-mown hay. You can add a few sprigs of freshly cut woodruff to a bottle of sweet white wine. Recork the wine, and after a week or so you have the traditional Mei Wein (May wine) drink of Alsace-Lorraine and Germany. This is traditionally served on May 1 as a punch with sliced strawberries and the like floating atop.

Wild Raspberry and Strawberry

On the edge of the wood, in a long forgotten and overgrown spot, we are likely to find a precious stray wild raspberry bush or two *(Rubus strigosus)*. The fruit of wild raspberry is small and scant, but, if picked on a warm and sunny afternoon with the hum of bees as the only background noise, wild raspberries have a depth of flavor unmatched by their more available cultivated cousin.

Unfortunately, wild raspberries are rarely found in enough abundance to make jams and jellies. In fact, they are best simply eaten fresh from the bush. Further, the leaf of this plant has gained a great following in recent years when taken as a tea during pregnancy.

Along with our wild raspberries, we may find a few wild strawberries *(Fragaria vesca)* growing in a sunny glade. Tiny scarlet gems less than an inch across, these are a delight best enjoyed eaten straight away or scattered to garnish a creamy dessert. Interestingly, the wild strawberry has properties valued by medical herbalists which are not to be found in the large, cultivated varieties.

Crab Apple and Blackberry

Finally, as our excursion ends, we may be lucky enough to find a crab apple tree *(Malus baccata)*. These miniature apples grow no more than an inch across and are extremely sour. They do, however, make a very good jelly for use, like the rowan jelly mentioned above, with cheeses and cold meats.

Alongside the crab apple tree is a blackberry *(Rubus villosus)* patch. Although cultivated blackberries can easily be found, their flavor does not compare with the wild variety. Found in abundance in temperate climes, blackberries should be on the plate of every child, whose right it is to get scratched and stained in the pursuit of a basket of these dark gems. A few added to an apple pie make a wonderful fall treat. And again, blackberries are another fruit which makes fine vitamin-rich jellies and cordials.

A bit of trivia: The old English name for the fruit is "bramble." This may, or may not, help if you are offered bramble jelly and would otherwise wonder what exotica is involved.

For Further Study

There are many books available to help you in your foraging through the countryside. Check listings under headings such as "wild flowers," "herbs," "wildcrafting," and "foraging." The following books are also well worth seeking out.

Partners in Life: A guide to cooking, gardening and healing with wild and cultivated plants. Adele Dawson. Inner Traditions, 2000.

The Foraging Gourmet. Katie Letcher Lyle. The Lyons Press, 1997.

Herbal Medicines on the Santa Fe Trail. Jim Long. Long Creek Herbs, 1996.

Flora Britannica. Richard Mabey. Trafalgar Square, 1998. (This book is based on the flora of Great Britain but is so comprehensive and applicable to temperate states that it is worth a look for U.S. readers).

In addition, there is an excellent article titled "Wildcrafting Tips" by Carly Wall in Llewellyn's *1999 Moon Sign Book*.

Wildcraft Gathering & Growing

≫ By Marguerite Elsbeth ≪

The Great Spirit is in all things: he is in the air we breathe. The Great Spirit is our Father, but the Earth is our Mother. She nourishes us; that which we put into the ground, she returns to us.

Big Thunder (Bedagi), Wabanaki Algonquin

Several summers ago, I had the privilege of gathering herbs with an elder woman from a northern New Mexico Pueblo Indian tribe, the *Keresan.* My friend is a die-hard wildcrafter. She was born and raised on the reservation, and knows much about survival in harsh conditions. Her belief is that we cannot buy what is sacred. She does not believe in growing medicinal herbs and plants in pots on the kitchen windowsill. It is the role of Mother Earth to provide healing plants to us, and it is my friend's role to receive these gifts of health and healing from her, if the Creator wills it.

The pueblo is set in what the locals say is the very beginning of the Chihuahua Desert, a shrub desert. Creosote bush *(Larrea tridentata)* is everywhere, and it is used to fight herpes and cold sores. Tarbush *(Flourensia cernua)*, a marker species for the Chihuahuan Desert, is used historically in northern New Mexico to make a decoction for treating indigestion. Other common plants in the northern portions of the desert include four-winged saltbush *(Atriplex canescens)*, used as greens in stews, and honey mesquite *(Prosopis glandulosa)*, used as food by the Indians native to the region. Several edible succulents—cacti, yuccas *(Yucca elata, Yucca torreyi)*, and the agaves of Mezcal wine fame—are also common here.

Many of us are also familiar with juniper *(Juniperus monosperma)*, or sacred cedar, which is very common in the Chihuahua Desert and across the Southwest. It, along with sweet grass, sage, and wild mountain tobacco, is found on the medicine wheels of many Indian nations. Those of us who follow Wiccan or Pagan traditions burn the leaves and berries of the juniper tree, so that the aromatic smoke will carry our prayers to the Creator. The smoke also purifies a negative atmosphere in the home, and blesses and protects us. Juniper has been utilized for centuries by the Pueblo, Apache, Navajo, Paiute, Shoshone, Tewa, and Zuni peoples as a gynecological aid, as a diuretic, emetic, and disinfectant, for colds and coughs, and as a cure-all for a variety of diseases.

Gathering Herbs

Not all American Indian people gather herbs in the same way. In fact; there are as many different methods for collecting botanical plants as there are cultures, customs, and religious traditions. Consider, for instance, that in central Germany, a man who sows flax (a herb used to relieve constipation, lower the risk of heart disease, and prevent cancer) carries the seed in a long bag that reaches from his shoulders to his knees. He walks in long strides, so the bag sways to and fro on his back and the flax waves in the wind; if the flax receives the blessing of the winds, the plants will grow tall and strong.

The women of Sumatra let their hair hang loose down their backs when they are sowing herbs, so the plants will have long stalks. Ugandan people believe that a barren wife infects her husband's garden with her own sterility, and prevents the herbs from growing. In the United States, we think nothing of going to the local health store and buying herbs that have already been dried, pulverized, encapsulated, and placed in plastic containers. There is nothing wrong with this, provided we approach the spirit of the plants with reverence prior to ingesting them.

With my friend, I traveled on foot, bringing only a brown paper bag in which to place the harvested plants. We did not have to walk very far. On this day, we searched for bearberry, also known as *uva-ursi*. The leaves of this small shrub have been used as a herbal folk medicine among Keresan-speaking peoples for centuries as a mild diuretic and astringent, and in the treatment of urinary tract infections such as cystitis, urethritis, and nephritis. Bearberry is currently a popular remedy for menopausal women to help remove excess water that is retained in the body due to hormonal imbalances.

We located a bearberry plant amid a wide circle of juniper trees. Following a few muttered prayers and a sprinkling of cornmeal, we pulled the bearberry conscientiously from the ground and placed it into the sack. The juniper was then attended with more ceremony—my friend declared that these trees were sacred cedar, and she approached the trees, speaking prayers in her native language. She then carefully and respectfully took leaves and bark and bundled them in her shawl. She later explained to me that she had asked the Creator, the Earth Mother, and the trees, for permission to use their hair and limbs for healing.

Plant Spirits

A herb becomes sacred through proper spiritual use of its given powers. In fact, many cultures around the world have a long-standing tradition of herbal medicine that is closely inter-twined with spiritual beliefs and customs. Thus, plants have been used for centuries in conjunction with magic to heal, purify, and strengthen the body, mind, and emotions.

Plants respond to our thoughts and feelings; they are sentient beings, animated by the same universal life-giving spirit that ensouls all creatures and things. This makes plants sympathetic to our bodies just as we are sensitive to their healing properties. The scientific approach to herbs serves us well in determining the chemical constituents, active ingredients, and biomolecules in plants, as well as how and why various cultures use plants for medicinal purposes. Wildcrafting, on the other hand, is a natural approach to growing and gathering herbs based on practical experience rather than rational, established laws and principles.

When we choose to follow a natural philosophy regarding herbal remedies, we need not concern ourselves about the processes involved or why these medicines work to keep us healthy and fit. The bottom line is they work. We believe the plant spirits will cure what ails us because we are recipients and witnesses to their curative properties. The Druids, for example, believed that trees such as the rowan and the oak possessed great mysterious powers. Now we know that the rowan tree, or mountain ash *(Sorbus aucuparia)*, has certain curative powers, as its berries, fruits, and seeds contain chemicals that prevent scurvy, reduce hemorrhoids, and treat stomach and duodenal ulcers. Likewise, the astringent effects of the oak were well-known to the ancients, as they made a decoction from the tree's bark to staunch hemorrhage, reduce fever, and treat chronic diarrhea and dysentery.

Indigenous peoples treat plants with great respect, because they believe that plants have supernatural powers, or may be inhabited by gods, goddesses, spirits, or the ancestors. This is why people who live close to nature choose to purify themselves before they partake of its medicine. The herb that is dropped in the cook pot and simmered to release its medicine may in fact shelter the soul of a deceased relation. The plant spirit may be offended, and the user may be deprived of its benefits, if the plant is not given proper reverence.

Wildcrafting Your Herbs

Wildcrafting is becoming ever more popular as many people choose wild herbs over ones that have been refined and developed for the marketplace. Personally, I believe that herbs gathered from the wild have more power and inherent healing qualities. Furthermore, gathering herbs in this way is a productive step towards fostering our relationship with Mother Earth. It is essential, therefore, to perform this task in synchronization with nature and avoid further destruction to our ecosystems.

All around the world, corporate interests and careless individuals, who see the value of the land only in terms of how it can be exploited for its resources, endanger our environment. The Earth, which once provided valuable botanical medicines seemingly without end, is facing a serious crisis. Our natural resources are nearing exhaustion from careless depletion. We must act now to help preserve our natural resources before many rare medicinal plant species disappear forever. I am also concerned about governmental agencies that, working hand in hand with major pharmaceutical companies, seek proposals to license all herbal remedies. They claim this is for our safety. However, in my opinion, the real reason for these laws is to protect corporate interest from losing market share as more people turn to herbal remedies and limit their intake of pharmaceutical drugs.

Wildcrafting is the most direct way of getting in touch with the healing powers of Mother Earth. Moreover, by learning to wildcraft, you can be assured that you may always find the herbs you need in nature, should the government step in and take away our ability to purchase these natural remedies.

Following are some simple guidelines to help you get started wildcrafting.

1. Study the environment before you begin gathering any herbs. Does it look pure and healthy, or is it diseased or polluted by chemicals?

2. Wildcrafting is a spiritual activity. Therefore, remember to ask the plant spirits for permission before you take them. Also, it is important to give something back in the way of an offering. For instance, traditional indigenous people offer wild mountain tobacco as a gift to the healing spirits of the earth. You may also offer copper coins, seeds, or a prayer of gratitude and thanksgiving while you are harvesting.

3. It is best to never take more than you need. Keep in mind that others may also require the herbs that you are gathering. Moreover, please consider that animals and insects help with pollination and seed distribution and may also rely on the plants you are harvesting for food.

4. Handle the plants gently and respectfully. Never touch the plants with metal, other than a knife or scissors to sever the plants or the leaves and bark from the rest of the plant. It is best to wear gloves and use your hands. Papers, or cloth made from natural fiber, make the best containers for transport, and your cookware should be constructed of wood, enamel, glass, or stoneware.

5. Be aware of the dangers of herbs. Misidentification, mislabeling, misinformation, and self-medication without a diagnosis from a qualified practitioner can place you in harm's way. Some herbs are poisonous; others may make you deathly ill.

6. Learn to correctly identify the plants you wish to harvest. Your local museum may have a herbarium, where many different kinds of plants have been collected and pressed. You can choose to take a course in botany at your local night school or college, or buy a book that will guide you

in identifying herbs and flowers. There are also many websites that have pictures and descriptionsm of herbs.

Once you begin your wildcrafting, here are some additional things you should keep in mind:

Collect your herbs in dry weather.

Grow your herbs in organic soil. Use crushed kelp or organic compost to feed the plants. Be sure to include some well-rotted straw manure or shredded leaves in the mix.

Annuals, plants that complete their growth in one growing season, should be cut to the ground.

Biennials, which require two growing seasons, should be cut about halfway down.

Perennials, which die back seasonally and produce new growth, should also be cut about halfway down.

Leaves should be collected in the early morning on a clear dry day, because this is when the fragrant oils are at their greatest strength.

Flowers are best used medicinally when they have just opened.

Barks may be gathered in the spring or fall when the plant is at least two years old. Age bark for about two years before using.

Seeds must be gathered as soon as they are ripe and fully developed.

Dry your herbs by tying them in small bunches and hanging them upside down in a warm dry place. Or wrap the herbs loosely in newspaper, tying a string around the middle of the paper, and hang them in a warm dry room or closet. The herbs will be dry in a few days.

Never store dried herbs in plastic. Instead, use glass jars or bottles, and keep them in the refrigerator or a cool dark place.

Do not use plants that have been sprayed with insecticides or tampered with in any way. Sprayed plants can poison you if used in teas or ointments.

Homegrown Wild Herbs

Growing herbs at home is easy and very rewarding. True, it's not exactly wildcrafting—after all, we do not all have access to wide-open spaces, mountain meadows, or the forest floor. However, we can, by revering the spirits of the plants we choose to grow, still employ the spiritual principles of wildcrafting at home. So, if you are feeling the call of the wild herb, and are unable to get out in nature, use these wild growing tips:

Outdoor Herbs

Grow in raised beds or containers for better drainage.

Plant angelica (for digestive and bronchial problems), beebalm (for nausea and menstrual cramps), lovage (for headaches and rheumatism), and assorted mints (for muscle spasms) in damp soil.

If your garden is shady, try sweet cicely (to increase appetite), lemon balm (to calm the nerves), chervil (for eczema and high blood pressure), valerian (for sound sleep), ginseng (to increase physical endurance), evening primrose (to regulate hormonal balance), or goldenseal (for good circulation).

If you are growing lavender (an antiseptic), thyme (for coughs and asthma), or rue (to promote menstruation), increase the soil's acidity by adding dolomite, wood ash, bonemeal, or eggshells.

Start your herbs from seed and plant them directly in your garden.

Indoor Herbs

Prepare flats or pots by lining the bottom with one white paper towel, and then add a layer of small rock for drainage.

Next, add organic potting soil mixed with compost.

Plant seeds in rows about two inches apart, or in clusters of three for individual pots.

Label each container with the types of herbs and the date of sowing.

Most seeds, such as chamomile (for inflammation and indigestion), feverfew (for migraine headache and arthritis), mugwort (for use in the bath to relieve aches and pains), and yarrow (for earache and bowel complaints), germinate in darkness, so press them lightly against the soil, and cover the container with glass or damp newspapers.

Place the containers in an area that remains 65 to 70 degrees day and night.

Once the seedlings are up, move them to a sunny windowsill. Turn the containers several times a day if you are using overhead lighting.

Finally, following is a list of the best herbs for indoors, including their medicinal virtues, a little folklore, and some helpful hints for growing them properly:

Aloe Vera *(Aloe vera, Aloe* spp.)

Medicinal Value: The gel inside the leaves may be used to treat burns, skin rashes, and insect bites. Rubbing aloe on the face and neck will help keep skin fresh and supple.

Aloe vera juice may take internally to soothe digestion and keep the bowels functioning smoothly.

Folklore: Growing aloe vera in the kitchen protects against burns and mishaps while cooking. It also guards against evil and prevents household accidents.

Cultivation: Aloe is best grown indoors in a wide clay pot. It thrives outdoors in hot and humid climates. Aloe is a succulent, so it needs water to keep its leaves fleshy and juicy.

Basil *(Ocimum basilicum)*

Medicinal Value: Use basil for stomach cramps, vomiting, fevers, colds, flu, headaches, whooping cough, and menstrual pains. The leaves can be applied on insect bites to draw out the poisons. The oil from basil leaves may be rubbed on the skin to enhance the complexion.

Folklore: Basil protects against negativity and aids in attracting and keeping love. Sprinkling powdered basil over your mate while he or she sleeps may eliminate a tendency to stray. Basil may also be used to purify the bath water, or to attract wealth and prosperity.

Cultivation: Basil grows in any well-drained and rich soil, and needs full Sun. Pinch off the tips of the flowering buds to make the plant bushy and promote growth.

Chives *(Allium schoenoprasum)*

Medicinal Value: Chive oil is antiseptic and helps to lower blood pressure if taken in large quantities.

Folklore: Chives may drive away diseases and evil influences when bunches of the plants are hung in the home.

Cultivation: Chives need a consistent temperature and constant moisture. Place the plants in full Sun.

Dill *(Anethum graveolens)*

Medicinal Value: Dill may be used to increase mother's milk, treat breast congestion due to nursing, and ease babies with colic. It also stimulates the appetite, relieves gas and indigestion, and induces sleep.

Folklore: Dill is used in love and protection sachets. Hang the dried seeds over doorways and above cradles for protection. Add dill to your bath to make you irresistible.

Cultivation: Plant dill in rich, well-drained soil, place in full Sun, and water frequently. New plants will shoot up every year if the flowers are allowed to go to seed.

Fennel *(Foeniculum vulgare)*

Medicinal Value: Fennel is a weak diuretic and mild stimulant. It suppresses appetite and may improve digestion and ease coughs. It may be safely used as a sedative for small children, and is also used to heal cancer patients after radiation and chemotherapy treatments.

Folklore: Grow fennel in the home to ward off negativity.

Cultivation: Fennel prefers dry, sunny areas, and grows in most average to poor soils.

Ginger *(Zingiber officinale)*

Medicinal Value: Ginger is a mild stimulant and promotes good circulation. It is excellent for strengthening and healing the respiratory system, as well as fighting off colds and flu. It removes congestion, soothes sore throats, relieves headaches and body aches, and soothes indigestion. This herb is also very effective against motion sickness and nausea.

Folklore: Ginger is used in passion spells to "heat up" a cooled-down relationship. It is also used in prosperity spells or to ensure the success of spells in general.

Cultivation: Give ginger plenty of warmth, moisture, and humidity. During warm months, move the plants to a semishaded outdoor area.

Marigold *(Calendula* spp.)

Medicinal Value: Marigold is a great first-aid remedy for headaches, earaches, and fevers. It strengthens the heart muscle and increases the circulation, and it may also be used externally to heal wounds and bruises.

Folklore: Fresh marigold heightens the energy in any room. Placed under the pillow before bed, marigolds induce clairvoyance. Under the bed, it protects you during sleep. Add to bath water to win recognition and respect.

Cultivation: Marigold is an annual plant that comes in many sizes and colors. It is adaptable to many soils. Give plenty of water, and place in full Sun.

Marjoram *(Origanum majorana)*

Medicinal Value: Marjoram is useful for treating asthma, coughs, toothache, conjunctivitis, sinus congestion, and hay fever. It also strengthens the stomach and intestines.

Folklore: Marjoram should be added to all love charms. A bit of marjoram in each room of the home will aid in protecting the family from harm. Marjoram will bring happiness to a grieving or depressed person.

Cultivation: Marjoram likes all kinds of rich soils, and prefers full Sun. It is grown as an annual or wintered indoors in cold regions.

Oregano *(Origanum vulgare)*

Medicinal Value: Oregano is used to promote perspiration as a treatment for colds, flu, and fevers. Oregano tea may bring on the menses and relieve menstrual discomfort, and is used in baths and inhalations. Taken internally and used externally, it can help alleviate dry, itchy skin. The essential oil is used to treat viral infections, respiratory ailments, and muscle aches. Pregnant women should not ingest large amounts of oregano.

Folklore: This herb may help you to forget unpleasant memories or let go of a former partner. Burn oregano as an incense or drink the tea for releasing the past.

Cultivation: Oregano prefers well-drained, slightly alkaline soil and full Sun. Seeding, root division, or cuttings propagate it. Harvest just as the plant is about to bloom.

Parsley *(Petroselinum lativum)*

Medicinal Value: Parsley is filled with chlorophyll, and contains vitamins A, C, several B vitamins, calcium, and iron. It is a helpful laxative, and may be used to treat respiratory, liver, kidney, and bladder problems.

Folklore: Add parsley to funeral bouquets, as this herb is associated with death and the afterlife.

Cultivation: Plant parsley in moderately rich, moist, well-drained soil in full Sun to partial shade. Parsley is hard to transplant, so it should be sown where it is to grow.

Rosemary *(Rosemarinus officinalis)*

Medicinal Value: Use rosemary internally to treat migraines and bad breath, and to stimulate the sexual organs and circulatory system. It is also used to treat nervous disorders, stomach upset, and menstral cramps. Mix the crushed leaves generously into meats, fish, and potato salads to prevent food poisoning. Use externally to treat insect bites and stings. The essential oil may be used as an inhalant and decongestant, and to enhance memory. It is also used in lotions to ease arthritis and muscle pain.

Folklore: Rosemary is used for protection and banishment. Rosemary leaves under your pillow will banish evil spirits and bad dreams. Hang rosemary bouquets on the doors and windows to keep thieves out. Tap someone on the shoulder with a fresh sprig to capture their love.

Cultivation: Rosemary likes a mild climate, and is tolerable of poor soil. Cut back after flowering.

Sage *(Salvia officinalis)*

Medicinal Value: Sage eases mental exhaustion. It may be used to relieve excess mucus, to treat sores and skin eruptions, and to stop bleeding. Chewing fresh leaves or drinking tea soothes mouth sores and sore throats. Sage is good for stomach troubles, diarrhea, gas, flu, and colds. It regulates the menstrual cycle, decreases milk flow in lactating women, and aids with hot flashes. Use sage tea as a hair rinse to remove dandruff.

Folklore: Sage is used in healing amulets and sachets. It may be burned as an incense to increase prosperity. Burned in the home, sage removes impurities, banishes evil, and provides protection.

Cultivation: Sage does best in sandy, limey soil, and should be placed in full Sun.

For Further Study

The Bootstrap Guide to Medicinal Herbs in the Garden, Field & Marketplace. Lee Sturdivant, Tim Blakley, and Peggy McRae. San Juan Naturals, 1998.

The Complete Medicinal Herbal. Penelope Ody. DK Publishing, 1993.

Cunningham's Encyclopedia of Magical Herbs. Scott Cunningham. Llewellyn Publications, 1985.

Making Soil Beds for Herbs

❧ By Penny Kelly ❧

S ince many herbs are natural healers and soil-balancers, it is hard to say whether it is more important for you to prepare soil beds for herbs, or allow the herbs to prepare the soil for you.

That is to say, when a soil is disturbed or out of balance, it is usually because one or two elements predominate in it. For instance, let's imagine there is too much magnesium and too little calcium in your soil. You could add calcium and a neutral element to the soil in an effort to balance the soil, or you could let nature take over. Plants that love soils with lots of magnesium will germinate, grow, and out-do all the others in your yard because the environment is perfect for them. After a couple of years, they will have used the high amounts of magnesium to flourish, while at the same time the plant's roots will have brought up calcium from the deeper subsoils. In

time, the soil will become naturally balanced and healthy, thanks to the remarkable abilities of simple plants.

If you were to turn over the soil in a garden patch, then leave it alone and just observe what happens over the next two or three years, you would notice that a different kind of "weed" would dominate the patch each successive year. Seven or eight years ago my husband was going to plant corn in a field that had been mostly covered with grass for the previous few years. He went out, plowed the field, and for some reason he never got the corn planted.

The following year the field stood out like a beautiful yellow jewel in a sea of green grasses. It was full of wild cabbage and mustards. Then, in the next year, a different plant was dominant in the field. Its flowers were feathery purple ones with yellow centers. The year after that something else was dominant and the flowers were now white. The only ones I recognized were wild sweet clover and fleabane, and when I walked out to the field I could see that more and more grasses were moving in.

When I finally discovered the reason for the flowery succession, it changed the way I treated my garden's soil. And it is this: Some plants act as soil-balancers. They add carbon in the form of their own bodies to make humus, to hold water, or absorb and transform toxins, and so give of themselves for future generations of plants.

Soil-Balancing Plants

One of the shocking discoveries I made when I first started to grow herbs was that I was already familiar with quite a few of them, except I knew them as "weeds." I made the discovery at the nursery, as many seedlings were plants that I had formerly tried to remove from my garden and yard. Ironically, when I brought the cultivated seedlings home and planted them, they were a great disappointment. The plants grew to gigantic proportions, and were stringy-looking and sprawling. In the rich soil of my garden beds they grew too quickly and soon could not stand upright. They produced smaller leaves, fewer flowers, and a few became mildewed and lost all fragrance. In the end I didn't even harvest them. Instead I went in search of their wild cousins at the side of the field and along the lane. These were full of oils and intensely fragrant.

Eventually, through years of trial and error, I discovered that, just as in raising children, you can't raise your herbs using the same technique for all. What works for some is the framework for failure with others.

In the field my husband plowed, the first wild plants that grew there were those that thrive in very high levels of magnesium and very low levels of calcium—namely, dandelion, stinging nettle, burdock, and mustards. After these yellow-flowered plants have thrived for a year or two, they will have used up some of the magnesium and brought up enough calcium from the deeper soils to change the soil composition just a bit.

Now another kind of weed moved into position as the dominant plant. This next group of plants was composed mostly of purple-flowered Canadian thistle, vetch, Queen Anne's lace, and bindweed. These will grow quite successfully for a year or two, and when the soil has been balanced a little more its composition changes again and such white-flowered plants as lambsquarter, catnip, evening primrose, and potentilla become abundant.

In my husband's field, after a few years grasses such as timothy, perennial rye, bromegrass, and bramble will eventually move in again. About this time, understory trees such as sassafras, sumac, cedar, mulberry, and poplar will be seeded by birds and begin to grow. These early, fast growing trees not only mine the subsoil for additional minerals, they provide the diffuse light and cooler environment for the big hardwood trees that come up much more slowly.

In Mother Nature's plan, this process continues until the elements in the soil are well balanced. When this happens, there will be a hardy and diversified community of grasses, herbs, and other plant species, all designed to work in harmony within the local microclimate, and to survive in the greater environment of the region. Each species of plant thrives in a specific kind of environment. One likes it hot; another likes it cool. Some do well in highly acidic soils, others need alkaline soil. A few prefer sand; many need something with a little clay and humus in it. Some like it wet, and others prefer it dust-dry.

If you want to coddle and fuss with the soil for some herbs, you'll want to do this mainly with your culinary herbs. Most of them—basil, parsley, oregano, marjoram, rosemary, sage, thyme, dill, chives, garlic, and onion—love to get their roots into good, composted soil. Put them in clay or sand and you may not get a harvest at all.

Setting up a Balanced Soil

I have found that the best way to grow herbs is to set up several beds of manageable size in three or four locations and copy Mother Nature as much as possible. At Lily Hill Farm, I have two main gardens: the kitchen garden and the crop garden. In addition, I have a seed garden, a greenhouse, and two small wild herb gardens. I grow various kinds of herbs in all of them, managing the soil in each using a variety of methods.

I start by dividing the herbs into two classes—medicinal herbs and culinary herbs. My experience has been that most medicinal herbs do well in the poorer soils of the two small herb gardens, while the culinary herbs do better in the richer soils of the kitchen garden and the crop garden. While there are exceptions to this concept, this has been a useful, if general, rule of thumb.

The Kitchen Garden

The kitchen garden consists of eight raised beds made of one-by-twelve cedar planks. Each bed is five feet wide, twenty feet long, and is surrounded by a thick layer of wood chips that make it possible to fetch something out of the garden without getting muddy. The bed is filled with compost made from a mixture of cow manure, chicken manure, weeds, wood chips, mushroom compost, bagged leaves, fruits and vegetables being thrown out by a local grocer because they were outdated, and Bio-Dynamic "preps." The compost was a year old when it went into the raised beds, and because it had never been used, I tested the pH level of the soil just out of curiosity. I found it to be a bit too high at the time, ranging from 7.8 to 8.2 on the pH scale (I would have prefered for it to be down in the range between 6.5 and 6.8).

Using mostly guesswork, I put one cup of vinegar in a three-gallon sprayer, filled the sprayer with water, and sprayed the beds with roughly equal amounts of the vinegar spray. As it turned out, that was not enough, though it did lower the pH to just above 7. I did not want to put any more vinegar into the soil, however, until I saw how the plants actually grew. I also knew that plain old water would likely change the soil's pH level in due time, so I left things alone at that point and soaked the beds, hoping things would work out.

A few days later I transplanted my twelve beloved thyme plants into the beds. At the same time, I sprinkled about five or six handfuls of montmorillonite clay onto the surface of each bed to add what I hoped would be a good beginning supply of minerals. I intended to put a sprinkling of paramagnetic rock into each bed to catalyze the soil's overall chemisty and fuel enzyme reactions, but I never quite got to it before the summer ended. And in fact, the plants didn't seem to notice the difference at all.

We chose to plant culinary herbs in the kitchen garden that we planned to use regularly through the season, that were not too aggressive and did not tend to spread, and that did not become stringy in good soils.

Kitchen Garden Herbs

Parsley	Thyme	Sweet Basil
Chive	Dill	Lemon Basil
Marjoram	Coriander	Ginger Root
Onion	Purple Ruffles Basil	Cinnamon Basil
Winter Savory	Garlic	Holy Basil
Summer Savory	Chervil	Bush Basil
Lavender	Cayenne & Chilis	Oregano

We planted annuals and perennials that we never seem to have enough of in the beds. We hoped to coax higher production out of fewer plants by putting them in excellent soil and harvesting them in a timely manner so as not to lose a single leaf, flower, or seed. The strategy worked beautifully.

At this writing, more than two gallons of dried parsley sit on the pantry shelf, harvested from a mere six plants. (And this was over and above the fresh parsley we harvested regularly to make tabouli salad.) We have one quart of dill seed from a mere twelve plants, five quarts of thyme from ten plants, three quarts of sweet basil, two quarts of cinnamon basil, three quarts of lemon basil, one pint of holy basil, two quarts of opal basil, one pint of marjoram, one pint of chervil, one quart of oregano, three pints of winter savory, and one quart of summer savory. Overall, the harvest was excellent considering that in most cases it came from only one or two plants.

The Crop Garden

In the crop garden there are no raised beds, and we follow a different soil preparation plan. Namely, we do not apply compost every year, choosing instead to spray compost tea, manure tea, and raw milk from our cows regularly on our crops. This year we did spread paramagnetic rock dust with montmorillonite clay and tilled to keep weeds down and to incorporate the young weeds into the soil as green manure.

Crop Garden Herbs

Echinacea	Tobacco	Lavender
Sage	Lemon Balm	Catnip
Hyssop	Salad Burnet	Yarrow
Potato	Red Raspberry	Black Raspberry
Chocolate Mint	Peppermint	Spearmint
Strawberry	Tomato	Chamomile
Borage	Sunflower	Horseradish
Lilac	Fennel	Corn
Cornflower	Blueberry	Elderberry

As already mentioned, part of the reason that these herbs go into the crop garden is that a number of them are quite invasive. We have discovered that the easiest way to deal with them is keep them well tilled and in bounds. I don't mind chamomile growing freely among the raspberries, but I do mind the raspberries coming up in the potatoes, the strawberries taking over the lavender, or the mints trying to take over the strawberries. As for controlling mints, a lone spearmint plant escaped from the crop garden some years ago and established itself behind the house. Eventually it spread around the steps and into the rock wall that borders the driveway. At first I was irritated by this invasiveness, but it in time I realized it beautified a rocky area and came to think truly belonged there.

The arrangement in the crop garden has worked quite well for several years, and although several of the rows are permanent perennials, the annuals move around each growing season, making the entire garden seem different and challenging each year.

The Wild Herb Gardens

In addition to the very cultured and controlled environments in the kitchen and crop hardens, we have two other locations where herbs are grown. One of these runs along the outer perimeter of the fence that surrounds the kitchen garden. The other runs along the west side of the greenhouse. I call these two areas the wild herb hardens, partly because I consider the herbs growing in them to be more wild and less cultivated, and partly because the herbs in them tend to get wildly out of control if you let them. There is also an air of mystery about these gardens, because I never know what new things I'll find growing there thanks to the effects of natural forces.

Wild Garden Herbs

Valerian	Mullein	Poppy
St. John's Wort	Caraway	Horehound
Marshmallow	Lovage	Rue
Tansy	Wormwood	Red Clover
Feverfew	Burdock	Yellow Dock
Soapwort	Stinging Nettle	Motherwort
Milk Thistle	Dandelion	Plantain

Many of the herbs I grow in my wild herb gardens are important additions to the compost, as well as to my daily use. Some of them are potent blood cleansers, and some are medicinally useful as well as beautiful. A few of these herbs, namely the nettles, wormwood, mullein, and horehound, were keys in my growing understanding that not every herb loved rich soil. The nettles grew tall and stringy, and then fell over and became mildewed when grown in rich soil. The wormwood died after I tried to feed it compost—and instead it thrived in the scant dirt of the old driveway, germinating easily in a complete absence of topsoil. The mullein behaves similarly to the nettles—it fell over in the first good wind while its wild relatives growing in the field remained upright. In good soil, horehound becomes so overgrown with branches it forgets to make any leaves with oil.

Herbs growing in dry, acidic, boggy, or depleted soils are able to do so because they can utilize the minerals and nutrients they find there in unique ways. In unique habitats and conditions, these herbs can produce the individualized plants oils they are known for. A plant's structure, chemistry, oils, flowers, leaves, seeds, and roots are all expressions of that plant's life intelligence.

Each herb plant adapts itself to certain conditions and responds to the nutrients at hand. In some ways, it is similar to the difference between humans and fish. Both live on the earth, but move the human off the land and put him in the water and he doesn't accomplish as much. In addition he needs special supports because he is adapted to live on the land. Vice versa with the fish, who would not do well on the land. Herbs are the same way. They do best in the environment they are adapted to and that allow them to produce their unique oils.

Special Cases

Besides those growing in the gardens, there are a few special herbs that I treat with highly individualized care. One of these is rosemary. The other is aloe vera.

Rosemary has a permanent home in one of the garden beds in my greenhouse. This plant is big and beautiful, and her aroma greets you the moment you step into the greenhouse. She grows well in one-hundred percent compost, but she lives a sheltered life because she is a tender perennial. But rosemary is well worth the extra effort. The aloe vera plants, meanwhile, live in pots in the house and thrive on very little water and relatively poor soil.

There are also a handful of beautiful herbs that grow near this or that doorstep. Honeysuckle frames the west entrance of our Learning Center, while several violets have sprung up from an unknown source under the maple tree at the same doorway. Climbing roses have made a home next to the door of the garden shed, along with some volunteer flax and foxglove. Bergamot has spread widely across an old flower garden left untended from ten years earlier. And clove pinks have appeared in the seed garden several years in a row not very far from the lilacs. These may sound like flowers, but they're not—clove pinks are actually very useful and powerful herbs masquerading as delicate sweet-things.

To Sum Up

Overall, you should let Mother Nature be your guide in preparing soil beds for your herbs. I recall long ago reading herbal references and endless descriptions of herbs—where they would grow best, how they should be treated. Again and again I found herbs that were relegated to the "waste places, or the "disturbed places." Naïve, I remember feeling sorry for these herbs, and thinking it was too bad they were called weeds and had nowhere nice to reside.

It was only after many years that I began to see the extraordinary service these herbs provide in helping to restore balance to disturbed soil. These are the missionaries of the fields and forests. Put some of these healing herbs into rich situations containing compost, and you won't get any healing properties in their roots, leaves, flowers, or seeds—if they even survive.

My own herb cupboard is now filled with herbs for another year, all of them grown organically here on the farm. I can't imagine cooking without a variety of herbs and spices to add deep flavor and extra nutrition to our meals. With the right environment, an attentive eye, and the correct soil for each kind of herb, you can grow your own right in your own back yard.

Culinary Herbs

The Magic of Herbal Tea

≫ By Mindy Houston ≪

A ll of us have sat down at one time or another with a hot cup of tea. Be it for medicinal purposes, for relaxation, or for warmth against the chill of a cold winter's day, tea has a number of useful qualities—from enhancing everyday well-being to treating the simplemaladies and complaints that plague us. And tea varieties come in endless numbers from all over the world.

Beginning with Tea

To start at the beginning, you should be aware that tea can be brewed from the roots, bark, flowers, leaves, seeds, and crushed berries of certain plants. In general, the flowers and leaves are steeped in water brought just under the boiling point. This is known as an infusion. For the roots, bark, and seeds of plants, you generally add the herbs to boiling water and allow the mixture

to simmer for a certain amount of time. This method is known as a decoction. (See below for further information about these two brewing methods.)

When brewing an infusion or decoction, it is best to use ceramic, glass, or stainless steel containers. Pots made of other metals risk causing chemicals to leach into the tea. You should always use bottled or spring water when you brew tea for the same reason. Tap water contains too much chlorine and other pollutants, and it can alter the taste of your tea. Be sure to carefully follow the directions provided with your herbs when making infusions and decoctions.

When making teas with loose herbs, a cotton bag or tea ball is recommended. These can be purchased through mail-order catalogs, or tea or coffee shops. Tea balls tend to be easier to find and to use. They come in all sorts of shapes and sizes—the best are the round ball type with a fine mesh screen and a chain that attaches to your cup or pot. These have a metal clip that allows the tea ball to open in half—the herb put in on one side and then locked shut. The mesh screen keeps small particles of herbs from leaking into your tea.

If you are interested in pursuing herbs, you should research extensively by visiting your local herb dealers and stores, and by reading (see the "For Further Study" list at the end of this article). For starting out, simple teas are best. For example, chamomile, raspberry, strawberry, and mint are staples of every culture. They are easy to start with, and can be easily found at your local grocery and health food store. There are many brands and blends to choose from. Choose a good quality brand for the best results.

Once you become familiar with the teas and their properties then you can blend selected herbs for a specific purpose. I advise becoming very familiar and comfortable with the simple herbs before progressing onward. Herbs are natural, but some can still cause harm if not used carefully. Read whatever you can on herbs, as there is a wealth of information out there—in books and on the Internet. But beware; once you start incorporating herbs into your life, you can easily become obsessed.

If you find that working with herbs is right up your alley, you may decide to look into a correspondence school. There are many different schools out there that offer a wide range of degrees in alternative fields such as herbalism and alternative medicine. This is good for the person who does not have a school nearby, or their local school does not offer these courses.

Infusions

For infusions, always use freshly boiled water when you brew your tea. Do not add your herbs to the boiling water—remove the water from heat first, then add the herbs. For a large infusion, you need one ounce of dried herb to every two cups of water, and two ounces of fresh herbs per two cups of water. When making a small infusion—that is, a single serving—pour eight ounces of hot water over one teaspoon dried herb or one tablespoon of fresh herbs. Steep your tea for about ten minutes, covered so the volatile properties are not lost.

You may steep the herbs from fifteen minutes up to several hours—this depends on the type of herb you use and how strong an infusion you want. When brewing your tea, check to see if you can smell the aroma. If so, cover with a lid until the brewing time has passed. This prevents the volatile oils from escaping and makes your infusion more effective. In most herbs, the essential oils are the active ingredient. You may add honey or stevia (a natural sweetener) to improve the taste of certain bitter herbs.

Decoctions

With the roots, bark, and other woody parts of a plant, it is necessary to use the decoction method in order to brew a tea. That is, these coarse plant parts require a higher heat than in the infusion method.

To start, use bottled or distilled water for a decoction. In this method, you need one ounce of dried herb to each pint of water. Place the water in a medium-sized stainless steel pan, and add the herbs to water that has been brought to a boil. Simmer the herbs at just below boiling for about thirty minutes. Once cooled, strain off the herbs and refrigerate the liquid. Honey or stevia can be added as some decoctions can prove rather bitter tasting. This brew will keep in the refrigerator for about three days.

Often, decoctions are the basis for tonics and syrups. That is, you will add this concentrated herbal brew to soda water or sugar syrup to make effective remedies for common ailments.

Choosing Herbs

The following list examines some of the properties of common herbal teas. You can easily make a start by mixing some of the herbs from this list for your teas.

Catnip

Catnip leaves, brewed as a tea, are useful as a sedative and as a digestive aid. It blends well with chamomile and is good for bringing on sleep and calming nerves. People who suffer from nausea or IBS (irritable bowel syndrome) will find this herb beneficial. Catnip has antispasmodic properties that calm the digestive system.

More than likely you will not find catnip prepackaged in a tea. But this herb can be purchased through mail-order catalogs, herb shops, and health food stores. You do want to be careful when using this herb as a tea. Excessive amounts will cause nausea. Pregnant women should avoid catnip as it can stimulate uterine contractions. I recommend blending it with other herbs. A bonus: Sprinkling a little on the floor will make cats go nuts.

German Chamomile

The flowering tops of the chamomile plant have an apple-like aroma that tastes delightful as a tea. This herb is used for its calming, soothing, digestive, anti-inflammatory, and antispasmodic properties. Chamomile is extremely versatile and is good for anxiety, tension, insomnia, restlessness, overexcited children, fevers, and teething babies. (Note: Always consult a qualified herbalist before using herbs on infants. Still, chamomile is generally regarded as safe and good for colicky babies.) When taken before mealtime it can help to stimulate the appetite. For this, take up to three cups daily. A compress soaked in lukewarm tea or teabags can relieve eye pain, eyestrain, and inflammation. Place on eyes for a few minutes. If you suffer from allergies due to ragweed, use caution with this herb. It is closely related to asters, ragweed, and chrysanthemums. Be sure to watch for an allergic reaction if you use it.

Chamomile tea comes prepackaged at the store, but you can also find bulk dried flowers of the herb. Another variety of chamomile is Roman chamomile—this is used in cosmetics only.

Dandelion

The leaves, flowers, and roots of the dandelion can be used in making tea. All parts of the plant are good as a liver tonic, act as a diuretic, and promote digestion. Dandelion helps to increase the production of bile, saliva, and gastric juices. The roots and leaves make an excellent tonic for a sluggish system, especially after a long or particularly cold winter. The root preparations are not recommended for use if you have gall bladder disease unless you are under the direct supervision of a physician. Mail-order catalogs and herb stores carry dried dandelion leaves and dandelion roots. You can also harvest the plant from your backyard—just be sure the lawn has not been sprayed with herbicide or pesticide.

Wines and jellies are made out of the flowers. The young leaves can be blanched and used in salads or dried for use in tea form. The leaves have a high nutritional value. The root can be dried, ground, and brewed as a coffee substitute.

Lemon Balm

The leaves of lemon balm can be used fresh or dried for a tea, and can be added to your bath for an uplifting effect. When you crush a fresh leaf of this herb between your fingers it produces a refreshing lemon-mint scent. Lemon balm is useful in alleviating nervous, digestive, and heart disorders, and in promoting sleep. Lemon balm tea contains flavonoids, which strengthen the heart and circulatory system. The bitter constituents and tannin of its tea soothe nausea, diarrhea, and flatulence. Lemon balm is most effective if you grow your own, but it can be purchased in dried form through catalogs and herb shops.

When making iced tea, crush the leaves and add to the hot water when brewing. This creates a refreshing drink for a hot summer's day. Lemon balm is perfectly safe for everyday use.

Peppermint

There are over twenty species of peppermint, but true peppermint is the variety of herb called *Metha piperita*. This herb has potent active agents such as menthol which make it good for nausea, vomiting, flatulence, stomach spasms, and digestive problems. Peppermint is chock full of B vitamins such as riboflavin, niacin, and folic acid. Fresh peppermint leaves are best whenever possible. Combined with lemon balm, peppermint tea can help calm frazzled nerves. Peppermint is not recommended in large doses for pregnant women or for people who suffer from heartburn or stomach problems due to gastro-esophageal reflux disease (GERD). It can aggravate the symptoms of such disorders. Do not give peppermint to infants and small children, as they can have an adverse reaction to the menthol.

Peppermint tea can be found ready to buy at your local grocery or health food store. You can use both the fresh or dried leaves of this plant. It is also very easy to grow your own peppermint, though if you do be sure to keep it contained—all mint varieties are creepers, an invasive plant that will take over your yard or garden.

Raspberry

Raspberry leaf tea is often called the "woman's herb." Pregnant women drink it in their third trimester to tone the uterus and strengthen the pelvic and uterine muscles—it will help to ease birthing pains and slow the flow of blood. Researchers have discovered an alkaloid in the tea that may be responsible for this. Pregnant women should avoid this tea in early pregnancy as it may cause a miscarriage. Consult a qualified herbalist if you have any doubts. Tannins are also present in the leaves, which gives the tea an astringent affect as an effective antidiarrhea and anti-inflammatory medicine. The tea is packed with lots of potassium, calcium, phosphorus, vitamin A, and vitamin C.

Please note: The leaves of the raspberry bush are used in making tea. Do not be confused—this is not a raspberry-flavored tea. Raspberry leaves are available at your grocery or health food store.

Strawberry

The roots, leaves, and berries are used to make strawberry tea. This tea is not strawberry-flavored, though a hint of the berry will be present from the leaves and natural flavorings. Strawberry tea is a very good source of minerals such as iron, potassium, sulfur, and calcium. The berries also contain a good dose of vitamin C. Strawberry tea is effective particularly for bringing on the menses. Women may choose to drink up to three hot cups a day to help induce late or abnormally light menstrual bleeding. Do not drink more than three cups, or too-heavy bleeding may be the result; raspberry tea can conversely help slow the flow of blood. If you have any doubts whatsoever please consult a qualified herbalist for advice.

You can harvest strawberry plants for use as tea. Just make sure the plant does not does not come from the side of a road or is sprayed with chemicals. Grocery and health food stores carry tea made from the leaves.

Enjoy Your Herb Tea

The teas I have listed here are simple to make and use. They have been used by people as medicine and as enjoyment for thousands of years. They are a wonderful addition to your alternative lifestyle.

If you get hungry for more information, there are many good books available on herbs. Please refer to the list of recommended titles below if you want to do some further research. There are thousands of books in print on the subject. Enjoy!

For Further Study

101 Medicinal Herbs: An illustrated guide. Stephen Foster. Interweave Press, 1998.

The Herbal Home Remedy Book. Joyce Wardwell. Storey Publishing, 1998.

Herbal Teas. Kathleen Brown, Storey Books, 1999.

Holistic Woman's Herbal. Kitty Campion. Journey Editions, 1995.

Jude's Herbal Home Remedies. Jude Williams. Llewellyn Publications, 1992.

The New Age Herbalist. Richard Mabley, editor. Collier Books, 1988.

World Spice Blends

⁓ By K. D. Spitzer ⁓

W e tend to think of herbs as indigenous plant tops or leaves that are grown for human consumption. We see this happening commonly in backyard gardens, along wild roadsides, or in open woodland groves.

But more intriguingly, we can also think of herbs as exotic spices made from roots, barks, and berries grown in far away and mysterious lands. In fact, the trade of exotic spices comprises a long, romantic, and often bloody chapter in human history. Originally brought by caravan from the Far East through roads in the Middle East to the peoples of the Mediterranean, herbal spices played a key role in the spread and growth of civilization. It is difficult to imagine— now that such herbs are now nearly omnipresent in even the most remote

corners of the planet—that there was a time when they were not entirely known everywhere.

Herbs in World Cuisine

Some historians have thought that the medicinal efficacy of herbs came before their use as flavorings, but just the opposite is probably true. People were eating greens long before they moved into settlements; they actually probably dried them in order to carry these flavorful plants more easily on their nomadic wanderings. The Romans carried seeds all the way to Britain, and the Brits brought them to the New World. It was a fair exchange because the Americas returned allspice, chilies, cayenne and paprika, sweet and hot peppers, and chocolate and vanilla to the Old World. Today these flavors are found in cuisines around the world.

Before refrigeration, herbs and spices were used not only to mask the odors of rotting meats, but also to preserve meat, dairy products, even bread in hot climates. We think of cinnamon as a sweet spice, but it was first used for its antibacterial qualities in the preparation of meats in India and the Middle East. Drop a stick into your beef stew, and people will question the surprising magic you have wrought.

A key ingredient in Mediterranean cooking, thyme, was rubbed on or used in the process of smoking meat in order to keep all kinds of vermin from entering the larder. And in fact, its name in Greek means "to fumigate." Today, thyme's reputation as an antibacterial is long standing as the distilled tops produce a strong disinfectant more potent than carbolic acid.

Caraway, meanwhile, was and is commonly used to season cabbage and pork dishes. It is also useful for its help with the indigestible side effects of a fatty dish. Its marriage with these ingredients is ambrosial, and its reduction of flatulence after dinner makes it a gift of the Goddess.

Specific herbs and spices have an affinity for one another. These classic combinations even stretch back several thousand years. Many of these mixtures are used in cooking food, such as meats, that require cooking over a long slow fire. Other mixtures are used in pickling, another useful and traditional food preservation method.

In any herb combination, be sure to use freshly dried spices and herbs. If purchasing such mixtures from a natural food store or herb shop where the prices are assuredly cheaper, be certain the herbs have not been on the shelf for a long time. Buy a good quality product instead, and make it organic if you can find it. Do not store containers on your stovetop or in the sunlight. Keep the lid tightly secured, and rotate your stock of herbs regularly to help maintain freshness.

Buying whole spices or peppercorns and grinding them yourself can produce a greater flavor sensation than purchasing the preground ones. For this, a marble or granite mortar and pestle grinds seeds and roots more readily than a wooden one. An electric grinder is even better if you grind in short bursts. Be aware, however: If the blade gets hot it will heat up and affect the oils of the herb or spice, thus ruining its flavor and properties. You can also place your herbs in a plastic bag and crush with a rolling pin or edge of an iron skillet. Some herbs, especially seeds, are toasted in a dry skillet to bring out their full flavor before grinding.

Recipes

The distinction among world cuisine relies not upon differing ingredients but in the subtle use of them. Chicken, rice, onions, garlic, and tomatoes can make your supper in Rome or New York, Calcutta, or Mexico City, but the use of herbs in differing proportions will blend these ingredients into an entirely unique ways—and bring a completely different taste to your mouth! And long-distance differences are not the only ones you will find. In

France, an experienced palette can tell the region by the flavor of the dinner. This is true in many countries, where regional differences have much to do with the local variance in traditional herbs and spices.

Below are some recipes you can sample to begin your exploration of the great diversity of flavor in herbal spices. You can use these as a starting point to examine the use of herbs in the endless and exotic cuisines around the world. Happy hunting!

Garam Masala

Aromatic garam masala is a spice blend from northern India. Your homemade version of garam masala will be far superior to anything you have bought in a store. Also, because of the variety of herbs and complicated flavor in the mixture—and the possible variations of flavor ranging from subtle to fierce—it is worth experimenting to produce a combination of spices in this mixture that is suitable to your own palate.

In Indian dishes, you can also add one part garam masala to three parts curry for a depth of flavor unobtainable by just using curry. The following is fairly mild, but still suitable for a meat curry. Indian spice blends are always best when used fresh.

(Makes about ⅓ cup)

20	green cardamom pods
3	cinnamon sticks
4	bay leaves
2	tbsp black peppercorns
4	tsp cumin seeds
2	tsp whole cloves
2	tsp freshly grated nutmeg

Remove the small dark seeds from the cardamom pods. Discard the papery outer husk. Crush the seeds. Break the cinnamon sticks into smaller pieces. Crumble the bay leaves.

Add all the spices except the ground nutmeg to a dry skillet and shake over medium heat for 2–3 minutes. Shaking or stirring with a wooden implement will prevent burning. If you can take the mouthwatering scent, you can also toast the spices in a 200-degree oven for 35–40 minutes, stirring occasionally. Place the mixture in a bowl and let cool completely. Add the nutmeg and then grind to a fine powder in small batches in a mortar and pestle or electric grinder. Store the spice mixture in a sterilized jar, seal, and then label. Refrigerate if you are not going to use it right away.

Note: The freshly grated nutmeg is well worth the slight extra effort. You will immediately realize the superiority of scent and flavor of this fresh spice.

Hot Curry Powder

(Makes about 1½ cups)

½	cup ground turmeric
½	cup coriander seeds
5	tbsp black peppercorns
1	tbsp whole cloves
2	tbsp cumin seeds
2	tbsp decorticated cardamom seeds
1	tbsp mace
1	tbsp ground cinnamon
1	tbsp ground fenugreek seeds
1½	tsp ground ginger
1	tsp ground cayenne pepper

Shake all ingredients in a heavy skillet for 5 minutes, or toast in a 350-degree oven for 20 minutes. Let cool and then grind coarsely. Store in a sterilized jar, seal, and label. Refrigerate. You don't need to cook it before using.

Herbes de Provence

The French have added several herb blends to world cuisine. Probably the most famous and expensive is the imported herbes de Provence. Made up of herbs commonly grown in the soil of Provence, this herbal bouquet is marked in particular for its inclusion of highly fragrant lavender. In fact, the province is well known for this flowery herb.

You can use herbes de Provence by tying it up in tiny cheese-cloth bags, or by measuring a teaspoon or so into a tea bell and tossing it into a stew along with some red wine. It is also use suitable for use as a rub on a roast.

(Makes about 1 cup—use freshly dried herbs if available)

3	tbsp summer savory
3	tbsp thyme
3	tbsp marjoram
1	tbsp rosemary
1	tbsp basil
1	tsp sage
1	tsp fennel seed
½	tsp lavender

Mix all of the herbs well. Store the mixture in a sterilized jar, seal and label.

Italian Seasoning

The Italians have their own wonderful herb blend that is perfect for throwing into a minestrone, rubbing on a lamb roast, tossing into a cannelini bean soup, or using to season a pizza. You can add fresh minced garlic to the mixure as you use it to bring out the flavors of the green herbs.

(Makes about 1 cup)

8–12	bay leaves
3	tbsp Greek oregano
3	tbsp Italian (flat-leaf) parsley
3	tbsp thyme
3	tbsp sage
3	tbsp freshly ground black pepper
2	tbsp hot Hungarian paprika (optional—you can use less if you choose)

Crush the bay leaves until a fine powder. Mix all the ingredients together and pack in a sterilized jar, seal, and label.

Note: Dry fresh flat Italian parsley in the microwave in 30-second bursts until dry. This has better flavor than the dried curly parsley sold in glass jars. Lemon thyme plants can be grown in small containers and have wonderful flavor. Dry this herb in the microwave.

Multipurpose Sweet Spice Blend

Spice up your pies and cookies with your own spice blend. Sweet spice mixtures have been popular for centuries. Try this one as it's written, and then next time change the proportions to suit your own tastes. Add in place of the cinnamon and other spices when making a pie, or instead of the spices in a cookie recipe.

(Makes about ½ cup)

2	cinnamon sticks
2	tbsp coriander seeds
2	tbsp allspice berries
2	tsp whole cloves
1½	tbsp ground ginger
1	tsp freshly ground nutmeg

Break up the cinnamon sticks and add to the allspice, coriander, and cloves. Grind to a fine powder. Blend in the ginger and nutmeg. Pack the mixture into a sterilized jar, seal, and label.

Sources for Dried Herbs

J. Crow Company
P.O. Box 172
New Ipswich, NH 03071
Phone: (800) 878-1965

Featherfew Herbs
9 North Main Street
Farmington, NH 03835
Phone: (603) 755-2177

Penzey's Spices
18900 W. Bluemound Rd.
Brookfield, WI 53045
Phone: (800) 741-7787
www.penzeys.com

Herbal Honeys & Honey-Candied Herbs

≫ By Sara Greer ≪

For thousands of years, healers have been endlessly praising the medicinal virtues of honey. Some have also added to these virtues by infusing honey with aromatic healing herbs, producing honeys that gave a one-two punch to ailments ranging from sore throats to upset stomachs, from influenza to the grippe.

Sweet Herbal Medicine

It's relatively easy to make herbal honeys for your home medicine chest, or for your kitchen pantry. These honeys will serve a wide range of purposes, from medicinal to culinary. Furthermore, herbal honeys have important advantages as a way to administer natural medications to toddlers and older children who would otherwise resist your doctoring efforts.

(Note: Honey should never be given to children under the age of one year.) Herbal honeys also have the advantage of creating two products with a single process. The herb themselves, candied by the honey, also can be useful in cooking, healing, or beautifying.

You should begin this process by selecting the honey you want to use. Many different varieties are available, depending on the season of the year and your local area. But any type of honey will do—delicate and light orange blossom honey and dark and intensely flavored buckwheat honey both can make excellent herbal honeys. Farmers' markets are a great place to hunt for honeys, and many health food stores and grocery co-ops sell honey in bulk. Plus, there are a number of good mail-order companies that specialize in honeys—from the exotic and unusual to the plain and ordinary.

If you are feeling particularly creative, you may try to match the flavor and texture of the honey to the flavor and texture of the herb you plan to use. This way, you can achieve a more harmonious marriage in your herb and honey mixture. For example, a strong herb such as lavender matches the strength of buckwheat honey, while a lighter herb such as rose petal mates well with orange blossom honey. Or, a hearty herb such as ginger root or thyme goes best with an exotic variety like carrot honey.

When in doubt, however, about which honey will match up with a particular herb, you should generally use a fairly neutral honey such as clover or wildflower—all of which work well with most aromatic herbs. Whatever honey you select, it should be at or above room temperature and should flow freely while you are working with it. If you have chosen a thick honey or one that crystallizes easily, such as buckwheat or star thistle, you may need to warm it gently until it thins or liquefies enough to pour readily. You will need at least a cup of honey to experiment with, and a quart would not be too much to buy at one time if you are likely to try more than one herbal honey.

Preparing Your Herbs

Once you have your honey, you should begin to prepare your herbs. The best herbs to use are the strongly aromatic and woody herbs such as rosemary, thyme, hyssop, and sage; very fragrant flowers such as rose and lavender; or strongly flavored roots and seeds such as ginger root and fennel seed. Avoid moist and juicy herbs such as comfrey and borage, and tonic bitter herbs such as gentian.

You may use either fresh or dried herbs for this project, though fresh herbs yield a stronger product. Make sure before you begin that your herbs are clean; wash and rewash fresh herbs to remove impurities such as dirt. If, as with many roots, you need to wash them just prior to using, and be sure to dry them thoroughly. Small-leaved fresh herbs may be used whole or even in sprig form. Larger leaves should be chopped coarsely. With roses, the petals alone are used; remove the white areas. Lavender buds are used whole. Seeds should always be thoroughly bruised, and roots should be sliced or chopped. Dried herbs can be used as small pieces.

In general, to go with a quart of honey you will need about one to two cups of fresh herbs or one-half to three-quarters cup dried herbs. If you are using roots and seeds, use the smaller amount; if leaves and flowers, the larger amount. For smaller batches of honey, reduce the amount of herbs accordingly.

When you are ready to make your herbal honey, you will need a clean and dry quart-sized glass jar to steep the mixture in. If the inside of the jar lid is unlined metal, use a layer or two of plastic wrap between the jar lid and the jar. This will keep the honey and herbs from coming into contact with the metal. Chemicals can leach into your honey if this occurs.

Making Your Herbal Honey

Now that you've got everything assembled, choose one of the methods outlined below to make your herbal honey. Base your choice of method on the herb you're using—its type and variety, and its freshness and form (that is, leaf or seed, dried or fresh, and so on).

Cold Method for Fresh Herbs

If you are using fresh herbs, the honey should be at room temperature. Place the prepared herbs in the bottom of a clean and dry quart glass jar. Pour the honey over the herbs, taking care to leave one inch of headspace at the top of the jar to discourage overflow. Cover the jar, tuck it into a cool dark place, and leave it undisturbed for one to two months. If you are using a highly aromatic herb, such as thyme, the honey is likely to thin out and may overflow from the jar in spite of the headspace. Place a saucer or small plate under the jar to protect your shelf from overspill, and check the honey every few days.

Warm Method for Seeds, Woody Roots, and Dried Herbs

Warm the honey until it reaches about 100 degrees. Proceed as with the cold method, except allow the jar of honey and herbs to cool completely before covering it and putting it away to steep. This product takes a little longer to finish. I generally leave the mixture to steep for two or three months to give the seeds the maximum amount of time to release their medicinal qualities into the honey.

Hot Method for Fresh Roots

Gently heat the honey until it is very liquid and begins to steam slightly. Follow the details of the recipe for ginger honey given below. This usually is ready in two to three weeks.

As the mixture steeps, the honey, with its unique property of being able to draw moisture out of plants, will force all of the juices and essential oils out of the herbs you've used. Note: Many herbs in turn will thin the honey, although some (lavender, for example) will not. The honey may change color as well as texture.

If you want to taste your herbal honey now and then during the waiting period, go right ahead. Just be sure to use a clean dry spoon—not your fingers. Often a layer of herbs will float to the surface, and you may want to dig down below this. It won't hurt to stir the herbs back in when you're done.

Herbal honeys in general make a great base for syrups, and a soother for sore throat or mouth. Ginger honey is a good tonic for upset stomachs, and with added lemon juice it helps to reduce the discomfort of colds. Hyssop or sage-infused honeys are wonderful for treating cold and flu symptoms. Honey-based salves are useful for rashes and dry skin. Honey infused with a soothing herb such as lavender is a pleasant treatment for healing a burn scar, and it does not have the warming effect of an oil base. Oxymel, a mixture of honey and vinegar which often included herbs, is an ancient remedy, and herbal honeys make excellent oxymels. Herbal honey makes a useful substitute for plain honey in homemade cosmetics or soaps. And herbal honeys can be cooked with or eaten out of hand. They're also great for sweetening medicinal teas.

The shelf life of many herbal honeys is in the six-month to two-year range, depending on the moisture content of the herb used. Honey itself, having antibacterial properties, rarely spoils or molds, but added moisture naturally dilutes honey's keeping qualities. When in doubt, store the honey in the refrigerator and use it within six to twelve months. Any honey or herb that develops an off color or odor, or any other signs of mold or spoilage, should be discarded. Never taste a suspicious product!

A Byproduct of the Process: Candied Herbs

Once the honey is finished steeping, you have two options. You can simply leave it as it is, herbs and all, dipping into it as desired. On the other hand, you can warm it gently and pour it through a strainer to remove the herbs. Then set the herbs aside and bottle the honey. Any herbal honey made with fresh soft flowers or juicy roots should be stored in the refrigerator. Honeys made with dried herbs, or with fresh woody aromatics like thyme, can be stored in your pantry or on a closet shelf. If the honey crystallizes, use it in crystalline form or warm it gently until it reliquefies. If you warm it, though, I'd recommend storing it in the fridge from that point on.

Either after straining the honey, or after using it up, you'll have a batch of candied herbs to enjoy. You can use or store them just as you take them out of the honey, since they keep well refrigerated. Alternatively, you can spread them out to dry and crystallize on a sheet of waxed paper or on a plate. If you choose this second option, allow the herbs to air-dry until either they crystallize at least partially, or they reach a texture you like. Some honeys don't crystallize readily, or tend to absorb moisture from the air, and humid climates also tend to discourage crystallization—so your herbs may not actually end up covered with crystals of honey. Even so, the herbs will still dry out somewhat, and if you want this effect you should be able to achieve it. In either form, honey-candied herbs should be refrigerated.

What can you do with honey-candied herbs? You can always eat them out of hand—ginger root, angelica stem, fennel seeds, and a number of other candied herbs make delicious healthy snacks. You can also brew teas from them, especially the intensely aromatic herbs such as thyme, sage, or lavender. Candied hyssop makes a pleasant tea to soothe coughs and congestion, and candied lavender tea helps soothe a tension headache. You can also cook with the herbs. Add them to salads, salad dressings, soups, stews, and baked goods. One of the tastiest uses is to enhance a simple dough—shortbread or biscuit—with lively herbal flavors and a touch of sweetness by adding candied herbs. See the recipe for Herb Shortbread listed below for a quick and easy way to take advantage of these delicate flavors.

Recipes

Herbal honeys are a lot of fun to fix, particularly if you enjoy cooking or medicine-making. You can share the pastime with children, who love to have tasting privileges, or you can revel in some solitary creative time with your herbs and honeys. The recipes below are my personal favorites, to start you on the road to inventing your own herbal honey delicacies and remedies. Enjoy!

Ginger Honey

8   oz fresh ginger root
3   lbs honey (about 1 qt) in a glass jar
1   clean quart (or slightly larger) jar with lid
     Stockpot or large saucepan

Fill the saucepan or stockpot about 4 inches deep with warm water. Put the open jar of honey in the saucepan. Add more water if necessary to bring the depth of the water halfway up the side of the honey jar. Warm the saucepan on low heat.

While the honey heats, peel the ginger and slice it into more or less square chunks ¼ to ½ inch thick. Put it into the quart jar. By now the honey should be fairly hot and liquid. Carefully lift the honey jar out of the saucepan, dry it off, and let it stand for about 5 minutes to cool slightly. Even after cooling the jar will still be hot, so either wear oven mitts for the next step or use a ladle. Pour or ladle the hot honey over the ginger root in the quart jar. Leave about 1 inch of empty space at the top of the jar.

The ginger will rise to the top of the jar and release its juice into the honey. The level of the honey may drop slightly as hidden air bubbles emerge and rise to the top of the jar. If this happens, add a little more honey to bring the level back up to the one-inch mark. You'll have about a cup of warm honey left over which you can use for something else, perhaps a small batch of lavender honey.

Now set the jar of ginger and honey aside to cool uncovered. Once it is completely cool—that is, back to room temperature—you can put the lid on the jar. If you must cover it before you can safely put the lid on, lay a piece of muslin or a flour-sack towel over the top of the jar instead of using the lid. This will allow steam to escape. If the jar is lidded too soon, the steam will condense and drip back into the honey, significantly increasing the risk of spoilage.

Once the jar is cool and you have put the lid on tightly, turn the jar upside down. This helps blend the ginger juice into the honey, and although it seems a bizarre method it works better than stirring. Put the upside-down jar into your refrigerator. After about 24 hours, turn the jar right side up; a day later, turn it upside down again. Repeat this process every day for the next 2 weeks. At the end of this time, the ginger juice and honey will have completely blended into a fragrant liquid with the consistency of maple syrup. You can remove the now-candied ginger pieces, or you can leave them in the jar until the honey is gone. Both the ginger and the honey are ready to be used in cooking, medicine, and so on. The ginger pieces are an excellent nausea remedy for travelers or flu sufferers. Watch out, though—the ginger pieces are much hotter than you would expect. Use tiny pieces only until you get used to the strong flavor.

Herb Shortbread

1	cup butter or margarine, at room temperature
¼	cup honey (may be omitted)
2½	cups flour
2	tbsp honey-candied herbs

Cream the butter or margarine. When it is soft, cream the honey and the candied herbs into it. Stir the flour into the honey/butter mixture, beginning with the lesser amount and adding more if necessary. Mix until the flour is thoroughly incorporated and a stiff dough forms. Shape the dough into a sausage shape about 7 to 8 inches long and 1½ to 2 inches across. Wrap this in waxed paper and chill it in the fridge until it is quite firm. Slice this "sausage" into ½-inch pieces and bake on a cookie sheet at 325 degrees until just beginning to brown, about 20 to 25 minutes.

I usually use lavender or hyssop in these cookies, but you can also make a delicious savory version by using sage or thyme, omitting the ¼ cup of honey, and cutting the flour down by ¼ to ½ cup. If you have crystallized honey, this recipe is a great place to use some of it—the crystals improve the texture of the cookies.

Honey Salve

1	tbsp herbal honey
3	tbsp extra-virgin cold-pressed olive oil
¼	oz beeswax
3	drops tincture of benzoin

Warm the honey and oil together until the honey is liquid and no longer clumps to itself in the pan. Grate the beeswax into the mixture and let it melt. Take the pan off the heat and stir in the tincture of benzoin. Pour into a 2-oz salve jar. Stir the salve every

10 to 15 minutes as it cools, or more often if the honey appears to be separating out. I use a plastic chopstick for this task. When the salve becomes stiff, you can stop stirring. When it is entirely cool, cover and label the jar.

For Further Study

Herbal Antibiotics. Stephen Harrod Buhner. Storey Books, 1999.

Herbal Gold. Madonna Sophia Compton. Llewellyn Publications, 2000.

Herbal Rituals. Judith Berger. St Martin's Press, 1998.

Herbs, Partners in Life. Adele Godchaux Dawson. Healing Arts Press, 1991.

Cooking with Lovage

⪼ By Carly Wall, C.A. ⪻

My introduction to lovage (*Levisticum officinale*) occurred when I picked up a tiny plant at a garden center while I was on the road traveling years ago. I have a habit of just dropping into garden centers or nurseries whenever I travel, just on the off chance that I will discover an unusual or unique herb that I have not seen before. Most of the time, of course, I don't find any herbs. But very occasionally, I sometimes do hit the jackpot, and find a tiny nursery brimming with all kinds of exotic plants with exotic scents and lovely leaves and flowers.

On this occasion, I found lovage. I was a relative beginning gardener then, just getting into herbs, and I didn't know much about anything. The only thing I did know, at least as far as lovage was concerned, was that its name was beautiful and its leaves were dark. So, it was with a trusting heart that I decided to take the little fellow home and plant him in a place of honor in my herb garden, near the entrance to the garden very close to a walking path. I hoped that I might in time perhaps learn a little more about him.

Little did I know—the lovage grew so fast I could not keep track. It seemed one minute it was six inches high, and a few minutes later it was climbing toward six feet in height. Very quickly, I came to know that this was a plant to be reckoned with, at least in terms of growth, and that it was very lovely to look at, though I still did not know much about its background— what was it useful for, how did it taste? There wasn't much information to be found on lovage in contemporary sources; it seemed to have fallen by the wayside in usage.

The History of Lovage

In actuality, lovage is one of the world's oldest known salad greens and has been in cultivation for several millennia. Native to the Mediterranean region, it grows wild in mountainous areas of France, northern Greece, and in the Balkans. It is a perennial herb that comes from the carrot family, and was actually one of the most popular herbs during the Middle Ages. Its seeds were long used in cordials and confections, as well as in a number of medicines. The Emperor Charlemagne required it in his gardens, and most monasteries were known to plant it. Monks often placed lovage leaves in the shoes of travelers in the belief that it soothed weary feet. The colonists brought the herb to the United States. Thomas Jefferson's home and famous gardens, Monticello, has a patch of lovage growing there to this day still. After learning about this surprising herb I tried it, and eventually lovage became a staple of my kitchen, appearing in my soups and salads regularly.

Medicinal Considerations

Lovage has many uses as a medicinal herb. First and foremost, it has been used as a diuretic. The infused leaves or seeds help reduce water retention and act as deodorizers. An old remedy for an upset stomach contained lovage, brandy, and sugar. It is also said to be good for relieving skin problems, and a preparation made from the roots was added to bath water or made into a salve. This herb was helpful for rheumatism and migraine when the leaves and stalks were made into a tea, and it is said the tea is helpful in relieving stomach pains caused by gas. Lovage has also been used as an aphrodisiac or "love charm," and so has been called "love parsley," or, by extension, "lovage."

Long ago, lovage cordial was a popular drink with country people, who took it as a rememdy for sore throats. John Gerarde, the noted author and herbalist, wrote in 1597 that lovage was one of the wonder drugs of the time.

Growing and Harvesting Lovage

One or two plants of lovage are probably all you need, as a little goes a long way with this particular herb. Lovage is a perennial that grows to six feet in height, though it may die back in winter and shoot up again in the spring.

Grow lovage in full Sun or partial shade. The plant is easily propagated by seed, or by root division. But when you plant it, be sure to give it plenty of room for it will want to spread out. Place the young plant in a sunny plot in rich, well-tended soil. Lovage is a heavy feeder and will reward good soil preparation with rampant dark-green growth. If your plants have sickly looking pale-green leaves, then you need to add fertilizer to the soil. If you want to keep your plant well groomed, meanwhile, you have to cut it back regularly. This will cause a beautiful compact plant to form; however, this will hinder flower growth. If you let your lovage grow free instead, you will get beautiful yellow blooms, and in second and each subsequent year thereafter, you will also get ample and sturdy bloom stalks.

To assure yourself of bringing in a good crop of lovage, it is best to plant the seed in the very earliest of spring, as lovage requires a long cool period to germinate—usually around 70 degrees for three weeks. In setting seedlings, give much room between them—often as much as twelve feet. Work aged compost into each planting hole, water it well, and then mulch. The roots can be divided and planted in autumn to expand the lovage bed.

Lovage is a stout plant, resembling in some aspects the herb angelica. Lovage has a thick, fleshy root that grows up to six inches long and has a strong aromatic smell and taste. The thick, hollow stems grow three to six feet in height, and the plant's leaves are dark green and not unlike the leaves of a celery plant. When bruised, the scent of the leaves of a lovage plant is very strongly similar to celery with an anise undertone.

In the summer, when the seeds ripen, they should be collected. You should later sow the seeds in autumn or very early spring. The lovage plants should last several years, if well cared for. And if left to self-seed, lovage should be carefree in coming up by itself.

Cooking with Lovage

The wonderful thing about cooking with lovage is that you can flavor any food with it just as you would flavor with celery. The flavor of lovage is very similar to celery, yet it is much more concentrated. And since celery is so hard to cultivate, while lovage grows with abandon, this will ultimately make things much easier for you in your garden. Keep in mind, though, that all parts of the lovage plant can be used in cooking— including the roots and seeds. This is somewhat unusual in a plant.

You can blanch and freeze the leaves and stalks of lovage if you have more than you need, or you can dry them to save for later. To save the seeds, cut off the flowering stalks when the seeds are ripe, and dry them upside-down with a brown paper bag tied over the seed-heads. As the seeds dry and fall off, they will gather in the bag and you will not lose them. After the plant has flowered, lovage leaves become a little bitter—so be sure to harvest lovage leaves early on in the summer months if you want to use them in your cooking. The roots can be harvested from two to three-year-old plants in late autumn.

If you use lovage in cooking, always be sure to err on the light side when adding for flavor. The flavor of lovage is very strongly concentrated, therefore, a little goes a long way. Add just a pinch at first and carefully taste to see how much more may be needed.

Lovage Seeds

Use the seed like celery seed in soups, stews, sauces, or dressings. Queen Victoria commonly had a hankering for lovage seeds in candied form. They are also good added to breads or meatloaf—adding an unusual flavor to these old-fashioned traditional dishes.

Lovage Leaves

The leaves can be added fresh or dried to salads, soups, or sauces.

Lovage Stems

Young stems can be candied. The celery-like stalks are a welcome addition to soups and stews. They can survive long cooking times without losing flavor. The stems can also make naturally flavored drinking straws that are fun for the whole family to use.

Lovage Roots

The roots are good added to the stockpot, or powdered and used for a seasoning. The roots can also be chopped and dried to use in a tea.

Recipes

Lovage is very versatile. It can be used in general to flavor tomatoes, potatoes, and rice dishes. It can be tossed into soups, stews, or pasta recipes. Lovage is also good with chicken, in stuffing, or in omelets. And this is a herb that works well in recipes with many other herbs—partnering especially well with such varieties as with chives, thyme, and bayleaf.

Here are a few recipes of my favorite ways to use lovage.

Lovage Bloody Mary

1	quart tomato juice
½	cup lime juice
1½	cups vodka
1	tbsp Worcestershire sauce
1	tbsp Tobasco sauce
1	tsp black pepper
6	8-inch lovage stalk "straws"

Combine all ingredients except the lovage in a pitcher, and stir well. Pour the mixture over ice in six glasses, and garnish with the lovage straws.

Fresh Tomato Lovage Chutney

2	lb tomatoes
1	cup honey
2	tbsp peeled, chopped ginger root
2	tsp dried basil leaves
2	tsp dried lovage
1½	tsp salt
½	tsp ground cloves

Dice the tomatoes. In a medium-sized saucepan, combine all the ingredients. Over medium-high heat, bring to a boil. Reduce heat to low; cook, uncovered, about 45 minutes or until thickened, stirring frequently. Put the mixture into hot, sterilized half-pint canning jars, filling to within ¼ inch of the tops. Seal with lids and screw bands. Place the jars on the rack of a canner. Pour in enough boiling water to reach 2 inches above jar tops. Process jars in a boiling water bath for 10 minutes. With tongs, remove from canner and place on thick cloth or wire rack; cool away from drafts.

After 12 hours, test the lids to make sure they have a proper seal; remove the rings from the sealed jars, and store them in a cool, dark place.

Potato Salad with Lovage

2	lb potatoes cooked in skins, then peeled and diced
½	cup mayonnaise
½	cup sour cream
3	tbsp chopped chives
½	cup chopped fresh parsley

½   cup chopped lovage leaves

Salt and pepper to taste

1   tbsp sugar

In a small bowl, combine everything except for the potatoes. Gently toss in the potatoes to cover, then season with salt and pepper.

Lovage Vinegar

Wash some fresh lovage, and place it in a glass bottle. Cover with a good wine vinegar. Close tightly and let sit for at least a month. Decant into another container, straining it first through a cheesecloth. Use in salads, soups, or sauces to add a little zip.

Lovage Tea

Make an infusion as follows.

Place 2 or 3 teaspoons of dried lovage in a cup of boiled water. Let the infusion steep for 10 to 15 minutes, then strain the herb away. Drink 2 or 3 times a day for diuretic action and to strengthen the body. People who are either pregnant or infirm should not take this tea because of its strong diuretic action.

Chicken Lovage Soup

2   cups chicken stock

2   cups chopped potatoes

2   cups fresh corn kernels

2   cups chopped cooked chicken

½   cup finely chopped fresh marjoram

2   tsp finely chopped lovage

Salt and pepper to taste

Bring the chicken stock to a boil, add potatoes, cover, and cook until potatoes are barely tender. Add corn and cook for 5 minutes. Stir in the chicken, lovage, and marjoram. Add salt and pepper to taste. Cook at a simmer for about another 10 minutes.

Candied Lovage

American colonists, who could not run to the store to buy candy when they had a sweet tooth, made their own sweet treats out of herbs. They candied young angelica stems and ginger, and also lovage stems and seeds, too, thus preserving the herbs and bringing out their flavor in a crystal sugar shell. These are wonderful to use as dessert garnishes or as edible decorations on cakes and pastries.

Cookbooks of the 1700s recommended the following process for candying lovage.

| 1 | lb lovage stalks |
| 1 | lb granulated sugar |

The most important thing about candied lovage is to choose stalks that are young and tender. You are only able to candy lovage in April or May when the shoots are new and softly colored. Trim the young shoots into 3- or 4-inch lengths, put them into a pan, cover with water, and bring them to a boil. Drain and scrape away tough skin and fibrous threads with a potato peeler, rather as you might prepare celery.

Return the lovage to the pan, pour on the fresh boiling water, and cook until green and tender. If the shoots are properly youthful, this process will take 5 minutes or less. Drain the stalks and dry them. Put them into a bowl and sprinkle granulated sugar between layers, allowing 1 pound of sugar for every pound of lovage. Cover and leave for 2 to 3 days.

Slide the contents of the bowl into a heavy-based pan. Bring very slowly to a boil and then simmer until the lovage feels perfectly tender and looks clear.

Drain, then roll or toss the shoots on greaseproof paper thickly strewn with sugar, letting the lovage take up as much sugar as will stick to it. Then dry off the lovage—without letting it become hard—in the oven, using the lowest possible temperature. I place the stalks directly on the oven shelves (with trays underneath to catch any falling sugar) and find they need about 3 hours to completely dry. Wrap and store the candied herb after it has cooled completely.

The Herbs & Spices of India

≫ By Carolyn Moss ≪

T here are so many books, magazine articles, and television programs around today about herbs that most of us are aware that the Italians use a lot of basil and oregano and the French favor tarragon and thyme. However, when it comes to experimenting with Indian food many of us just reach for a jar of curry powder without considering what goes into it.

But in fact it is easy, and very rewarding, to make your own curry powders and other fresh spice mixes from fresh ingredients. I'd like to encourage you, by talking about some of the flavorings used commonly in India, Pakistan, and in the wonderful but troubled island off India's southern tip, Sri Lanka, to take a plunge of your own and learn more about some of the herbs and spices of this region.

You will find that many of the herbs and spices in the following list are familiar friends—though a few will likely be new to you. Although supermarkets are getting better and better in their range of exotic spices, some of you may have to use the Yellow Pages to locate some ethnic markets (try Chinese as well as Indian, Sri Lankan, or Pakistani; in parentheses I have included the Indian name of the item). If you live in a more remote location, and are unable to find Asian markets, you might want to explore mail order—a good place to locate such suppliers are the back pages of food magazines.

And just one more thing—if you don't like hot food and have an impulse to skip over this article, then please don't. Much food from the subcontinent is fragrant and spicy rather than just plain hot. The use of such foods has also been found to do wonders for the immune system—so perhaps all of our lives could all use a little spicing up from time to time.

Asafoetida (Heeng)

This is one herb that you will only find in specialist stores. I have to admit to including this item for interest value possibly more than for practical use. It is found in Asian cooking from Afghanistan and Kashmir in the north to Sri Lanka in the south. It is to be found in the form of a block of resin, and has, to the average Western nose, the most appalling smell. The irreplaceable doyen of American cookery writers, James Beard, likened it to truffles, although I would say he was being charitable. However, a pinch thrown into recipes when spices are being fried in oil adds a certain depth and authenticity to the food. It also has the property of relieving gas and flatulence and aiding digestion.

Bay (Tej Patta)

An aromatic leaf from a tree which will grow to twenty or more feet in the right conditions, bay is used in many cuisines of the world. It is normally used whole and, unlike many herbs, dries well. Occasionally, recipes will call for ground bay, in which case pound it in a pestle and mortar or grind it in a spice grinder.

Cardamom (Elaichi)

Cardamom is to be found in three forms: ground to a powder, in small pale-green pods, and, less commonly, in larger rough dark brown pods (usually found only in ethnic stores). The two forms of pod are interchangeable in recipes. They must be pounded in a pestle and mortar (or with the bottom of a bottle) to extract the seeds, which should then be lightly crushed. The pod can be included in cooking for extra flavor but must be fished out before serving. Ideally if a recipe calls for ground cardamom you would pound up some seeds yourself. Spices purchased in powdered form never give as good a flavor and deteriorate very quickly.

Cardamom is used in savory meat, vegetable, and rice dishes on the subcontinent, and is also found in sweet preparations such as rice pudding or festive candy. Interestingly, cardamom also crops up in Scandinavian baking as a cake and cookie flavoring.

Cayenne Pepper (Pisi hui lal mirch)

This is one of the hottest preparations available and is made from powdered dried red chilies of the fieriest variety. It is freely available in supermarkets and should be used in great moderation. It will, of course, be familiar to those who enjoy Tex-Mex food as well as Asian cookery. It is a product where the powdered form is the norm and perfectly acceptable.

Fresh Green Chilies (Hari mirch)

It is the use of fresh chili which has given Asian food its reputation for fighting bacteria. These chilies also contain vitamins A and C although, of course, one cannot consume huge quantities of chili. Although it is tempting to think that where a recipe calls for fresh chili, dried will do—surely it is only to add heat—there is a real difference in the freshness and vibrancy of a dish to which the fresh spice has been added. So do try to find them. There are, of course, many varieties of chili about, and, in broad terms, the larger the variety, the milder it is—with the tiny red pea chilies and the little round habanero being the fiercest. If you aren't sure, proceed with caution. And always be vigilant in handling chili—do not touch your face, especially your eyes, while working with them and for a short time afterward. Just deal with the chili and then wash your hands well when you are done.

Red Dried Chili (Sabut lal mirch)

Again, one could use powder to get the kick into a dish, but dried whole chilies gives a different spicing effect in dishes. A tip: If you are concerned about heat then cut the pod open and throw away the seeds.

Cinnamon (Dar cheeni)

Cinnamon is a very familiar spice. It is a bit unusual, however, as it comes from the bark of the cinnamon tree. Most herbs and spices are leaves or seeds and pods. Cinnamon is often found in powdered form which is fine for sweet dishes. For Indian rice and curries one needs the actual small bits of bark, which look like small hollow sticks, to be included in cooking and fished out before eating.

Cloves (Lavang)

Cloves are another Asian spice which has settled itself well into Western baking. An English Christmas cake would certainly not be complete without a pinch of clove powder. Again, for Indian cooking we want to use the whole clove, which is actually the entire tiny dried bud of the clove flower. The cloves must be removed before eating as biting on a whole one is not too pleasant an experience for the inexperienced. Indians do, however, suck on them as breath fresheners. The concentrated essential oil of cloves has slightly anaesthetic properties and is recommended (diluted and on a cotton pad) for treating toothaches.

Coriander (Dhaniya)

This lovely spice is used widely throughout the subcontinent and is found in recipes in three forms: the fresh leaves, the whole seeds, and a ground powder. The leaves are closely related to the cilantro used, of course, in Mexican food. In Asia, these are normally added near or at the end of cooking almost like a parsley garnish although with a much more pungent effect. The whole seeds can be ground at home most easily in an electric coffee or spice grinder. Where a recipe calls for whole seeds, they need to be crushed lightly before using. I would mention that coriander is extremely easy to grow from seed. It is an annual and will grow outside in the summer months anywhere in the United States (other than Alaska), and all year round in the more southerly states.

Cumin (Zeera)

Cumin can be used as a whole seed or ground into a powder. Many recipes call for the seeds to be roasted before using. This is done by placing the seeds in a small dry pan over a medium heat. Do not use any fat, and do not leave the pan unattended. Stir the seeds until they start popping and emit a lovely, spicy fragrance. Remove them from the heat and continue with your recipe or store for future use.

Curry Leaf (Kari Phulia, Kari Patta)

The curry leaf is widely used in southern India and Sri Lanka to flavor everything from egg dishes to soups and rice. It gives a citrusy, and not, as you would expect, a curry flavor. Likely, you won't find this ingredient in the supermarket. Ethnic stores may have the dried leaf, and, on occasion, you will find the fresh leaf imported from Kenya rather than from the subcontinent.

Fennel (Soonf)

Whereas in Western cooking we enjoy the bulb and leaf of the fennel, Asian recipes require only the seed. Fennel tastes like its close relative the aniseed, and is used in spice mixes as a garnish. It is also useful as a breath freshener chewed after a meal. Fennel has digestive qualities and is used in babies' "gripe water" to soothe and placate them.

Fenugreek (Methi)

With fenugreek, both the rather odd little seeds, which are almost like tiny cubes, and the fresh leaves, are called for in recipes. The leaves will probably only be found in ethnic stores, and so are out of the range of many of us. The seeds are easier to come by, and you may also come across the dried leaf—although I am not a fan of dried leaves. This ingredient, leaves or seeds, is found throughout Indian cookery and is a major ingredient in the Balti recipes which have been popular with some Indian restaurants in recent years. Balti is a strange phenomenon, which, like much Chinese food, has evolved in restaurants and has little to do with what is actually served in people's homes in India itself, although it is still rather delicious.

Garam masala

I have included this item because you may well come across it while shopping for your other herbs and spices. The words simply mean "hot spices" and are a form of authentic curry powder used in India, Pakistan, and Sri Lanka. There is no fixed recipe and each manufacturer and family will have their own version. They will normally include cardamom, cinnamon, cumin, cloves, pepper, coriander, and possibly something extra such as nutmeg. As you will see from this list, and despite the translation of the name, the effect of garam masala is aromatic rather than hot. Garam masala is sometimes simply sprinkled onto a dish after cooking.

Fresh Ginger (Adrak)

Although the dried powder is sometimes called for in Eastern cooking, more common is the wide use of fresh ginger. Ginger is a wonderful knobbly root which is peeled and grated, sliced, or pounded to a paste. It adds a great pungency and freshness to recipes. Fresh ginger also has considerable medicinal properties and, made into a tea, sweetened to taste, has been found to cure chronic sickness and nausea, such as morning sickness during pregnancy, that will not respond to any other kind of treatments.

When you buy a lump of ginger root and only want to use a small piece, plant the rest in a small pot of sandy soil on your kitchen window sill. Water from time to time. It will keep fresh—just dig up, wash, and cut off whatever you require each time. It will also sprout new knobs and may even send up leaves.

Mint (Podina)

Another ingredient which will need little introduction, mint is used occasionally as a fresh leaf. It is also used dried in many curry paste mixtures. Be sure only to use dried mint if the recipe specifically asks for it. It is generally not a good substitute for fresh. FYI—mint is one of the easiest herbs to grow in a garden or pot.

Mustard Seeds (Sarson)

We are all familiar with mustard, but here we are talking about the whole black, or dark or reddish brown, seeds of the mustard plant. They give off a marvellous flavor when fried in oil and used as directed in Indian recipes, and they are great just fried in some good oil and spinkled over salads of mixed green leaves or grated carrot.

Nutmeg (Jaiphat)

Another friend from the bakery cupboard, the whole nutmeg should always be used freshly grated in Asian food. You can even purchase darling little nutmeg graters with their own lidded box attached at the back for keeping the nutmegs in. Whole nutmegs look rather like tiny brains, particularly in cross section, and under the old Law of Similiars, where the early medicinal herbalists thought plants cured that which they most resembled, nutmeg was recommended for head problems.

Paprika

This is the Hungarian name for a form of powdered chili that is used for depth of flavor and color rather than heat. However, you may find brands labelled mild or hot, in which case just experiment according to your preference.

Saffron (Kesar)

Another unusual part of the plant is used here—saffron threads are the stamens of the saffron crocus which is grown widely in parts of northern India and Spain. It is the most expensive spice in the world by weight although a tiny box should last for a good few recipes. It gives off a beautiful yellow coloring that can be replacated by turmeric (see below). However, its flavor cannot be reproduced, so do try to use whenever possible. Recipes will say how to use the spice, whether it is to be pounded first or soaked in water or milk. Just a pinch added to good basmati rice raises a simple dish onto an altogether higher plane. Saffron is, of course, used in Western cooking—particularly in gourmet sauces and Italian risotti.

Sesame (Til)

Associated more with oriental food and burger buns, sesame seeds are readily available and are often found in sweet and savory Indian recipes, sometimes just dry roasted in a frying pan and added as a flavorful garnish at the end.

Turmeric (Haldi)

This spice is normally found preground and adds a bright yellow color to rice or curries. It has digestive properties, and although it brings a mild flavor it is mostly used for coloring. Fresh turmeric is a root and looks like a yellow, thin ginger root. It is rarely to be found in its fresh form in the West, so the powder will do just fine.

Recipes

Space forbids me giving you a lot of recipes with which to try out the above spices, but books abound in the stores and libraries—so you should easily be able to find something to suit you. Some people are put off Indian recipes by the long lists of ingredients. What I will do, then, is give you a couple of recipes which you can make up in advance and keep in your cupboard or refrigerator and then have the means to cook up something good and spicy at very short notice.

Garam Masala

1	tbsp cardamom seeds (removed from pods)
1	2-inch cinnamon stick
1	tsp cummin seeds
1	tsp black peppercorns
½	tsp whole cloves
½	tsp coriander
½	whole nutmeg seed, grated

Put all the ingredients into an electric coffee grinder and whiz until everything is finely ground. Sieve if you wish, although it is not necessary if you have managed to grind things to a reasonably fine powder. Store in an airtight jar away from heat or light.

Curry (Balti) Paste

4	tbsp coriander, ground
2	tbsp cumin, ground
2	tbsp fenugreek seeds
2	tbsp garlic powder
2	tbsp paprika
2	tbsp turmeric
5	tbsp garam masala (see above)
1	tsp bay leaf, ground

1	tsp ginger, ground
1	tsp chili powder
1	tsp black pepper
1	tsp cinnamon, powder
1	tsp asafoetida (optional)
	Vinegar
½	cup light vegetable oil

If all ingredients are already powdered, simply mix. Otherwise, mix and grind them finely. Add enough vinegar to make a thick paste. Heat the oil in a frying pan. Add the paste and fry, stirring continuously until the color has darkened and the oil separates. Store in a lidded jar making sure the paste is covered with oil. Simply use 1 or 2 tablespoons of the paste when you stir-fry meat, chicken, or vegetables, or add when a recipe calls for curry paste or powder.

Finding Out More about Asian Food

I hope this short explanation of some, although by no means all, of the ingredients of Indian cookery has tempted you to experiment. If you want more detailed recipes one of the most widely available authors to look out for is Madhur Jaffrey. She has produced a wide range of books and television programs, and your bookshop or library should be able to get hold of her books for you. One of her first books, *Indian Cookery* (Barrons Educational Series, 1983), is probably the best to start with. She has also produced vegetarian cookbooks.

The Art of Cold Maceration

≈ By Sara Greer ≈

Your best friend calls you to announce she is pregnant. After you hang up the phone, you go to your herb cupboard and get out dried calendula flowers. You place some of the flowers into a clean canning jar, and perhaps you mash them up with a pestle or the back of a spoon. Then you reach for your bottle of extra-virgin cold-pressed olive oil and pour enough over the flowers to cover them completely, plus another inch for *lagniappe*. You put a lid on the jar, label it with the date and contents, and tuck it away on a closet shelf where it will stand in cool darkness until needed.

Eight months later, a few days before the baby is due, you get down the jar of now golden oil. You lay cotton muslin over a strainer, set it over a fresh jar, and pour the maceration into it. The oil passes freely through the cloth, leaving behind any particulates. You press the flowers gently but firmly, squeezing out as much oil as you can. Eventually, when the drip of oil into the new jar has slowed and no more oil can be squeezed out, you take your harvest into the kitchen. There you divide the oil, bottling a part of it, placing the rest into a glass saucepan. You grate beeswax into the pan as it warms gently on the stove. Perhaps you add a few drops of essential oil of lavender, or a tincture of balsam poplar buds, or some angelica flower essence. When the wax has melted, you add several drops of tincture of benzoin as a preservative and pour the fresh salve into small jars. It will cool into a soft soothing substance to smooth on mother and baby's skin. The oil, too, will moisturize skin and heal minor ailments for both recipients. You add decorative labels to the jars and bottles, pack them into a pretty basket, and present it to your friend after the birth. She is delighted with your gift.

Many natural processes take place gradually, over a more or less long period of time. The gestation of a child is one; cold maceration of herbs in oil is another. Crusaders in medieval times would fill a flask with olive oil and St. John's wort flowers when they took to the road, knowing that they would have a potent red oil by the time they arrived in the Holy Land. Modern herbalists, following a slightly different road, can use cold maceration to prepare weeks or months in advance for the ailments and injuries of daily life—anticipate the colds and flus of winter with warming oil rubs begun in May, prepare for June's sunburns with violet vinegar you've been steeping since February.

Or say you decide to make a healing oil with some fresh St. John's wort from your garden. You put it to macerate in olive oil and go about your summer business. After four weeks your maceration has taken on the ruby hue of a successful fresh St. John's wort oil. As this oil is for your dog, who has developed a tendency to get infected ulcerations on her back, you want this batch to be really strong. Just filter out the herbs from the oil, put a fresh batch of herbs into a clean jar, add the oil, label it, and tuck it back onto its shelf for another month or two. In time you'll have a jar of oil that you could use as a stop light, and your dog will be feeling better just from sniffing it.

The Process

The process of cold maceration is as simple as the description above. To start, take a clean glass jar, preferably with a lined or nonmetal lid. Select your herbs, making sure they won't fill the jar more than two-thirds of the way. If you are using dried herbs, you can crush or break them up a little. If you are using fresh herbs, pack them gently down. Fresh or dried leaves and flowers may be left whole, but seeds should be bruised and roots sliced or broken up. Pour your oil over the herbs, making sure to cover them by a depth of an inch or more. If the herbs tend to float, or if you see a lot of air bubbles among them, stir the herbs into the oil with a clean nonmetal spoon or chopstick. A few tiny air bubbles are nothing to worry about, since the oil will usually percolate throughout the mass of herb.

Cover your maceration tightly. If your jar has a metal lid, put a layer of plastic wrap over the mouth of the jar to keep the maceration from contacting the metal. Label your jar with the contents and date it, putting it on a shelf in a cool dark place. In my experience closets are great, as long as they don't contain a hot water heater. You might want to check the maceration after a day or two. Some dried herbs tend to absorb a lot of oil, so depending on which herbs you have used you may need to pour more oil into the jar. On the other hand some fresh herbs may cause a very full jar to overflow, and any signs of leakage can be countered by putting a plate under the jar to catch drips.

After four to eight weeks, you can go peek at your work. Fresh herb macerations will probably be ready by now, but if you used dried herbs or really tough fresh roots you may want to leave it at least a month longer. I normally leave dry herb and seed or root macerations for up to nine months, leaves or flowers for around four months. If the oil has changed color and taken on a strong scent of the herbs, you're probably looking at a finished maceration. Many herbalists also develop a sixth sense that tells them very clearly whether something is ready or not, so if you get that familiar tug at your awareness listen to it.

The Advantages of Cold Maceration

The difference between cold maceration and other methods of extracting the properties of herbs is that cold maceration uses no added heat in the extraction process. Hot maceration uses moderate amounts of heat on the stove top to extract the herb's constituents in a few hours time. Warm maceration, which normally involves a Crock-pot or simmer-pot, uses low heat to hold the maceration at 110 to 120 degrees continuously for several days. Cold maceration extracts the plant constituents at room temperature, taking approximately one to six months depending on the herb and plant part used. It is similar to the tincturing process, but with oil as the solvent.

The unassisted process of extraction sums up the essential qualities of cold maceration. As the maceration rests on its cool dark shelf, the constituents of the plant matter percolate gradually into the oil. The oil's color, scent, and sometimes even texture change bit by bit as the weeks pass. The results are dramatically visible if you put a jar of maceration away in June and look at it next in October. That dried plantain leaf has turned the oil an intense green so dark it looks black, and the calendula maceration is an incredible orange-gold. Then there's the arnica/cayenne blend, which practically glows in the dark...

Cold maceration by its very nature has certain advantages. The primary advantage is that cold maceration maximizes the usefulness of dried herbs. Dried plant material gives up its medicine more slowly than fresh material. Over the time periods normally used in cold maceration, the oil thoroughly penetrates the dried plant matter and extracts the constituents. As long as the dried herb is still potent, you can get excellent results with cold maceration. This makes it a good technique for people who want to make their own herbal remedies but need to rely on dried herbs purchased from a shop or catalog. Plenty of urban herbalists have little or no garden and are unable to purchase fresh herbs. They can make a lot of effective medicines using cold maceration.

Another advantage is shelf life. Extraction by gradual percolation instead of by added heat doesn't "cook" the oil or plant matter. Since this reduces the risk of rancidity, it can prolong the shelf life of the product. If spoilage is one of your concerns, cold maceration can help—a properly made and properly stored cold-macerated salve can keep for as long as six to eight years. If you are using cold maceration for this reason, though, I would advise making your maceration with dried or partially dried herbs. The extra moisture content from a fresh herb would offset the keeping advantages of an uncooked product.

Cold maceration has another good point: It doesn't require much tending. This can make your life as a herbalist much easier, particularly if you travel a lot, work unpredictable hours, or have kids. Even if you're busy and stressed, you can get a cold maceration going in less than ten minutes and stash it on the closet shelf. A few months later, having ignored your maceration all the while, you can strain and bottle the oil in approximately half an hour. If something complicates your schedule at the time you had intended to filter out your oil, just leave the maceration on the shelf until you are able to finish it. Due to a series of unexpected events, I once left a jar of maceration sitting for almost two years. Not only was it still good when I filtered it, it yielded one of the best salves I've ever produced.

Cold maceration also has a couple of natural disadvantages, however. One is its mixed performance with fresh herbs. The high moisture content of some fresh herbs can result in mold or other spoilage while your maceration soaks. It does well with oily or woody herbs, such as rosemary or St. John's wort, but cold maceration is a poor method for making infused oils with soft succulent herbs like comfrey or fresh flowers. You can partially offset this by letting fresh herbs dry for a day or two before putting them into your maceration, or by floating a layer of vodka on top of the oil to soak up moisture. But frankly, your best bet is to infuse most juicy fresh herbs with warm or hot maceration instead of the cold technique. The heat drives off any extra moisture, or leaves it in a separate layer on the bottom of the pot.

Another disadvantage is that some oils don't work well as a medium for cold maceration. Any oil with a fairly short shelf life should not be used for cold maceration since the oil itself may spoil before the maceration is finished. I always use extra-virgin cold-pressed olive oil, which keeps well for a long time under the approximately 60-degree temperature in my herb closet.

Overall, cold maceration is a wonderfully flexible oil infusion technique. During my hectic summers, I need only one quiet weekend to get my whole winter's stock of oils going. I can filter them out during the year on an as-needed basis, and can easily control the strength of each maceration. Since the oils have a long shelf life, I can filter an oil in a few spare minutes and make salve out of it weeks or months later. My cold macerations fit into the changing rhythm of my life, as these oils develop at the same gentle steady pace as the year itself—the same pace that creates the rhythms of birth, growth, and death in the plant realm.

For Further Study

Handmade Medicines: Simple recipes for herbal health. Christopher Hobbs. Interwave Press, 1998.

The Herbal Medicine Cabinet. Debra St. Claire. Celestial Arts, 1997.

Herbs for Health

Herbal Antioxidants

⤳ By Mary Czap ⤶

W e have all noticed the "rusting apple" phenomenon. That is, you take a bite of an apple, set it aside for some reason, and the return to it later to find the flesh of the fruit has turned an unappetizing and dull brown color. The oxidation of the apple is a good metaphor for what can happen to our cells when they are assaulted by free radicals.

Free radicals are unstable oxygen molecules that have lost an electron. In an effort to seek out another electron to pair up with, free radicals wreak destruction by damaging cell membranes and tissues and by negatively reconfiguring our DNA. This havoc can eventually cause cancer, heart disease, and overall body entropy. That is, in plain English, our bodies start to rust.

The Good News

There is hope, however, in the human battle against oxidation. Nature has provided us with an array of herbs and plants that counter the damage caused by free radicals. These plants, known as antioxidants, are heart-healthy because they prevent the oxidation of the LDLs (low density lipoproteins), or "bad" cholesterol, present in the body. Antioxidants strengthen arterial walls while preventing the platelet clumping that generally leads to arterial blockage and heart disease.

Fortunately, one need not trek to parts unknown to include powerful antioxidants into your diet. In fact, some of the most effective tools in fighting free radicals, heart disease, and general bad health are available at your local supermarket. The following foods and herbs are among the most powerful antioxidants available to general consumers.

Garlic

Garlic is famous for its ability to ward off vampires, but aside from this garlic is a redolent seasoning. Neither a spice, herb, nor vegetable, garlic can be used as all three. A member of the lily family, *Alium sativum*, or pejoratively "the stinking rose," has been used throughout the world for culinary and medicinal purposes for 5,000 years. It was written about in Sanskrit, the earliest known written language, and it has sometimes been called the second most popular spice in all of North America, after pepper.

Garlic was grown in the Hanging Gardens of Babylon, and some was even found in King Tut's tomb. Workers on the great pyramids in Egypt were fed garlic to increase their stamina. During both World Wars field surgeons used it to arrest gangrene. In 1944, chemist Chester Cavalitto identified the fragrant compound in garlic called allacin and proved it was a highly effective antibiotic. Tests have shown garlic is a powerful germ killer. The microbes that garlic can wipe out include botulism, tuberculosis, staph, pneumonia, and various parasites. Cooking neutralizes allacin so to get the most out of its powerful properties eat it raw whenever possible.

An analysis by the USDA proves garlic acts as an antiseptic, fights infection, thins the blood, reduces cholesterol, controls triglycerides, and acts as a decongestant and expectorant. According to medical experts there is evidence garlic is actually capable of inducing tumor regression. Further studies are currently being conducted by the American Lung Association.

Green Tea

Several years ago, a landmark study found that while Japan had more smokers per capita than any other country, Japanese men had the lowest incidence of lung and esophageal cancer in the world. Scientists were baffled by this fact until research found that the common denominator was green tea.

Recent studies have found a potent antioxidant found in green tea called EGCG (epigallocatechin gallate) which inhibits an enzyme that cancer cells need to grow. Black tea also contains EGCG; but in much lower concentrations. Another antioxidant found in both black and green tea are known as catechins. These are flavonoids—compounds that occur naturally in plants, citrus fruits, tea, and wine. Green tea is also high in vitamin K, a nutrient needed for normal blood clotting. Both black and green teas contain hundreds of compounds called polyphenols. These are natural antioxidants that neutralize the renegade oxygen molecules rampaging our cells. These polyphenols prevent cholesterol from oxidizing our blood vessels five times more effectively than vitamin C.

In experiments at Case Western University School of Medicine in Cleveland, researchers have seen tea stop cancer at every stage in its life cycle. If you are sensitive to caffeine, don't worry. Decaffeinated green tea has only a slightly lower level of polyphenol content than regular green tea.

Carotenoids

Carotenoids in vegetables act under the same premise as polyphenols do in tea. All yellow, orange, and red vegetables are healthy sources of natural anticarcinogenics. These vegetables include cantaloupe, carrots, kale, leafy greens, oranges, peaches, pumpkin, spinach, sweet potatoes, and tomatoes.

Ginko Biloba

Imported from mainland China in the 1700s, this herb is mentioned in Chinese texts dating back 3,000 years. While many folks use it to improve their cognitive ability or to prevent onset dementia, ginko is thought to derail free radical damage through its abundant flavonoids and terpenoids.

Elder Flower

Used in ancient times as a compound to induce menstruation, this herb is rich in two flavonoids, quercetin and rutin, and is an extraordinary antioxidant.

For Futher Study

Nature is abundant with healing plants and herbs. The following titles are good sources for further study.

The Honest Herbal, A sensible guide to the use of herbs and related remedies. Varro E. Tyler. Pharmaceutical Products Press, 1992.

Jude's Herbal Home Remedies. Jude Williams. Llewellyn Publications, 1998.

PDR For Herbal Medicines, 1st edition. Medical Economics Company, 1999.

Herbal Care for Expecting Mothers & for Infants

⫷ By D. J. Cobb ⫸

As an expecting mother's belly swells with the promise of new life, her garden grows green and abundant with herbs that bless her and her child through this cycle. That is, through the stages of pregnancy a good gardener will bend and weed, nurture and harvest her plant, thus stretching and strengthening the birthing muscles, and sharing the peace of the garden with the growing fetus. Cultivating a fertile garden heals and blesses the life-giving process, and assures that the child will be healed and blessed by the same herbs and entities that care for the mother—comfrey, calendula, and chamomile.

The following article details the health-giving use of three common garden herbs for expecting mothers and young infants. Using comfrey, calendula, and chamomile during pregnancy and with your infant can bring a wealth of healing, beauty and abundance, joy and radiance, and calm and peace to your life.

For internal use, teas and infusions are recommended. For external use, ointments, compresses, and oil infusions are recommended. However, because of their concentrated properties, essential oils are not recommended for use during pregnancy or with infants, unless properly diluted.

Comfrey *(Symphytum officinale)*

Standing tall and strong in the back of the garden, mighty comfrey forms a rustling prickly barrier that deters local wildlife. Blooming from May to September, comfrey's purple-blue flowers attract bees and butterflies, drawing beauty and abundance to the garden. Each spring it returns magically, poking small shoots up through the chaff of old stalks. Containing allantoin, comfrey aids in the rebuilding and regeneration of skin cells. It naturally heals, soothes, and repairs rashes, bumps, bites, and wounds. The folk name for comfrey hints at the powers it possesses: "All Heal and Knitbone."

While oral ingestion of comfrey during pregnancy is not recommended, topical application of ointment, infusion, bath, or poultice is useful and safe. Used on the belly during pregnancy, comfrey root ointment soothes and strengthens skin, enabling it to expand while reducing stretch marks. Comfrey root ointment strengthens the aureola and nipple in preparation for breast-feeding, and it helps heal and soothe caked or sore nipples once your milk is in. For babies, comfrey root ointment is a soothing blessing, providing relief and healing from diaper rash burns and chaff.

Comfrey leaf is used less frequently, as it is not as rich in allantoin and therefore has a less potent healing capacity.

Calendula or Pot Marigold
(Calendula officinalis)

Spread throughout the garden is self-seeding calendula. Its hardy orange flowers bloom continually from late spring through early frost, bringing joy and radiance to the garden. Ever fertile, calendula seeds scatter and will sprout the following year wherever they have fallen. Calendula is very abundant in fertility and versatility, making it a brilliant blessing for mother and child.

The edible flowers of calendula brighten up salads—brilliant orange adorning the greens. It can be added to oils, bringing a warm copper glow to salad dressings. As a healing herb, calendula possesses remarkable strength and versatility and is known for help it lends in calming and soothing irritated skin and tissue. During pregnancy, calendula ointment is excellent for soothing stretching belly skin and for calming rashes caused by raging hormones.

An ointment made from calendula is excellent for strengthening nipples during pregnancy and healing cracked nipples caused by breast feeding. For babies, calendula ointment is gentle and calming, easing skin irritations such as cradle cap and diaper rash. With its antiseptic, antibacterial, antiviral, and antifungal properties, calendula is valuable externally as a wound healer and in preventing infection.

Chamomile *(Chamomilla recutita)*

Delicate chamomile scents the garden with soft promise. Generally blooming from late spring to early fall, the golden buttons of chamomile open into delicate white flowers resembling daisies. Chamomile brings calm and peace to the garden and carries these properties into healing work. Chamomile is an excellent remedy for ailments requiring healing, soothing, calming, and brightening. As a soother and calmer, in fact, there are few herbs that parallel chamomile. It promotes sleep, relieves pain, and facilitates mental and emotional relaxation.

During pregnancy, mild chamomile is a calming tea to be sipped morning and night. It helps overcome morning sickness, calm a delicate stomach, and promote a sound night's sleep. While breast feeding, chamomile is recommended for both mother and child to promote calm and relaxation. Excellent for colic, indigestion, and diarrhea, chamomile is a soothing and calming influence for the delicate digestive systems of babies. Its anodyne (pain relieving) qualities make chamomile a wonder for teething infants. The healing properties of chamomile are antifungal, antibacterial, anti-inflammatory, and anti-allergenic. Taken internally as a tea or infusion, chamomile acts as a relaxant, calming the digestive system. It dispels nausea and has a mildly sedative effect on the nervous system.

Used externally as an ointment or oil infusion, chamomile has emollient and anti-allergenic qualities, making it invaluable for use with babies and nursing mothers.

Herbal Remedies During Pregnancy

Pregnancy brings an abundance of changes—physical ones as a mother grows large and ripe; emotional ones as they flux and change with the hormones and feelings of pregnancy; and spiritual ones as they come into conscious contact with creation and the new life cradled within them. Through the centuries, women have long turned to herbs for assistance with minor ailments associated with pregnancy. Follows are some of the more common remedies used through the ages.

Hair

Many women experience changes to their hair during a pregnancy. Due to stress on the body and an abundance of hormones, hair can thin, become dry and brittle, or exhibit a lack of luster and shine. Most hair care products on the market contain numerous artificial and harmful chemicals, but herbal remedies that are natural and nontoxic can generally protect you and your growing child.

To guard against hair thinning and hair loss, use a rosemary rinse after shampooing, and leave the rosemary in the hair. Gently massage the scalp to promote good circulation, and avoid perms or chemical sets. To create the illusion of thicker hair, try braiding the hair at night off of the top of your head, and release the braid in the morning. Kinky hair appears full and robust and will cover any thinning. To add color and luster to your hair without chemicals, use a chamomile rinse to brighten blond and red hair. A rosemary rinse will add warmth and brightness to brown and black hair. Natural henna can also be used safely without concern for the child you are carrying.

Hemorrhoids

Weight gain and the added pressure of the fetus in the abdomen will often cause hemorrhoids to develop. Herbal sitz baths are effective in relieving and healing hemorrhoids. To reduce the pain and swelling of hemorrhoids, and to stop bleeding, apply Caring Comfrey Root Ointment carefully to the delicate tissue after each bath.

Morning Sickness

Hormonal changes and low blood sugar during early pregnancy can cause morning sickness. Drinking a sweet tea of chamomile before rising can calm the agitated stomach, providing nausea relief. Try to eat small meals rich in proteins and complex carbohydrates.

Pregnancy Rash

Some women develop abdominal and chest rashes during pregnancy. In the first trimester, the liver is actively working to process the increased levels of hormones in your system. In the second trimester, with a decease in the amount of hormones being secreted, the liver often continues to overfunction, causing a rash that is itchy, uncomfortable, and sometimes painful. To soothe the raw and irritated skin, immerse yourself in a soothing oatmeal and chamomile bath, and apply Calming Calendula Ointment after.

Perineal Pain, Stretching, and Tearing

The perineum can be massaged frequently prior to labor to soften and strengthen the tissue. Use comfrey-infused oil or comfrey ointment to massage and stretch the perineum. During labor, warm comfrey compresses can both soothe and encourage the stretching of the perineum.

Stretch Marks

As a mother grows ripe and round, her skin stretches to accommodate the growing fetus. Pregnant women often develop dark red or purple marks around breasts, belly and hips, caused by the stretching of skin. With proper nourishment and lubrication we can prevent or reduce stretch marks.

A diet rich in vitamins A, C, and E can help to reduce the effects of stretch marks. Vitamin A aids in the growth and repair of body tissues. It helps keep skin in a smooth, soft, disease-free state, and helps protect the mucous membrane. Good herbal sources of vitamin A include comfrey, nettles, raspberry leaf, cayenne, and paprika. Good food sources of vitamin A include leafy greens, yellow and orange vegetables, eggs, whole milk, and lettuce.

Vitamin C helps maintain collagen which is crucial to the formation of connective tissues in skin. It helps in wound healing and infection fighting, and keeps tissues elastic. Vitamin C also aids vitamins A and E.

Herbal sources of vitamin C include comfrey, red clover, rosehips, dandelion greens, nettles, and parsley. Food sources of vitamin C include citrus fruits, pineapple, tomatoes, leafy greens, and potatoes.

Vitamin E protects tissues from abnormal breakdown. It helps in the formation and function of red blood cells, muscles, and other tissues. It strengthens capillary walls and helps prevent scar formation. It especially increases the elasticity and expandability of skin and vaginal tissues, aiding the effective function of full-term pregnancy hormones. Herbal sources include raspberry leaf, rosehips, seaweed, and alfalfa. Food sources include whole grains, wheat germ, vegetable oils, and lettuce. Good quality vitamin E capsules or oil can also be used as a good natural source.

Other remedies useful for preventing or reducing stretchmarks include Caring Comfrey Root Ointment and stretch mark ointment, available in many herbal or health food stores in most areas.

Sore Breasts

Prior to giving birth, use herbal remedies to prepare your skin. In the last month of pregnancy, strengthen and prepare the tissues by regularly rubbing your nipples with comfrey ointment or warm comfrey-infused almond or olive oil.

Postpartum Herbal Remedies

After birthing, a mother needs the care and comfort of nature in order to heal and recover. Herbal remedies and ointments can help with a large number of postpartum ailments and minor needs.

Exhaustion

Birthing babies is hard work. After expending vast energy on labor, many women are exhausted and depleted of vital energy. To calm nerves and to facilitate relaxation after giving birth, drink chamomile tea. Several cups will promote sleep. A gentle massage oil infused with lavender, or Pregnancy Pick-Up Massage Oil, will bring comfort and calmness.

Perineal Pain, Stretching, and Tearing

To relieve the discomfort of perineal tearing or stretching, use a sitz bath containing sea salts and comfrey leaf. Sea salt is naturally antiseptic, and the allantoin in comfrey promotes healing. After bathing, apply oil infused with goldenseal, yarrow, or rosemary to prevent infection and lessen pain.

Vitamin C can help prevent the tearing of the perineum, and can also raise resistance to infection. Vitamin C also assists in wound healing and infection fighting, and it keeps skin and vaginal tissues elastic.

Sore Breasts

After the baby arrives there are several painful conditions that can afflict the breasts. All can be eased with herbs.

For engorged breasts, cold compresses can provide relief and contain enlargement. Keep the baby feeding. Though uncomfortable, this is one of the best remedies for engorgement. A hot compress of comfrey leaves can help to draw the breast and establish proper flow. Sore or cracked nipples is a common effect of breast feeding.

Use Caring Comfrey Root Ointment to soothe nipples, and use vitamin E oil to heal them. Apply oil or ointment liberally after nursing. In general, you should use only a natural source of pure vitamin E. Remember to wipe away any residue of oil or ointment before breast feeding again, enabling your baby to securely latch onto the nipple. Caring Comfrey Root Ointment heals any cracks to the skin. Calming Calendula Ointment soothes dry, rough skin. Another traditional remedy is to rub a small amount of breastmilk into your nipples each time after breast feeding.

Herbal Remedies For Infants

Infants mostly require the comfort and care of their parents, but they can also benefit from the continuing care and nurturing of nature. Many herbal remedies and ointments bless the baby with a natural source of comfort and relief for common ailments. Be sure to dilute any herbal infusions you give to an infant.

Colic

A tea made of chamomile is helpful in relieving colic. It can be consumed by the breastfeeding mother, or bottle-fed as a soothing supplement for colicky babies.

Cradle Cap

After gently bathing the baby in Baby's Blessing Bath, smooth Calming Calendula Ointment on the area where cradle cap is prevalent. Gently loosen the flakes of dried skin when they soften and wipe them away.

Diaper Rash

While all babies' bottoms are prone to diaper rash, the use of disposable diapers makes diaper rash more prevalent. Consider using nondisposable diapers until the rash has cleared, and use herbal remedies to soothe the inflamed skin.

When bathing the baby, use oatmeal and chamomile bath to soothe and cool the hot red rash. When you are done, pat dry the baby's bottom and gently apply Caring Comfrey Root Ointment or chamomile and lavender-infused oil to the irritated or abraded area.

Eye Irritations

New babies are prone to eye irritations as they acclimatize to their new environment outside the womb. To remedy eye irritation, brew an infusion of chamomile leaf, then cool and strain the infusion. Use the warm fluid to rinse the baby's eyes, and use the otherwise discarded herbs as a compress to soothe.

Hair

When we bathe the gentle skin of the newborn, we must be conscious of the needs for natural, nontoxic products. A baby's hair can be washed with a mixture of oatmeal and a chamomile infusion. This is cleansing and calmingly gentle to the baby's hair and scalp.

Teething

Chamomile provides pain relief and soothing calm for teething babies. It can be made into a tea and sipped by the mother during breast-feeding to pass on to her child, or brewed and cooled and bottled to be given to the baby. Alternately, chamomile tea can be frozen into ice cubes and rubbed gently on the gums of teething babies to provide a soothing effect from its cold temperature and the magic of chamomile.

Herbal Recipes

The following recipes help mothers and infants in coping with their minor birthing-related ailments.

Herbal Infusions

To make the herbal infusions necessary in the following recipes, place one ounce of herb in a large jar. Fill the jar with boiling water, then place a lid on the jar and allow herbs to infuse fifteen to thirty minutes.

Variations

Roots: Use dried roots (approximately one big handful) and a pint-sized jar. Let infuse for eight hours.

Leaves: Use dried leaves (two and a half handfuls) and a quart jar. Let infuse for four hours.

Flowers: Use dried flowers (three handfuls) and a quart jar. Let infuse for two hours.

Many herbs, such as chamomile and calendula, are delicate and should infuse for no more than thirty minutes.

Baby's Blessing Bath

½   cup powdered milk

1   tbsp cornstarch

3   drops essential orange oil

1   cup calendula infusion

Mix into runny paste. Use 1 tablespoon of mix for a bassinet, or ¼ cup in the bath.

Baby Shampoo

¼   cup ground oatmeal

     Chamomile infusion

Mix enough chamomile infusion to moisten the oatmeal into a runny paste. Use it to lather the baby's head. Rinse completely afterwards.

Chamomile Hair Rinse

Make a chamomile infusion, making sure not to let it sit longer than 30 minutes. Rinse your hair with the infusion after shampooing. Leave the rinse on to dry.

Rosemary Hair Rinse

Follow the above recipe for chamomile hair rinse, substituting rosemary for chamomile. Use the infusion to rinse hair after shampooing. Leave the rinse on to dry.

Herbal Oil Infusions

Harvest herbal leaves or roots at the peak of their potency. Be sure to thoroughly clean the roots using a soft dry brush, but do not wash leaves or roots.

Coarsely chop plant materials and fill clean dry jars with them. Pour oil over chopped herbs, filling the jars. Olive and almond or a mix of the two are commonly used as infusion oils. Seal, label, and store the oil at room temperature for 6 weeks. Strain oil from plant materials using cheese cloth or a clean thin cotton cloth. Dispose of the plant material, and store the oil at room temperature or refrigerate.

Baby Massage Oil

Using the recipe above, put equal parts chamomile flowers and lavender flowers into the jar of oil to infuse. Add 4 drops of geranium essential oil. When ready, warm a small amount of the oil in your palms to gently massage into your baby's delicate skin.

Calendula Infused Oil

Using the recipe for herbal oil infusions above, place coarsely chopped calendula flowers into the jar of oil. The calendula flowers should be harvested at the peak of their bloom, and used fresh or carefully dried and stored for later use.

Chamomile and Lavender Infused Oil

Using the recipe for herbal oil infusions above, place equal parts chamomile and lavender flowers into the jar of oil to infuse. Follow the directions for finishing and storing.

Comfrey Root Infused Oil

Using the recipe for herbal oil infusions above, place coarsely chopped comfrey root into a jar of oil to infuse. The comfrey roots should be harvested when the leaves of the plant have died back at the end of the active growing season, when the cold weather sets in. Thoroughly clean the roots using a soft dry brush before adding to the oil.

Perineum Massage Oil

Using the recipe for herbal oil infusions from the previous page, first place coarsely chopped comfrey root in a jar of oil to infuse. Use the infusion daily to massage the perineum, stretching the area with your two index fingers as you do so.

Your partner can do this massage for you as well—it is best done using two thumbs to provide a larger, softer surface of contact with this delicate area of the body. Stretch the perineum until it tingles.

Pregnancy Pick-up Massage Oil

Using the recipe for herbal oil infusions from the previous page, first place equal parts chamomile and lavender flowers in a jar of oil to infuse. Add four drops rose essential oil and 4 drops geranium essential oil. Have a partner or friend gently massage this oil into your back and thighs to alleviate any nagging aches, pains, or tiredness, and generally to uplift your flagging energy level.

Herbal Ointments

Ointments can be easily made from infused oils.

Basic Ointment

4   oz infused oil

1   tbsp beeswax

1   small widemouthed ointment jar

     Jar label

Place oil and beeswax in a small saucepan at low heat, until the wax is melted. Pour the liquid into the ointment jar. Allow the wax and oil mixture to cool until it solidifies. Label the ointment and store at room temperature or refrigerate.

Calming Calendula Ointment

Follow the recipe for a basic oinment as on previous page. Use calendula flower oil as the infused oil.

Caring Comfrey Root Ointment

Follow the recipe for a basic oinment as on previous page. Use comfrey root oil as the infused oil.

Stretch Mark Ointment

Follow the recipe for a basic oinment as on previous page. Use comfrey root oil as the infused oil, and add 20 drops of orange essential oil and 4 tablespoons of cocoa butter to the oil base.

Apply this ointment daily to your belly, breasts, and thighs, massaging gently but thoroughly. In general, after a warm bath or shower is an ideal time; this is a comforting activity to share with your partner.

Herbal Sitz Bath

Infuse 4 ounces of dried herbs in 8 cups of boiling water. Allow to steep for 8 hours. Strain plant material from the liquid. Pour the liquid into a shallow basin. Sit in this for 15 minutes several times each day.

Hemorrhoids Sitz Bath

Follow the recipe for a herbal sitz bath as above. Use comfrey root as your dried herb, and add a few drops of witch hazel to the water.

Perineum Sitz Bath

Follow the recipe for a herbal sitz bath as above. Use comfrey leaf as the dried herb, and add 1 cup of sea salt to the water.

Postpartum Calming Sitz Bath

Follow the recipe for a herbal sitz bath as on the previous page. Use 2 ounces of comfrey leaf, 1 ounce of lavender flowers, and 1 ounce of chamomile flowers as the dried herb in the bath.

Oatmeal and Chamomile Bath

For this bath, pour 3 cups of boiling water over 1 cup of oatmeal and 3 tablespoons of chamomile flowers. Allow this mixture to steep for 10 full minutes. Then, using a piece of cheesecloth or gauze, strain the flowers and oats out of the fluid, and tie the cloth firmly. Pour the fluid into your bath as the water runs, adding water to make the appropriate amount and temperature to bathe in. Take a moment to float the cloth containing the oats and chamomile in the bath water, and then squeeze it frequently to release more of the infused herbs and oatmeal.

Skin Itch Cream

¼   cup cocoa butter

1   tbsp chamomile infused oil

1   tbsp calendula infused oil

1   tsp vitamin E oil

Gently heat the cocoa butter in a sauce pan until it is melted. Remove it from heat, and add all the other ingredients. Mix the mass gently, and pour it into a clean wide-mouthed glass container. Label the containter, and store it in a cool dry place. When you belly and breast skin is itchy or irritated, take out and smear on as needed.

For Further Study

Aromatherapy for the Healthy Child: More than 300 natural, non-toxic, and fragrant essential oil blends. Valerie Ann Worwood. New World Library, 2000.

Field Guide to Medicinal Plants. Steven Foster and James A. Duke. Houghton Mifflin, 1990.

Herbal Gold. Madonna Sophia Compton. Llewellyn Publications, 2000.

Jude's Herbal Home Remedies. Jude Williams. Llewellyn Publications, 1998.

Wise Woman Herbal for the Childbearing Year. Susun Weed. Ash Tree Publishing, 1985.

Taking Business Stress in Stride with Flower Essences

≫ By Leeda Alleyn Pacotti ≪

A s a prelude to the twenty-first century, the 1990s gave us a turbulent ride into what some have glibly dubbed "a new business paradigm." While many of us prefer to reserve judgment, no one would describe the cataclysmic upheavals of massive lay-offs, the demise of middle management, kaleidoscopic corporate mergers, and the mushroom-like growth of dot-com companies as the business-as-usual of the previous ninety years. Employees on all levels, including some formerly untouchable executives, are now reeling from one surprising sandbag blow to the gut after another—as they lose their positions without warning, are promoted beyond their abilities, or are forced to compete amidst a burgeoning class of entrepreneurial scramblers.

A Legacy of Stress

Although no particular catchphrase or buzzword has yet succeeded in capturing the flavor of these strenuously busy years, one term worked its way into business, health, social, and marital conversations concerning stress: the "age of technology." That is, we are living in an age in which all positive meanings of stress—as emphasis, accentuation, or importance—have left us, and instead we are overwhelmed with a legacy of pressure, strain, and tension.

In recent years, two stress-related health conditions have gained prominence in medical diagnosis—migraine headaches and panic attacks. Previously, diagnoses of migraines often went with specific aberrant mental conditions or certain life phases, such as the teen years or menopause. Meanwhile, the insidious panic attack, which strongly resembles a heart attack in the placement and intensity of pain, was sloughed off as an hysterical reaction to the new pressures of workplace and career, primarly experienced by women. Health practitioners later observed that the panic attacks signalled an increased heart-attack risk in women, and so this disorder has become an important signal of a mental state which eventually can impinge on the body.

In reality, though, carefully utilized stress becomes an excellent tool by which we can confront our poor habits and make a conscious effort to change them. As such, we have never been "plagued" by stress, and indeed are not now. When we lift a grocery bag or toddler, when we push ourselves to jog an entire mile rather than run-walk, or while we exercise determination to maintain patience through a complicated task, we are simply acting out a directive to live out our potential.

Distress, meanwhile, which masks itself as stress, is the real culprit, receiving energy from those difficult moments we face throughout the business day. Distress gains stature and momentum in our minds, as we habitually replay the repulsive feelings it brings. Unfortunately, such habitual thinking, which we believe will remind us to avoid the same problem, succeeds in becoming a self-fulfilling prophecy the moment we encounter any circumstances similar to the ones that tend to cause us distress. That is, anyone who was badly unnerved and upset over a music recital in childhood may come to find all forms of public presentation an impossible agony in all circumstances. For those who dealt with mentally bombastic teachers or parents, they may find it difficult to relax and present themselves during an annual review of employment or before an interviewing panel. These repetitions of distress become a trial of control over anxiety and agitation. This can affect performance of day-to-day responsibilities on the job and create a vicious reinforcement of disquiet, worry, anguish, and misery in afflicted individuals who have yet to overcome their fears and worries.

These broad examples mirror the pioneering conclusion of Dr. Hans Seyle, who first studied stress in the 1930s, during which he found that "fight-or-flight" reactions, habitually triggered by repetitive emotions and life situations, seriously debilitate the nervous system. Furthermore, as these mental states and emotions take prominence in our thinking and reactions, they exact a desperate toll on our lives outside the workplace, contaminating our opinions, spoiling casual conversation, and damaging personal relationships. While the industrial world went into high gear over technology and vied for thinly veiled global dominance, mainstream health practices lagged in finding safe interventions for these ever-more-common mental difficulties.

The Discovery and Development of Flower Remedies

Fortunately for all of us who suffer in one degree or another from various distress-related disorders there is a natural and easy remedy available in the form of flower essences. In 1930, Dr. Edward Bach (pronounced "batch") withdrew from his homeopathic practice in London after observing the malingering effects of psychological shock suffered by soldiers returning from World War I. For the next six years, Dr. Bach occupied himself with a study of the role of emotions and attitudes on disease, and in time he developed thirty-eight essences from wildflowers growing in the English countryside, as well as one remedy mixed in one combination formula.

Using whole blossoms of each wildflower, Dr. Bach prepared a water infusion to capture the essences. Thereafter, he diluted the infusion once or twice, in a process somewhat resembling the potentization, or diluent, processes of making homeopathic remedies. Ultimately, alcohol—usually brandy—was added, as a preservative.

With Dr. Bach's death in 1936, at age 50, his formulae for various wildflower remedies went with him, thus creating a provocative mystery for future seekers. Except for the notes of his biographer, indicating his sensitivity toward plant form, growth, and habitat, Dr. Bach's few writings give no clue as to whether he delved into extensive trial-and-error or relied on an extraordinary insight. Furthermore, we are also left with no clear understanding as to why Dr. Bach believed that the essences of flowers would have any strong impact or effect on the emotions of humans.

Beyond the initial discoveries of Dr. Bach, modern research has begun to extend the scope of essences to encompass the wildflowers of North America. Today, a review of each candidate wildflower includes a plant study, incorporating the information from the notes of Dr. Bach's biographer, with clinical and therapeutic trials to verify the efficacy of each new essence. At this time, there are 103 North American wildflower essences, which, added to the original thirty-eight Bach English essences, makes for a wide-ranging treatment for a variety of emotional distresses and ills.

How Flower Essences Work

Each essence from a wildflower works as a vibrational remedy. That is, like light and sound, scents from flowers can evoke feelings or states of thought. Because feelings and thoughts have a direct impact on our autonomic processes—our breathing, pulse rate, and so on—we can observe the ultimate reaction to an essence and try to determine its health-giving properties.

A flower essence is taken into the body and used to settle and balance emotional states and energy fields, but without discernible effect on biochemistry. As mentioned earlier, the preparation of flower essences and homeopathic remedies have some things in common, but, unlike homeopathic remedies, flower essences do not generally stimulate physical healing. The concept of physical healing also exposes the difference between flower essences and herbal remedies. Herbs are selected for specific physical symptoms, while flower essences are chosen to treat emotional and mental symptoms.

Although flower essences are too dilute to have a physical effect on the body or a physiological process, each carries a subtle potency that acts on the various energy fields of the body. These energy fields, or flows—generally described as "chi" in the Orient, and "vital force" in the West—are what cause the animation of physical matter, or the state of being alive. During life, the energy fields continually influence mental states, emotions, and the sense of physical well-being or equilibrium. This mind-body connection, so poorly understood, is now a rich field of research to discern how we become ill and how we make ourselves well again.

Researchers who have investigated Dr. Bach's work cannot explain how he conceived the role of flower blossoms as factors in emotional and mental well-being. However, from a vibrational point-of-view the essences create an equilibrium or balance in the emotional or mental inner environment. A feeling or a way of thinking is not nullified or ended. Instead, the mind attains a neutral objectivity, able to review the validity of the emotion or feeling, through a rational process of inner debate about other ways to feel or think. Ultimately, the mind can reach a new conclusion about an emotion or thought, which causes the break-up of habitual response. As the habitual response eventually breaks apart, the physiological activities it triggers stop, permitting affected parts of the body to rest and commence self-healing.

Choosing Flower Essences for Workplace Woes

Over the last sixty-five years, flower essences have produced undeniable emotional alterations and targeted specific triggers in countless people willing to try them. As mentioned before, the general descriptives of anxiety, nervousness, stress, and tension commonly name the wide-ranging emotions to which we have become accustomed in the modern workplace.

The following brief indications can help you decide which flower essence suits your situation. While not a complete list, the essences suggested are intended to treat the most commonly described feelings or mental states that we encounter in the workplace. Each essence is marked to indicate whether it is the Bach English (E) or North American (NA) system.

Anxiety

Elm (E)—Perfectionism, especially the fear of letting others down.

Garlic (NA)—Chronic worry, strain, flushed face.

Golden Yarrow (NA)—Performance anxieties, often felt as stomach cramping.

Larch (E)—Paralyzing anxiety and fear of failure.

Mimulus (E)—Timidity; fretfulness and nervousness over daily life.

Nicotiana (NA)—Anxiety masked by a cool exterior.

Nervousness

Chamomile (NA)—Emotional tension felt in the stomach.

Cherry Plum (E)—Nervousness over losing control.

Cosmos (NA)—Rapid speech patterns; speaking and thoughts are out of synch.

Lavender (NA)—Frayed nerves; tension.

Vervain (E)—Frayed nerves; chronic overachieving.

Stress

Aloe Vera (NA)—Burn-out; overwork.

Cherry Plum (E)—Fear of a nervous breakdown.

Corn (NA)—Overwhelmed by crowds and city life.

Dill (NA)—Overwhelmed when starting new projects.

Elm (E)—Overwhelmed from too much responsibility.

Five-Flower Combination or "Rescue Remedy" (E)—Extreme stress; life threat; taking the first step into a new and unknown venture.

Hornbeam (E)—Lack of energy to carry on.

Impatiens (E)—Impatience; frustration.

Oak (E)—Pushing beyond natural limits or abilities.

Red Clover (NA)—Upset from group emotions, mob hysteria, or panic.

Star of Bethlehem (E)—Trauma from severe stress.

Yarrow (NA)—Stress from the negative intentions of others.

Tension

Dandelion (NA)—Emotional tension felt in various muscles; cramping.

Iris (NA)—Tension in the regions of the neck.

Snapdragon (NA)—Tension in the jaw; grinding teeth; clipped speech.

Yerba Santa (NA)—Emotional tension held in the region of the chest.

Note: By far the most well-known of Dr. Bach's flower essences is his "Rescue Remedy," the five-essence combination of cherry plum, clematis, impatiens, rock rose, and star of bethlehem flowers. During emergencies, prolonged high stress or life-threatening situations, this combination restores calm and mental stability, proving helpful during trauma, panic, disorientation, and loss of consciousness.

Obtaining and Using the Flower Essences

Because flower essences are not drugs or pharmaceuticals, stock bottles can be purchased over-the-counter at most health food stores, by mail order, or through the Internet. Some manufacturers sell in both 10 ml (⅓-ounce) and 30 ml (1-ounce) stock bottles. At stores, some manufacturers provide a short questionnaire to help you assess your feelings and determine the best essence to use.

Because they are named for the wildflower from which each essence is derived, confusion over a particular product is unlikely. However, Dr. Bach's "Rescue Remedy" is a trademarked product name, held by Nelson Bach USA, Ltd. Other flower essence companies also manufacture the five-flower combination, but use a proprietary name such as "Five Flower Formula" (Flower Essence Services), or "Calming Essence" (Ellon Botanicals, Inc).

Because essences are preserved in an alcohol solution, persons with an alcohol sensitivity or addiction can prepare a dosage bottle using a one-ounce bottle with a glass dropper. Fill the bottle about half full with vegetable glycerin as a preservative, adding two to four drops of the flower essence, then fill the remainder with spring water. Cap the bottle and shake well. This dosage bottle can be kept without refrigeration and is also an excellent dilution for pets and other domestic animals.

Individuals who have no alcohol sensitivities can make a dosage bottle by filling it three-quarters full of spring water, adding two to four drops of flower essence, and filling the remainder with brandy. This mixture must be shaken well. The dosage can be kept without refrigeration.

Several methods make use of the essences very discreet and practical, depending on the situation and your immediate need.

To break down long-term emotions or thinking, place four drops of the essence in a glass of water, stirring both clockwise and counterclockwise for about one minute. Sip the glass of water throughout the day. The essence in water can be taken daily for as long as necessary, until you notice an established change in your viewpoint.

When an unexpected event occurs, take four drops of the essence, directly under the tongue—before or immediately after the event—from either the original stock bottle or from a dosage bottle.

During a grueling work session or other stressful planned event, place a few drops from the stock or dosage bottle on your wrists. A few drops on a handkerchief will also fortify you through tough moments. When you know about such plans beforehand, use the sipping method above for several days prior to the event.

After an exhausting day, place twenty drops of essence from the stock bottle into a warm bath. Before entering the tub, stir the water in a figure-eight motion for one minute. After soaking for twenty minutes, pat the skin dry gently. Follow the bath with quiet rest, or go to sleep.

The modern idea that distress is a normal part of life isn't simply a fallacy; it's a health hazard. Disrupting patterns of thought and emotions, which reinforce distress, keeps the mind in imbalance. With a clear mind and a rested body, however, you are in a strong position to decide the direction of your career, and life, instead of being ruled by it.

For Further Study

Flower Essence Repertory. Patricia Kaminski & Richard Katz. Flower Essence Society, 1992. (Discusses both English and North American flower essences.)

The Healer's Manual: A beginner's guide to vibrational therapies. Ted Andrews, Llewellyn Publications, 1993.

Flower Essence Suppliers

Ellon Botanicals, Inc.
(800) 4BE-CALM
www.ellonbotanicals.com

Flower Essence Society
(530) 265-9163, www.flowersociety.org

Nelson Bach USA, Ltd.
(800) 314-BACH
www.nelsonbach.com

Preparing Herbal Remedies

⤳ By Anna Franklin ⤳

S trictly speaking, a herb is a non-woody plant that dies down after flowering. Generally, the term is applied to medicinal or culinary plants and trees.

As a rule, many different parts of a herb may be used by people interested in its properties as a medicine or as a flavoring. This includes the root, stem, rhizome, bulb, leaf, bark, flower, or fruit. In annual plants, the healing properties reside mostly in the seeds. In perennials, it is in the roots.

Depending on which part of the plant is used, herbal remedies are prepared in different ways, as described in further detail below.

Infusions—Teas and Tisanes

Herb tisanes, or teas, can be made from leaves, flowers, and green stems. Some seeds and barks can be crushed and made into teas. For this, use one

teaspoon, or one ounce, of dried herb per cup of boiling water. Pour the boiling water over the herb and let it infuse for fifteen to thirty minutes.

Cold Infusion

Some herbs have properties which are destroyed by heat, so a cold infusion is necessary. Use a nonmetal container, and add one ounce of the herb to one pint of cold water. Cover with a lid or other cover, such as cling film or foil, and leave to stand for five to six hours.

Decoction

Some seeds, roots, buds, and barks need to be boiled in water for a while. This is called a decoction. If they are dried they should first be pounded into a powder. Use one ounce of each dried herb, or two ounces of each fresh herb, to one pint of water. Bring the mixture to the boil in a nonaluminum pan and let simmer for ten to fifteen minutes. Strain before drinking.

Tinctures

Plant constituents are generally more soluble in alcohol than in water, so tinctures are made. They are stronger than infusions or decoctions—the dosage is usually from five to fifteen drops rather than a full cup.

Tinctures are generally mixed with water before drinking. Drops of the tincture can also be added to the bath or used to make an ointment. To make a tincture, put four ounces of dried herbs, or eight ounces of fresh herbs, into a clean jar, and pour one pint of vodka or cider vinegar over the herbs. Seal and keep in a warm place for two weeks, shaking daily. Strain and store in a dark bottle.

Syrups

Some herbs are bitter tasting and are more palatable when taken in the form of a syrup. This is particularly true for children. To make a syrup, for every one pint of infusion or decoction add one pound of sugar and heat gently until the sugar is dissolved. This will need to be kept in the fridge.

Baths

Add one pint of infusion or decoction to running bath water. Afterwards, pat yourself dry.

Ointments

Herbs can be worked into salves for topical application. To do so, melt eight ounces of petroleum jelly, or other fat, and add two tablespoons of the herb. Simmer the mixture for fifteen minutes; allow to cool completely before handling.

Compresses

To make a herbal compress, prepare a clean cotton cloth and soak it in a hot infusion or decoction. Make sure it is as hot as you can stand when you place it on the affected area. Change the compress as it cools down.

Poultice

To make a herbal poultice, bruise fresh herbs and apply directly to the skin. Cover them directly with a cloth.

Cold-Infused Oil

To make an infused oil, cut up the herb and cover with suitable vegetable oil such as olive or almond in a glass bottle or jar. Leave in a warm place for two to three weeks, shaking daily. Strain into a clean jar. These are applied to the skin or used in massage.

Essential Oils

Essential oils can be added directly to the bath, to massage oils, or in an evaporator. They cannot be made at home but are readily available from shops. They are very concentrated and must always be diluted with a vegetable carrier oil.

Author's Note

Herbal remedies are best used under the guidance of a qualified practitioner. In general, self-treatment can be dangerous. Consult a professional before you embark on any kind of regiment of herbal healing.

Caution: You May Want to Avoid These Herbs

⤳ By Diana Rajchel Olsen ⤵

H erbs have enhanced my life in more ways than I can count. I would never separate myself from them.

However, if used improperly, herbs can teach some vicious lessons. While often touted for their safety and mildness compared to synthesized drugs, herbs still contain chemicals that must be used with great caution. After all, many commonly used synthesized drugs originate from herbal sources.

In fact, according to chemists, a large enough dose of anything can poison a person. Which is to say, treat cautiously anything that you ingest, and if you engage in herbal practices seek formal training and advice from experts. Verbal descriptions of plants that are found in books often fail to include details necessary for complet safety in using certain plants.

The following lists include several relatively well-known herbs that can be dangerous if taken in high enough doses. Some of the herbs may be sold at your favorite herb shop, and some may be offered to you regularly by your naturopath or herbal healer in very small doses. My lists serve as a warning for you to take some care when using any of the herbs—I have included some of the dangers associated with each, but my list is by no means exhaustive.

I also encourage you to seek more information and learn as much as you can. Before trying a herb unfamiliar to you, cross-reference it with three or four different sources and ask a professional about it. Make sure you know what you are working with always. Herbs provide us a wonderful natural source of healing, magic, and joy so long as we regard them with the same caution we would any other chemical substance.

Black Cohosh

Cimicifuga racemosa

The dried rootstock of black cohosh is often used for female concerns, and as an antispasmodic and sedative. Although this has many medicinal uses, it is easy to overdose on this plant. Dosage should be carefully managed with the help of a health-care professional. Too large a dose will cause nausea and dizziness. Pregnant women should never use this herb.

Buttercup

Ranunculus acris

The fresh buttercup plant is poisonous, though at the same time it is effective medicinally. This herb is a classic example of the double-edged sword of herbalism: What makes it useful is also what makes it dangerous. Because of this poisonous effect, this herb should only be administered by a professional. The sap of all buttercups are dangerous, and some can cause blisters or ulcerous sores if touched with bare hands.

Foxglove
Digitalis purpurea

Often used as a decorative plant for its long lines of bell-shaped flowers, foxglove is used to create the heart medicine digitalis for adults suffering heart attack. It is also used magically as a protective house-guarding herb. While this medicine is potent treatment for heart attacks, in a healthy person it can also cause heart attacks. These plants should never be ingested, nor should they be handled with bare hands. Poisoning may include paralysis and sudden heart failure.

Goat's Rue
Galega officinalis

Goat's rue was formerly used to stimulate milkflow in nursing mothers and was considered useful for reducing blood sugar. Believed to cure bites from poisonous animals, in magical practice this herb may be added as an incense in healing rituals. Not used as commonly today, a person seeking goat's rue should know that this item is known to kill farm animals and likely would have similar effects on humans.

Hedge Garlic
Sisymbrium alliaria

Not overtly poisonous, hedge garlic has a high acidic content that can irritate the skin. It is most often used to treat asthma and rheumatism.

Hedge Hyssop
Gratiola officinalis

Hedge hyssop is used in extremely small doses for quitting smoking and as a purgative. However, it is very easy for a person to ingest too much and become ill.

Holly
Lex vomitoria

Considered one of the sacred herbs in Wiccan practice, there are about four types of holly in North America. The *Hex auifolium* or *I. opaca* may be handled with relative safety; all other forms are best avoided. Considered sacred as a protective and good luck herb, the berries on both of these types of holly can kill small children. Avoid for internal use, and if holly is needed, locate a person with formal training in plant identification.

Jimson weed
Datura stramonium

Found in waste places, pastures, and roadsides all over North and South America, jimson weed is potent as a narcotic and a hypnotic. It is very easy to overdose on the herb, though very small doses can be used in emergencies for respiratory problems. Poisoning can include dry mouth, dilated pupils, reddening of the face and neck, rapid heartbeat, and delirium. It is best handled by a health professional.

Lily of the Valley
Convallaria majalis

According to magical tradition, lily of the valley cheers a room and improves the memory. Considered the most valuable heart remedy presently available, what makes this herb valuable is also what makes it dangerous. The plant contains specific toxins that help an ailing heart but will also harm a perfectly healthy one. It contains chemicals that act similar to digitalis (the active ingredient in foxglove), and it can produce irregular heartbeat or upset stomach. Use only with medical supervision.

Mandrake
Podophyllum petatum, Mandragora ofcinarum
Applied historically in love spells and image magic, the human-like shape of the mandrake root has given it mythical qualities of magical power. It is used for protection, fertility, money, love, and health, as well to guard against demons and evil. However, when ingested it is extremely dangerous. At one time, mandrake was used for suicide. It is not for ingestion.

Mistletoe
Phoradendron flavescens, Viscum album
Mistletoe is considered a sacred herb in Wiccan practice. Used magically as a potent plant for protection, love, health, and exorcism, mistletoe medically treats convulsions, hysteria, and delirium. The berries are poisonous and can kill small children.

Monkshood
Aconitum napellusf, **also known as aconite**
A potent sedative and narcotic, monkshood is one of the most potent poisons in the plant world. Far too many people have ingested this assuming that because it is a herb, it is safe.

Mulberry
Morus rubra
Said to protect a garden from lightning and to protect people from evil, mulberry juice, if the berries are handled when not ripe, can cause hallucinations.

Ragwort
Senecio aureus
Considered by some a protective amulet against charms and spells, ragwort was said to provide material for Witches' brooms

during the days of the Inquisition. It also contains toxic alkaloids that have poisoned livestock.

Yew

Taxus baccata

A sacred plant to Wiccans, yew has traditionally been used to raise the dead. It is rarely used for any reason now: All parts of this plant except the fleshy seed covering are poisonous.

For Further Study

The Complete Illustrated Holistic Herbal. David Hoffman. Element Books, 1996.

Encyclopedia of Magical Herbs. Scott Cunningham. Llewellyn Publications, 1997.

Herbal Rituals. Judith Berger. St. Martin's Press, 1998.

The Herb Book. Mary Ann Dykes. Healing Link, 1996.

Magic and Medicine of Plants. Inge Dobelis, editor. The Reader's Digest Association, 1986.

Herbs
for
Beauty

Making Herbal Lotions

≫ By Carly Wall, C. A. ≪

B ack when I was a child living on the farm, my family was some-what isolated from civilization because we lived at the end of a dirt driveway a half mile from the road. That meant that in the summer, days were long and lazy—cut off from the unnatural bustle of modern society. In the early mornings, we picked things for Mother and Grandma to can—raspberries and beans and corn. The afternoons, meanwhile, were ours for us to pester the farm animals—horses, pigs, and rabbits—or to walk down the dirt road to our swimming hole.

Sometimes, when the other kids were off getting into mischief, I, being the oldest, would sometimes see what the grown-ups were doing. Because it was a problem getting into town back then, often I would find Mother and Grandma in the house, making their own cosmetics rather than having to wait for a chance to get to the store in town. And I saw them creating some wonderful stuff.

It was great fun to watch them smear honey masks on their faces and lie still with big cucumber slices covering their eyes. Afternoon was their time to relax in this way until it was time to start supper.

I enjoyed sitting and listening to their gossip. Sometimes they let me be a part of it all, and I loved it. I'd help mix a new facial wash and would get to splash it on my face. Or I would end up as the guinea pig for Mother to try a new cream she had invented.

The afternoons were a special time to relax, renew, and to beautify with home beauty products. The day's cares seemed to slip away when we gathered for these sessions. I always hated when that time had to end, and I could tell that both Mother and Grandma did, too.

Home Herbal Cosmetics Today

Edgar Cayce once said in a psychic reading: "To be able to remember the sunset, to be able to remember a beautiful conversation, a beautiful deed done where hope and faith were created, to remember the smile of a babe, the blush of a rose, the harmony of a song—a bird's call; these are creative. For if they are a part of thyself, they bring you closer and closer to God." I still enjoy making my own cosmetics, and some of the best can be made from herbs right from your garden.

The effort we make in decorating ourselves, in bringing more beauty into the world, is never wasted time. Sharing "beauty moments" with a neighbor, a friend, or a loved one is a creative way of giving. And what better way to catch up on family business than to plan visits around such times?

Making your own cosmetics at home isn't a big bother and can be a lot of fun. A big plus of the process is you know exactly what you are using, and that these products haven't been tested on innocent animals. Of course, it is unlikely that you will want to make all of your own cosmetics; such things as eyeliner and foundation are likely impossible to make yourself at home, but the many products you can make at home will enhance your appearance and save you money.

If you have a kitchen, you probably have all the equipment you'll need to start creating a wonderful array of products. But one of the best things you can make at home, and one of the most useful, is homemade herbal lotions.

Making Herbal Lotions

The tools you'll need to make rich and healthful herbal lotions are probably right in your kitchen now. If you have measuring cups, spoons, mixing bowls, a double boiler, a microwave, and a blender, in fact, you have everything you need to get started on the process.

You'll also need some herbs or essential oils, and some pretty containers, jars, or bottles to contain your creations.

Grandma would rather have walked on hot coals than have her beautiful rose cold cream slopped into an old mayonnaise jar. Her taste ran to beautiful cut glass and crystal containers. Whenever she went shopping at garage sales or junk shops, she diligently searched for any beautiful type of jar and bought those that struck her fancy. Her dressing table was a proper mix of elegant bottles and perfumes along with the everpresent fresh bouquet of flowers. This, she said, was her simple way of starting the day right. And I have followed her lead. It makes such a difference if you surround yourself with beautiful things. In this way, you are much more apt to use your homemade creations. And you will be in the right frame of mind to think of yourself as "beautiful."

I still treasure my own beauty breaks and wouldn't trade them for the world. The following are my own special recipes for homemade lotions and oils. They are guaranteed to bring a rosy glow to cheeks. Beauty is such an important part of life, we shouldn't let an opportunity pass us by to add a little beauty to our world.

Herbal Lotions

Rose Cream

Rose cream is a good facial moisturizer, perfect for removing makeup, as well as daily sweat, grease, and grime. Place this lotion in a pretty jar after you make it, and be sure to keep plenty on hand to smooth rough skin day or night.

1	oz beeswax
6	tbsp sweet almond oil
	Several drops castor oil or vitamin E
4	tbsp rose water (strong rose petal tea)
	Rose essential oil (optional), or use rose geranium essential oil as it is less costly

Melt the beeswax in the top of a double boiler. Blend in the oils. Remove from heat, and, stirring constantly, add the rose water. Beat the mixture vigorously until the mixture is cooled and is fluffy and white. You could choose to add rose essential oil for a more concentrated scent. The rose has been used for ages for beauty preparations because of its very strong cleansing and astringent qualities.

No-Wrinkle Lotion

For this recipe, mix all ingredients well at room temperature. Apply it to clean skin only. No-Wrinkle Lotion may be applied before bedtime to your entire face or to the area under your eyes only.

2	tbsp basil
2	tbsp strong lemon balm tea

2	tbsp castor oil
2	tsp honey

Beauty Cream

This is a fast-absorbing and richly creamy cosmetic to apply to your face and the skin of other body parts. Use distilled water to maintain its absolute purity.

⅔	cup herbal tea from distilled water (use mint, chamomile, or rosemary)
⅓	cup comfrey root tea
½	tsp vitamin E
½	tsp essential oil of choice (try jasmine, sandalwood, ylang ylang, or neroli)
½	cup almond oil
⅓	cup cocoa butter
1	tsp liquid lanolin
2	tbsp liquid lecithin
½	oz grated beeswax

Melt the oils and wax together, watching carefully that they don't burn. Set the mixture aside until it has cooled to room temperature. Add teas and essential oils to the blender in the meantime, and whip until frothy. Put the melted oils into a measuring cup with a spout so you can easily pour it. Turn the blender on high and slowly drizzle the oil into the blender. The mixture will change to a light color and then thicken considerably. When it is the consistency of mayonnaise, spoon it into jars. It should keep for quite awhile.

Wart or Mole Removing Cream

To make a cream that removes unsightly moles or warts, take fresh-picked violets or strawberry blooms and leaves (high in vitamin A), and place in a jar of castor oil. Let the jar soak in a sunny window one to two weeks, then strain. Rub the cream on warts or moles frequently. It will take some time, but eventually the warts will disappear, and the moles will peel off. This herbal remedy works wonders.

Lavender Lotion

This lotion is good for acne, and is generally very healthy for your skin.

4	oz vegetable shortening
2	oz beeswax
2	oz glycerine
2	tbsp liquid lecithin
4	oz distilled water

Melt all ingredients together just until it becomes liquid. Mix with a whisk until it begins to thicken. Add ½ teaspoon lavender essential oil and mix well. Pour into a jar and allow to cool. Use as needed.

Healing Lotion for Sore Skin

1	cup glycerin
1	cup rosewater
10	drops essential oil of sweet orange or ylang ylang
¼	tsp vitamin E oil

Put all of the ingredients into glass or plastic bottles. Portion out the ingredients according to the ounce capacity of each of the bottles you are using. Shake well until all the ingredients are completely combined.

If you are using the scent, shake the bottle well several times a day for two or three days before giving or using.

Beeswax Balm

Beeswax is very healing for the skin and protects it from the elements.

3	tbsp grated beeswax
1	tbsp liquid lanolin
½	cup peanut oil
2	tbsp strong mint tea
1	tbsp coconut oil
1	tsp honey
⅛	tsp baking soda

Combine all ingredients in a glass ovenproof container, and heat it in the microwave until all the wax and oils are melted. Do not allow the mixture to come to a boil. Pour the mixture into a jar or other glass container and allow to cool completely. Makes 4 ounces total.

Creamy Oatmeal and Almond Hand Lotion

½	cup strong rosemary tea
1	tsp almond extract
1½	cup oat water (see below)
1½	cup baking soda
½	cup beeswax

Mix all of the above ingredients very well to make the cream. This can be kept in a plastic or glass container to be used daily. (To make oat water, soak 1 cup of oats tied in cheesecloth in 2 cups water for several hours, then drain and use the water).

Herbal Massage Oils

A good massage is an invaluable tool to help you keep a balanced perspective in these often hectic times. Nothing can compare to the nurturing and healing ability of touch. Massage does much more than relax you. It has been found to relieve many physical disorders. It can reduce edema (swelling) and disperse cellulite. It also improves circulation and muscle tone, stimulates internal organs, and releases toxins stored in the body.

Although massage in itself is very beneficial and healing, when you use herbs and essential oils in massage oil you get the added action of the herbal scent—which soothes the senses and can dispel bad moods, headaches, and other minor ills—plus the physical healing properties contained within the plant itself. Some plants, for example, can pamper stressed muscles, be antiseptic, or act as a restorative to aging skin.

This healthful form of therapy is a good way to feel energized, relaxed, and peaceful—and it's also a delight to the senses. Overall, massage is a good way for couples to get and give affection and healing to one another. Massage can also be shared among friends.

The person receiving a massage may be experiencing such problems as a persistent headache, restless nights, severe stress, or low energy. A blend of different infused herbs and essential oils can be used with a most therapeutic effect in these instances.

Skin condition is also improved through this process, according to the type of oil and herb used. Castor oil, for example is most beneficial in healing minor skin growths and moles. Peanut oil helps improve the texture and tone of the skin. If you have dry skin, you may want to use chamomile, orange blossom, or rose oil; and use almond, castor, olive or peanut oil or a combination of these. For oily skin, use lavender, lemon balm, lemon verbena, or thyme in sesame or sunflower oil. If your skin type is normal, any of the herbs listed here can be used in combination with any oil. The lightest and fastest absorbing oils are the sesame and sunflower.

Infused oils, which have been used by civilizations for thousands of years, are a mixture of an unscented base oil and herbs or essential oils. They are used as a rub for massage or a daily lotion.

The fragrance-rich oils of the plant are obtained by soaking the flowers or leaves in a vegetable-based oil. The base oils you use should be of high quality for massage applications since they are absorbed into the skin through the pores. Thus, the scented oil of the plant is actually carried into the body, where it acts automatically according to specific therapeutic value. And many vegetable-based oils contain vitamins such as A and E which are nourishing to the skin.

Since highly processed oils lose their vitamin content, the best oils are cold-pressed, or virgin, types of oils.

As scented oil blends generally stay in peak condition no more than six months, you might want to add a little vitamin E (or a touch of wheatgerm oil since it contains high amounts of vitamin E), castor oil, or honey to your base oil to keep it fresh. These all act as preservatives. Generally, your oil is still good if it hasn't gotten cloudy or begun smelling rancid—if it has, it's time to make a new batch!

Castor oil is soothing and healing to the skin. Edgar Cayce, many of whose psychic readings suggested treatments for illness, recommended using castor oil almost universally directly applied as therapy for moles, warts, and other skin conditions, or in a compress or pack for internal ailments. We can also use castor oil's benefits in our herbal oil infusions. Since it is thick, you may want to mix it with a lighter base oil. Another possibility is jojoba oil, derived from a desert plant of the same name. This product is similar to a diluted wax, and it gives the skin a wonderful silky feel when applied. It has also been reported as being good for dry eczema.

Here are some basic recipes of infused herbal oils to get you started. You can use the ingredients individually or in combination in the proportions of your choice. You can use these as massage oils, as oils for very dry skin, or even add a bit to bathwater for a very moisturizing bath.

For Women

To relax and uplift mood: Rose, chamomile, rosemary

As an energizer: Peppermint, rose geranium

For muscle aches or as antiseptic: Lavender, peppermint

For Men

As an antiseptic or energizer: Peppermint, lemon balm

To relax muscles, soothe aches: Lavender, clary sage

To relax and uplift: Rosemary, orange blossom, basil

Making Infused Oils

To make an infused oil with concentrated essential oils purchased commercially, merely add two teaspoons per sixteen ounces (two cups) of base oil and shake well before use. It is ready immediately.

Alternatively, you can purchase dried herbs and add them to the oil before placing in a sunny window. Leave in the window (shaking at least once per day) for two weeks. Strain, then add more herbs and repeat the process until the oil is scented. After the oil is scented, strain completely and place in a tightly closed container to be placed in a cool dark place until ready to use.

Have fun experimenting and making your own perfect lotion or infused herbal oil. You may come up with a recipe that you can pass down in your family as a treasured herbal recipe. Perhaps you and your family can make a tradition of having a "beauty afternoon," concocting your own beauty recipes and trying them out. It's a great way to relax and unwind as well as make yourself feel terrific.

Nettle for Your Hair

⫷ By Roslyn Reid ⫸

T he idea of nettle in your hair might sound like a frightening prospect at first, but various formulations of this notoriously biting plant have been used for hair and skin care for hundreds of years.

Nowadays, of course, modern scientists know that this is because of the high vitamin A and vitamin C content in nettle—after all, our skin just loves vitamin C. But though the ancient Britons, Gypsies, Russians, and other people of antiquity did not realize why this plant was such an effective tonic, they still had a keen appreciation, and developed countless uses, for it.

Stinging nettle (of the genus *Urtica*) is also known as common nettle, so called because it is a weed that can be found just about everywhere. But because the word "nettle" comes from *netel* or *noetl*, which is the Anglo-Saxon word for needle, I prefer to play it safe and buy mine from someone who knows how to pick it!

Even world-famous herbalist Tom Brown recommends putting on gloves before you try picking your own nettle. Being one of the plants ruled by Mars (obviously), nettle is associated with the sign Aries—and both of these influences can be rather prickly.

In fact, considering how difficult it is to harvest nettle without harming yourself, ancient peoples must have been convinced that the plant had a remarkable effectiveness indeed, or no one would have even dared to try it.

The Uses of Nettle

Among the uses of nettle in ancient times was the application of a nettle tea as a hair and skin conditioner. Nettle plants seem to prefer wastelands, such as roadsides; but they will grow just about anywhere—including in your garden. The plants can reach heights of up to seven feet. In the U.S. and Europe, nettles produce flowers from June to September; these flowers grow in long yellowish hanging clusters. For culinary purposes, the leaves and stalks of the nettle are best when harvested before the flowers form.

A popular drink in Britain, nettle tea is thought to have been introduced to that country by the ancient Romans. According to renowned herbalist Juliette de Bairacli Levy, the Romans cultivated nettle extensively as a rheumatism remedy—flogging the affected joints with nettle was considered a good way to get the blood flowing to them. Whether this pain was better than that of arthritis is a subjective question, although right now you are probably glad you're not an ancient Roman.

Besides being an effective astringent which works well on cuts and bug bites, the juice of nettle leaves makes a great hair rinse—in addition to leaving the hair with a healthy luster, the application of various forms of nettle promotes hair growth. The following is my favorite recipe for such a hair rinse, using dried nettle leaves. It is easy and will work well on anyone's hair.

Nettle Hair Rinse Recipes

Place a teaspoon of dried nettle leaves into a tea infuser or muslin tea bag. Put this into a teacup, then fill the cup with boiling water. Steep the leaves for twenty minutes, then remove the infuser and set it aside. Pour this tea into a small saucepan and bring it to a boil. Use caution here and be sure to keep a judicious eye on the pot—this tea can boil away before you know it.

While waiting for the pot to boil, place the tea infuser back into the teacup. When the saucepan begins to boil, pour the hot liquid over the infuser and let this double-strength tea steep until it is cool enough to apply to your head.

As you would with any hair rinse, pour this nettle tea over your hair after shampooing. If you have long hair, you can immerse its ends into the cupful of tea first, then remove the ends from the cup and pour the remains of the rinse over the rest of your hair. Do not wash this nettle conditioner out of your hair, but leave it in and let it dry.

In addition to its leaves, the seeds of the nettle plant can be used for a hair and scalp treatment, not to mention a good home-made astringent wash for the coats of your pets after a bath. To make a rinse from nettle seeds, soak a teaspoon of them in hot water for twenty minutes. When cool, this liquid can be sponged onto the hair (or pet), or poured over it in the same way as described above, leaving it in the hair when drying.

American herbalist John Lust gives this recipe for hair rinse using fresh nettle leaves: Boil three to four ounces of fresh chopped leaves in two cups of water and two cups of vinegar for a short time, then cool and use on the hair. If you know how to pick nettle or know somebody who does, this recipe can be quite economical.

European herbalist Maria Treben uses both the leaves and the roots of the nettle for her hair rinse recipe. In addition to her rinse, another of her uses for nettle roots, which she recommends digging up in the spring or fall, is to make a tincture for rubbing into the scalp daily. Treben claims that the use of nettle rinse rids one of dandruff, makes the hair thick and soft, and imparts a beautiful sheen to it.

In her article "A Medicinal Herbal" in the Llewellyn's *2000 Herbal Almanac*, Ellen Evert Hopman recommends rubbing the fresh juice of nettles into the scalp as a hair tonic. British gardening writer Mary Brown mentions that this potion was a well-known old folk remedy which supposedly cured baldness; although these days one might be better advised to try Rogaine. Hopman's recipe for nettle hair conditioner is to simmer two teaspoons of the chopped root along with a cup of water in a saucepan for twenty minutes. She specifies that one should use a nonaluminum pot with a tight-fitting lid for this brew, because some substances are known to react badly with aluminum when heated in it.

Another benefit of making your own hair rinse from any kind of natural substance is that you can cook up as much of it as you want ahead of time, then refrigerate it until you're ready to use it. And if you or someone you know likes to eat fresh-cooked nettles—all species of nettle are edible—you can use the cooking water for a rinse, instead of boiling up the tea separately.

However, there is one drawback to using most homemade herbal beauty recipes: Since they do not contain preservatives, all of them must be refrigerated. So unless you think pouring cold water over your head is exhilarating, you might want to warm your premade hair rinse in the microwave before you use it.

Other Nettle Recipes

In addition to its use as a hair conditioner, strong nettle tea can be mixed with tallow, glycerin, or other similar waxy base to concoct a hand and body lotion. As mentioned above, though, the disadvantage to this lotion is the same as with the hair rinse:

To prevent spoiling, it must be refrigerated (brr!). It's a bit easier to warm up tea than it is lotion; rubbing a little dollop of lotion briskly between the hands before spreading it on the skin is probably the best way to deal with this problem.

According to de Bairacli Levy, nettle lotion is good for soothing aching feet. She also credits nettle tea hair rinse with improving the color and texture of the hair, and with the elimination of dandruff.

As you can probably deduce by now, nettle leaves are used in facial preparations, too. One can employ the old-fashioned steam technique of boiling the leaves in a pot of water and placing a wet towel over both head and pot to capture the vapors to condition the skin; or the leaves may be used overnight in a regular vaporizer. Either way, the use of nettle steam will soften, cleanse and nourish your face.

Nettle beauty preparations provide an easy, natural, cost-effective, and eco-friendly way to give your hair and skin a healthy, vibrant glow. And while you wait for your hair or lotion to dry, you can relax and enjoy a nice hot cup of nettle tea—drinking it promotes hair growth, too.

For Further Study

For more information on nettle, consult this website— http://www.botanical.com—which has an online hypertext version of Mrs. M. Grieve's time-honored reference book, *A Modern Herbal*. If you do not have Internet access, many libraries do; or they have either Grieve's famous *Herbal* in textbook form. This book contain exhaustive descriptions of all the different types of nettle and their uses.

Other books used in this article are:

Breast Cancer? Breast Health! The Wise Woman Way. Susun Weed. Ash Tree Publications, 1996.

Common Herbs for Natural Health. Juliette de Bairadi Levy. Ash Tree Publications, 1996.

Health from God's Garden: Herbal remedies for glowing health and well-being. Maria Treben. Healing Arts Press, 1988.

The Herb Book. John Lust. Lust Publications, 1974.

Llewellyn's Herbal Almanac, 2000–2001. Llewellyn Publications, 1999–2000.

Llewellyn's Organic Gardening Almanac, 1993–1996. Llewellyn Publications, 1992–1995.

Wise Woman Herbal Healing Wise. Susun Weed. Ash Tree Publications, 1989.

Herbs for Great Skin

By Penny Kelly

When I was a little girl I used to hear about a "strawberry-and-cream" facial mask, and I used to wonder why anyone would waste good strawberries by putting them on their face instead of in their tummy. Now that I'm older I can say I finally understand.

The effect of a strawberry-and-cream facial is a marvelous combination of cleansing, toning, and feeding the skin. Afterwards, you are left absolutely pink-cheeked and glowing.

I started taking regular daily care of my skin at the ripe age of ten when I took a Four-H course on personal care and hygiene. I loved the discipline and ritual of self-care.

My mother reinforced my early habits with her own daily routines. Although she had six children and never enough money or time, she spent time every single day to cleanse, massage, and feed her skin before putting on a touch of lipstick, maybe a bit of mascara or blush. I recall looking at her one night when she was thirty-six, and I was sixteen, her skin was clear and healthy looking. Finally, I asked her how she got her "rouge"—which was the term for blush in those days—to look so natural.

"It's just the color of my skin," she said, "I don't have any makeup on today."

"None?" I asked, disbelieving.

"None," she replied, continuing to look through a box of sewing supplies

"But how did you get your cheeks that color?" I pressed, unable to comprehend how someone could have such rosy cheeks without makeup.

"That's just good health and taking care of my skin," she said.

When I was in my twenties I used to spend a pretty penny on cleansers and facial masks that came in a jar or tube. There were all sorts of them, usually labeled with names like oatmeal or nutshell scrub, lemon and honey mask, willow bark and mint washes, or lavender and raspberry bubbles. Some of them worked well enough, although when I look back I can't imagine why I thought I needed to spend all that money on my skin.

Not until I was in my late forties and seriously interested in good health did I really come home to the fact that there is no facial mask that has as much effect as good health and a regular routine of daily care using natural skin-care products from herbs.

Natural Skin Care

Think of your skin as a savings account in a bank that regularly lets in a thief. The thief in this case is Time, and thus you have to put a little effort into your skin account every day to account for this theft. When you do this, the benefits to your skin will build. If you choose not to, the net effect on your skin account will be extremely draining. That is to say, the result of good skin care shows, as does the result of neglect.

If you eat sweets, smoke, or like to have a drink or two every night, these are particularly hard on the skin simply because they depress the activity of the liver. The liver is responsible for filtering toxins out of the blood and when it is working poorly the blood remains relatively "polluted." This waste matter gets deposited in the skin and the result is skin that loses its flexibility, and becomes wrinkled and spotty. Circulation slows, and your skin loses its natural color, becoming sallow and dull. Therefore the first step in creating skin that looks bright, unlined, and has good color is to change what you are eating. The next step is to get a bit of exercise to increase your blood flow and to improve the delivery of nutrients to your skin.

Along with these changes, a variety of facial masks and treatments can make a tremendous difference both in how you look and how you feel. My first encounter with "real" food products used on my face came unexpectedly about eight years ago. I was driving my parents back to Michigan from a cancer center in Houston, Texas, when we ran into a terrific rainstorm in Arkansas. It was late in the day, and we were all exhausted from weeks of hospital routine, hospital food, and the tension that comes with the effort to heal. So we pulled off the highway and headed to the closest town, which happened to be Hot Springs, Arkansas.

Somehow we found a Holiday Inn, and, upon checking in, discovered they had natural mineral baths. In a moment of uncharacteristic adventurousness, the three of us decided to splurge and immediately arranged baths, hoping to renew our tired bodies and minds. Upon arriving in the bathhouse, we were whisked into large tubs of steaming mineral water, soaked and scrubbed, and then removed to another room where we were wrapped up like mummies in a huge sheet and left to sweat.

But before our heads were wrapped—and this is the key part—a thick slice of cold cucumber was laid over each of our eyes. No words can ever convey the combination of feelings and thoughts that passed through my mind as I lay there, my heart pounding relentlessly in an attempt to disperse the heat, sweat pouring out of me carrying all kinds of toxins and waste products that had been stored in my skin. The two living pieces of cucumber were so cool, so comforting, so ironically and wonderfully present, that I was completely surprised.

From that moment on, things that came out of jars and tubes took second place to the real items they were named for. In time, I came to realize that all those oatmeal, lemon, honey, willow bark, lavender, and strawberry-and-cream creams were not just named after herbs and food items to make them sound natural or improve marketing. Rather, these facial cleansers, masks, and moisturizers were trying to incorporate and harness the power of these foods and herbs. After this realization, I began to experiment, and I continue to do so to this day. New ideas seem to arise every year during the garden season.

Cucumber Compress

In summer, the long hot days of Sun take their toll on your face. For a truly refreshing late afternoon break, cut two slices of cold cucumber, dip a small hand towel or washcloth in cold water, and squeeze it out just enough to keep it from dripping.

Next, find a sofa or reclining chair that allows you to lie as near to horizontal as possible. Lie down, put the cucumber slices over your closed eyes, fold the towel or washcloth so it covers your face from the tip of the nose up, and lay the cold cloth gently over the cucumber slices. Take three really deep breaths to fill your body with oxygen, then just let your breathing do its work while you lie there.

For the next fifteen to twenty minutes just relax, daydream, and let the skin and tissue around your eyes soak in the effects of the cucumber. When the time is up, get up, splash more cold water on your face, pat it dry, brush your hair, and go back to whatever you were doing. You'll feel amazingly calm and refreshed, and you'll look younger even though the day is getting old.

If you work in an office or a factory, you can still do this during your lunchbreak. Every workplace is required to have a lounge or place where people can lie down on their break. Skip your lunch and do this simple little cucumber facial. It will make the afternoon seem more pleasant, and you'll leave for home looking less haggard.

A Healing and Cleansing Facial

If you're at home on a weekend, you might want to try a series of facial treatments that are truly wonderful and health-giving. The first few steps are with oatmeal, the next couple involve steaming your face and using a choice of several herbs based on your individual skin conditions, and the final is the option of a face pack.

Step 1

Get a large towel and lay it across your bathroom sink, making sure to cover the drain and drape the ends out across the countertop. Next, put one to two cups of oatmeal in a large flat pan such as a cookie sheet or cake pan. It can be regular or quick oatmeal—either one works well, although regular is rougher than quick. Put the pan over the towel, across the sink.

Take off your blouse or shirt and wrap a towel around your chest, leaving your shoulders and arms bare. Then lean over the cookie sheet, scoop up the oatmeal in the palms of your hand and rub it briskly on your face, neck, shoulders, upper arms, and forearms. Rub until your skin feels quite smooth, as if it has been sanded. Don't rub until the skin is raw, just until your skin is bright pink and you have covered all areas. Be careful over the bony parts such as cheekbones, the bridge of your nose, the edge of your lower jaw, and the collarbones. There isn't much padding over these body parts, and you can damage nerve and bone if you are not careful.

Some of the oatmeal may bounce around the bathroom, but don't be too concerned about this. Try to keep most of it in the cookie sheet and just clean up the bathroom when you are finished.

Step 2

Move the cookie sheet—but don't dispose of the oatmeal yet—and carefully pick up the towel so that any oatmeal in it is not dumped down the drain. Gently shake the towel over the wastebasket, or go to the door and shake it outside. Spread the towel either over a favorite recliner chair or your bed. Now go back to the cookie sheet and scoop one to two tablespoons of oatmeal into the palm of one hand. Using warm water, make a spreadable oatmeal paste right in your hand. Then rub the paste around your face, wetting your fingertips just a bit now and then to massage the oatmeal in. Make a second or third handful, if needed, to rub into your neck, shoulders, and more for your arms. Now sit back and relax in the recliner or on your bed until the oatmeal is dry.

Step 3

Wash off the oatmeal using a washcloth and a bowl full of water. Try not to wash a lot of it down the drain or you may create plumbing problems for yourself. Pat your face dry. Dump the oatmeal-water outside or down a garbage disposal.

Step 4

This next step involves your choice of several herbs and some steam. If you don't have a face steamer, you can lean over a bowl with very hot water in it and put a towel over your head tent-style. Or you can plug the bathroom sink, fill it with boiling water and lean over it, again with the towel to trap steam.

At this point you have to decide what you most want to accomplish with your skin. What you're trying to do will determine your choice of herbs. The following list will give you some ideas of what to put in the water and how it will affect your skin. They are all good in one way or another. Once you've picked one, put about two heaping tablespoons of the selected herb in your steamer, bowl, or sink. Turn on the steamer, or pour a teakettle full of boiling water over the herbs in the bowl or the sink. If you are using a bowl or the sink, use about two to three quarts of boiling water. A smaller amount will cool off too quickly.

Rosemary—Corrects dull, sallow skin. Rosemary has great ability to improve circulation, bringing rosy color to your cheeks. Its fragrance is also very pleasant.

Rose petal—Has cleansing and astringent properties. If your skin tends to be oily and you want to balance it out, put a handful of rose petals in your hot water. And nothing is more elegant than the fragrance of roses.

Chervil or Yarrow—Both have the cleansing and astringent effects of rose petals, but without the elegant fragrance.

Bergamot—Good for acne or other skin troubles. Bergamot will help clean and clear pimples, prevent the infection that make them red and sore, and speed healing. If you have lady's mantle available, you can use it to do the same things as bergamot.

Fennel seed and leaf—Good for deep cleansing. Put two tablespoons fennel seed in a small grinder for ten to twenty seconds and add to your hot water. Let it work deep into your pores, cleaning and medicating. It works especially well for skin that has been damaged by smoking. If you have allergies or sensitive skin, fennel may bother you.

Geranium—Both astringent and stimulating, it is the thing to use if you have trouble with sebaceous glands or your skin has lost its tone and hangs in limp folds. The scented varieties—lemon, rose, apple, lime, nutmeg, and pine geranium—will give you a good aromatherapy effect.

Elderberry flower—A good choice if you want to lighten freckles or age spots

Chamomile flower—Does everything for skin. In summer it helps sunburned skin recover. In winter it helps with windburn. In any season it works to restore moisture to skin. If you have a rash or inflammation, use chamomile to speed healing. It is even used to help restore skin that has been irradiated and is suffering from severe burns. Chamomile is related to the ragweed family, so keep this in mind if you are allergic to ragweed.

Violet flower or leaf—Excellent for balancing skin in the case of chronic conditions like psoriasis, eczema, and other rashes. Though you don't hear much about violets, they have some amazing properties that range from fighting tumors to flavoring jellies. In a facial steamer, violets help reduce scarring from acne or recent surgery.

Hen-and-Chicken—Is particularly helpful for nourishing and softening skin. It can be used in facials or for soaking feet. It will soften corns, allowing you to begin rubbing them away, and it helps soften and remove old scar tissue.

Once your chosen herb has been added to the water in your steamer or bowl, lean into the steam, letting it flow over your face, neck, shoulders, and arms. Some people can stand only ten minutes worth of steam, others don't want to quit after thirty minutes. Take it at your own speed. Though to get the best results from the natural oils in the herb or flower you chose, try to keep steaming your face for at least fifteen minutes.

Step 5

Turn off the steamer or empty the bowl or sink that held your hot water. Now begin to splash your face with cold water, and continue this for at least one full minute. Finally, gently pat your skin dry.

If you look in the mirror at this point you will usually see a bright red face that looks perhaps a bit swollen or worse than usual. Don't panic. This means you have gotten all the way through the skin layer with your cleansing, healing efforts. When the color returns to normal and the skin loses some of its puffiness, you will be amazed at how beautiful your skin looks.

Step 6

You have two choices at this point. You can stop, apply a very light moisturizer, perhaps one with aloe vera in it, and go about the rest of your day. Or, you can continue with a third round of facial treatments if you are serious about healing and want one of the effects offered by a specific face pack. Consider the following suggestions.

Clay Pack

Used by people around the globe for thousands of years, clay is one of those "does everything" therapies. It doesn't just clean the surface of your skin; it literally draws waste and toxins out of the deep layers of skin and tissue and sucks them into the clay pack. When you remove the pack, the toxins go with it and the clay cannot be reused.

Clay comes in various colors—green, red, brown, gray, and white, to name a few—but the green clay is the best and most powerful. You can buy it in tubes at your local health food store, where it's quite expensive at around $10.00 per eight ounces. Or you can buy it in bulk powder and get twenty-five pounds for about $15.00, mix it with water, and use it for everything from insect bites, burns and bruises, to rashes, warts, and tumors.

Although scientists don't understand all the reasons why clay works the way it does, they do agree that it is loaded with minerals. This is one of the reasons to use it on your face. It actually feeds your face with minerals, and at the same time it deep cleans, shrinks pores tremendously, and removes dead skin so the deep layers of dermis can breathe better.

To tap into this healing, put the clay on your face as evenly as possible, in a layer about one-eighth to one-quarter inch thick. Lie back and rest until the clay is completely dry, which will take up to forty-five minutes depending on the temperature, humidity, and thickness of clay. You will definitely feel it pulling and working on your face as it dries.

When dry, remove the clay using a bowl of water and several disposable cosmetic pads. Do not wash the clay down the sink or you will plug up your drain. Throw the water and clay into your garden or lawn when you are finished with it. It does wonders for your plants because of the minerals it contains. Rinse your face and pat it dry.

Apply a light moisturizer and you are ready to finish your day. Don't use a moisturizer that is too greasy or heavy or you will block the ability of the skin to breathe after you just spent two hours clearing away dead skin and cleaning out pores and tissues.

If you are young and in your twenties, consider going bare-skinned for a few hours or the rest of the day. If your skin is too dry, or you are older, consider applying a bit of vitamin E oil, an avocado oil, or something else that the skin can use to repair itself. Above all, don't apply any makeup for at least two or three hours.

Strawberries and Cream

This kind of pack is a good follow-up to a facial steam bath for two main reasons. First, the strawberries tend to lighten freckles and age spots, thus giving your skin a clear and even tone. And second, the cream is an emollient that simply can't be beat. It feeds your skin like nothing else, and you won't believe how soft and supple and wrinkle-free it will be afterwards.

To make your own strawberry-and-cream pack, first cut one or two large strawberries in half, and holding them carefully, rub over your face, neck, shoulders, and arms. Next, mix about one cup of fresh, slightly mashed or finely chopped strawberries with two to four tablespoons of heavy cream. You don't want the mixture to be too juicy or it will run all over the place and refuse to stay on your face. If you're not allergic to wheat you can add a bit of whole-wheat flour to thicken it. If you are allergic to wheat, try a bit of tapioca flour, or some arrowroot.

Wrap a towel around your hair, pat the mixture onto your face, and lie back to let the strawberries and cream work their magic. Leave on for about twenty to thirty minutes, then wash off with cool water.

Gotu Kola

Known also as the herb centella, gotu kola has been a widely used alternative medicine for serious skin conditions. If you have had skin ulcers, grafts, burns (even second and third-degree burns), psoriasis, eczema, the appearance of small veins in your facial skin, or a variety of other debilitating skin conditions, you might want to do a facial pack using gotu kola.

To start, prepare a decoction of this herb the day before the facial pack by placing a handful of crushed gotu kola in two pints of water. If you can't get the dried leaves, your local health-food store can order a topical gotu kola salve for you.

Once you have the salve or decoction, do the facial cleansing and steaming as described generally above, then dip a clean cloth into the decoction, wring lightly, and put on your face, or apply the salve and massage it generously into your skin. Lie back, close your eyes, and let it work for at least half an hour. Then get up and use a warm washcloth to rinse out the remains of the herb or remove any excess salve. This will help your skin heal and rebuild itself.

Gotu kola triggers deep skin replacement, improves venous blood flow through the skin, and strengthens connective tissue. If you have skin problems elsewhere on your body, you might want to take a standardized extract of gotu kola on a regular basis.

Aloe Vera

Almost everyone is familiar with aloe vera, and if you choose to do an aloe vera face pack, all you really need to have available is a good aloe plant. Cut off one or two pieces of the plant's fleshy arm, each one about two inches long. Slit each one open carefully, exposing the luxurious gel inside, and force the flaps of the piece open so you can rub the gel all over your face, neck, and down onto your shoulders. If your two pieces run out of gel, cut another one and continue spreading the gel until you are covered. Then lie back and rest for fifteen to twenty minutes while the gel dries.

If you like you can dampen the gel with a bit of water and rub it in more deeply, allowing your skin to absorb as much of it as possible, then rest for another fifteen minutes or so. Or lay a warm wet towel with a flat weave over your entire face, neck, and shoulders and allow your skin to soak up the damp gel undisturbed for at least forty-five minutes. Aloe vera soothes skins, moisturizes it, kills bacteria and fungus, and reduces scarring. It protects against chapped skin, heals eczema, sunburn, and speeds cell regeneration when you do get burned. Aloe is used to heal radiation burns and as an anticancer agent for those who have had small skin cancers on their face.

When you emerge from under the towel, rinse the remains of the aloe vera off with cool water. Go bare-skinned if you can for a while, or apply a light coat of a nourishing oil, something that the skin can use to feed itself, like vitamin E or avocado oil. Brush your hair. Now you are ready to deal with the world.

Using herbs and natural foods to take care of your face, and completing the process of an entire facial, is like a meditation on life itself. When you are done it is quite obvious that a transformation has taken place. You are the same person, yet you look and feel differently about yourself. The ritual of rubbing away dead layers of the self, cleansing your deep unseen levels, and restoring vitality is something that needs to happen physically, mentally, emotionally, and spiritually. A good facial is not only an excellent symbol of renewal, it is the perfect place to start.

Henna: The Red Herb

≫ By K. D. Spitzer ≪

L awsonia inermis, commonly called henna, was named by a British explorer, John Lawson, in the early 1700's. This rather inexplicable fact belies its ancient history in North Africa and India. In fact, the use of this herb has been carbon dated back to 3500 BC, marking it as an important and continuing presence in human civilization for much of the past 5,000 years.

In Arabic countries, henna is also called *khanna*. The Hindus of India call it *mehedi* or *mehndi*. Ancient hieroglyphs in tombs in the Valley of the Nile gave the Egyptian name of *pouquer* to this dye that colored the fingernails of mummified remains. Today, plantings have been restored to the Nile Valley where it is called Egyptian privet.

The Use of Henna

Henna is a herbaceous shrub that grows from six to twenty-five inches in height. There are several varieties, but the *inermis* variety is the most commonly available for sale in the United States. Although the plant thrives in hot and dry climates, in the northern states it grows well indoors in bright light as a tub plant, though it can be carried outside during the warmer summer months.

The colors extracted from the leaves of the henna plant can range from white through rose to red; the best colors for dyes come from the top of the plant or from any area of new growth. Furthermore, the very fragrant flowers, which grow in clusters on the plant, are used in perfumes.

Indeed, the Romans called this perfume camphire. It is believed to be the base of Cleopatra's scent—the one into which she dipped her sails on her way up the Nile to seduce Marc Antony. This fragrance preceded her and gave perfumed intimations of her arrival.

In aromatherapy, this scent is an aphrodisiac—so poor Antony probably was ensnared by Cleopatra even before he met her. Today, Arab medicinal practitioners counsel people to inhale the scent of henna blossoms in order to prevent sterility and to enhance passion.

Indeed, the Bible's Song of Songs confides: "My beloved is unto me as a cluster of henna blossoms in the vineyard of En-gedi." This reference to henna as a perfume (camphire) suggests its use as far back as 250 BC. In India, it is still used as a perfume component; it is also distilled there for use as an essential oil.

The folklore surrounding this herb reveals how deeply ingrained it is in cultures stretching from Egypt and other Arab countries through India to the Far East. Henna is part of a social tradition of decoration of the body for celebration and rites of passage. It is the catalyst for age-transcending bonding among females in the tribal community or seraglio. Its application as body art is the ritual that eases a young girl's passage from virgin to wife and in this context serves as a medium for strengthening bonds among the generations—the experienced gives advice to the novice. It is also the beginning of the bond between wife and mother-in-law.

The mystique surrounding this plant probably dates back to early periods of world goddess fertility religions. The leaves from the top of the shrub were infused in oil and used to massage and stimulate the male phallus, mimicking the color of arousal and love-making. Its use then is reflected in modern times in its status as a symbol of love and as an aphrodisiac.

However, it is its ancient roots as a medicinal herb that has suggested its continuing use as a cosmetic. Living as we do in a temperate climate, we do have true understanding of the heat of the desert climate and the societal need for a plant that is cooling and soothing. Henna answers this need, as it is antipyretic (cooling) and antispasmodic (soothing). Additionally, it is antiseptic, astringent, antibacterial, and antifungal. If that did not ensure its place in the *materia medica* of the hot climates of the world, then its use as a sunscreen and sunburn soother will. Henna, furthermore, has even been used as a deodorant; its leaves carried under the arms or worn in sandals to protect against perspiration and to perfume, so that the feet and underarms of weary travelers are certain not offend.

Henna's history as an important medicine is recorded by the ancient Egyptians and Greeks. Its leaves, bark, and flowers are found in ayervedic formulas dating back thousands of years; its uses are in fact quite universal and widespread. As a beverage, henna is known to relieve headaches, soothe fevers and stomach pains; as a paste, henna protects and soothes skin ailments, and helps to heal wounds. The essential oil of henna is also used as a medicinal.

Henna's use as a hair dye stems from its ability to protect the head from the heat of the Sun. The leaves and flowers were placed on the head as a soothing screen. Perspiration wet the leaves, which in turn caused the hair to turn red. Eventually, it was discovered that henna also helped to prevent the hair from thinning.

It is not too difficult a leap to make that dark-eyed, dark-haired people would find red hair different and attractive, and so was born a beauty trademark that has spanned the entire world for centuries.

The use of henna in art traditions are a natural extension of its medicinal uses. The dyeing of the entire foot (like a shoe) with henna is called the "step in" design. This displays henna's basic ability to insulate the feet from hot desert sands, as well as its function as an adornment. Form follows function. Most cultures that use henna functionally have evolved a similar decorative art tradition.

In the Arabic world, artists have developed large floral patterns that are painted in red henna on the hands and feet. African traditions among the Berber tribes offer a deeper, almost black color, and large bold geometrics in skin patterning. It is in the Indian tribal patterns that we find the allure of bright red dyes on hands and forearms, shins, and feet. The designs are ornate and drawn with fine, lacy lines in small floral patterns. It shouldn't be surprising that the paisley is a favored theme.

The Magic of Henna

It goes without saying that a herb of such universal capability and use as henna is bound to have arrived in the twenty-first century with a long and certain history of magical powers. Even in an environment as inhospitable as the world's hot and arid regions, the need for protection from the vagaries of daily life is a given.

Henna's use as a textile dye and leather stain is, in fact, a natural byproduct of this herb's wide versatility and strong magical powers. If your wealth is tied up in livestock like horses or cattle, then dyeing the heads and horns of the animals with henna to protect from the evil eye may very well be a smart move. Naturally this is accompanied by incantation to recount the herb's past triumphs and to exhort the herb to newer and greater ones. It is not uncommon also to see doors painted red to invite prosperity to enter and to encourage prosperity to stay with those within.

The Egyptian queen Nefertiti who lived around 1350 BC was a famous beauty whose reputation for allure has lasted for centuries. She was a known to be a redhead, even though she is today often portrayed with a black wig. Her name translates as "the beautiful one comes." Like many other famous redheads, her hairdresser knew her secrets and one of them was henna.

Using Henna in Your Daily Life

Today you can avail yourself of this vegetable and nonallergic colorant without having to grow your own grove of trees. Most natural foods stores have safe henna coloring kits that are simple to apply. Henna protects hair from the harshness of the Sun and air, and gives elasticity and body to your hair. It is good for dark hair, making it glossy and shiny. It brightens fair hair and covers up unsightly grey hair. It helps with dandruff and relieves tension in your head and face muscles. Always test a strand of hair before proceeding when you plan to apply henna. An ounce of prevention is worth three weeks with a bag on your head.

As you get more facile with this hair dye, you can begin to experiment using powdered henna in bulk along with other herbs which can amend the shades of color depending upon the color and texture of your hair. Additions such as chamomile and calendula can alter color shading for blondes. Strong tea and grape juice can offer interesting alternative color changes for brunettes.

It is as a body stain that henna has shown great inroads into Western beauty ideals. A social phenomenon as well, women are having henna parties and decorating each other with finely drawn designs.

If this is a beauty attraction for you, then it is wise to practice technique before beginning the process. After using paper and pencil to work out your designs, you can use an icing gel to practice a smooth unbroken line. It also makes sense to do a test patch on the inside of your arm to be certain that you are not allergic to henna.

In general, you need to be sure that you purchase henna that is marketed for body staining and not as a hair colorant, as on your skin the henna must be pure and unadulterated. It is important to find the freshest henna that you can, and that it be very fine—much like flour, so you can sift it through an old nylon stocking.

There are many basic recipes for henna paste and you may want to experiment with them all. The following is simple, and a good place to start. The consistency of your paste should be similar to a soft toothpaste.

Henna Paste

1	tbsp powdered henna
1	tbsp freshly squeezed and strained lemon juice
6	drops eucalyptus essential oil
2	drops clove essential oil
	Brewed coffee, strong tea, or distilled water

Mix all ingredients in a ceramic or stainless steel bowl, and let sit overnight. Cover it but don't refrigerate. In the morning, stir; add drops of coffee, tea, or water to make a soft paste. If it is too soft, then stir in pinches of henna powder until it reaches the proper consistency. Let it sit until evening before applying, as the stain will be darker.

Before applying the henna paste, it is important that your skin is clean. Scrub with soap and water. Some henna artists recommend even patting the skin with eucalyptus oil.

Spoon the paste into a plastic baggie and snip off a tiny corner. You may need to enlarge this slightly until you become more expert. Twist the bag like an icing bag and proceed with the design.

The henna paste needs to stay moist on the skin for one to three hours. If it starts to dry, gently dab or mist on a solution of one tablespoon of lemon juice and one teaspoon of sugar. When you are ready to remove the paste, slosh on some olive oil, and scrap off the paste with a butter knife. It's a good idea to oil the design every day with almond or olive oil. Try not to use soap and water on it for a couple days.

Like any other art technique, practice makes perfect. Also, it is a good idea to experiment with the materials to achieve a better application.

Resources

You can find designs in a decorative arts book at your local library. You can also find plenty of ideas on the web. The web site for the Tap Dancing Lizard is a very valuable resource. It is located at: www.tapdancinglizard.com/mehandi/. Another good site is located at: www.mehandi.com.

If you want the designs without the trouble of mixing the paste, the Crayola company sells nontoxic markers in skin colors. Check their website at www.crayola.com.

If you are not very good at freehand designs and think that stencils are the way to go for you, then you'll want to be in touch with the Castle Art and Import Company. They are located in Green Bay, Wisconsin; their phone number is (888) 829-8018, and their website is at: www.castleart.com. They have a little bit of everything for mehndi practices.

Henna essential oil is also available and comes attractively packaged at a very reasonable price from Zinnia Worldly Goods. It is called Hina and you can find it online at: www.zinnia.ca. Herb's Daughter, in Centerville, Massachusetts, sells henna perfume similar to the scent that Cleopatra used. You can e-mail them at: herblady@ma.ultranet.com.

Finally, if you live near a metropolitan area, you may find a talented henna artist in a spa or salon who can do the work for you. Check your local Yellow Pages.

Herbs for Attractive Eyes

≈ By Leeda Alleyn Pacotti ≈

How often have we heard the old adage that the eyes are the windows of the soul? Certainly, the health and beauty of these extraordinary sensory organs impress each person we encounter, every time we meet them. In fact, when we look at ourselves in the morning mirror, our first assessment of how we are feel physically and emotionally comes from observing the condition of our eyes.

The strong effect of seeing our own eyes, of appreciating their allure, cannot be underestimated. Whereas baggy, bloodshot, or swollen eyes signal distress and cause a casual observer to withdraw from us, on the other hand soft lids and luminous eyes intimate warmth and caring and generate a desire in others to draw near and converse. Wide-open and bright eyes signal our interest in the daily flow

of people and events. Even when a person does not possess a perfect complement of pretty features, one's healthy eyes attract others, who will see the eyes as indications of inner balance, compassion, and beauty—a combination that creates irresistible attraction.

Ocular Anatomy

When it comes to appraising our eyes and eyesight, usually we are only concerned with the glistening exterior of the eyeball and the resilience of the surrounding eyelids. However, there is much more to eye health than ball and socket.

Attached to each eye are six muscles, four of which reach from the front of the eyeball to the back, and two of which surround the eye obliquely. All of these muscles perform as countering pairs, moving the eyeball up or down, from side to side, or around in arcs or circles. The alternating pull and relaxation of these muscles over the surface of the eyeball are what allow us to survey the surrounding environment rapidly.

Besides rapid movement, these muscles help the eye focus on what we see by applying pressure to flatten or shorten the eyeball as necessary. Most people believe the lens of the eye alters for focus, but it is the changed length of the eyeball that causes sharp visual perception. When we view objects close at hand, the muscles elongate the eyeball. When we look into the distance, the same muscles flatten the eyeball, permitting us to see distant objects clearly.

Also misunderstood is the fact that eyes don't actually see. Because our eyes are extraordinarily diverse and constantly active, we believe sight is centered in them. However, these organs merely function as receivers of light waves, with the eyeball being the equivalent of the adjustable lens of a camera. When light waves enter the pupil of the eye, they are concentrated together at the back of the eyeball onto the retinal wall, where the optical nerve of the brain attaches. Simultaneously, a chemical change occurs on the retina, stimulating the optic nerve to translate and carry those light wave signals deeply into the brain, where its visual center is located. At the visual center in the back of the head, we see a developed picture of the exterior world we are viewing.

Of course, good sight is impossible without the lens of the eye, which must be kept transparent for light waves to pass through it. Built in concentric layers, the clear lens contains channels for the passage of lymphatic fluid, which keeps the lens moist and resilient. That same lymphatic flow transports nutrition to the lens and carries off any debris that could accumulate and clutter the lens' clarity.

Eye Problems

As a nation of readers and computer-users, Americans are finding that sight impairments are a common byproduct of daily life and work. Most notable are the conditions of nearsightedness or myopia, farsightedness or presbyopia, and astigmatism.

Continual elongation or flattening of the eyeball causes, respectively, myopia and presbyopia. In both of these conditions, certain pairs of the muscles surrounding the eyes are in a constant state of tension, forcing the eyeball to maintain an unnatural length. The difference between these two conditions is the placement of the concentrated focus of light waves to the retinal wall. In myopia, because the eyeball is too long, light wave concentration is in front of the retinal wall. In presbyopia, the eyeball is too short, causing the light wave concentration to focus behind the retinal wall. Consequently, the unnaturally forced length of the eyeball prevents the alterable focus of light waves, causing clear vision only when objects are near, in myopia, or far, in presbyopia.

Astigmatism results when the pull and relaxation of muscles becomes unbalanced. Muscles that pull more strongly than their opposites reshape the eyeball from its natural roundness, creating an unequal pressure on its surface. The eyeball becomes lopsided, or flattened in some one portion. The result is blurred vision, as the received light waves are bent and distorted to accommodate the misshapen interior space of the eye.

Besides impairments, other conditions can temporarily affect the eyes. Cataracts, which are believed to be irreversible, diminish the clarity of sight. These begin when the fluid flow into and through the lens of the eye becomes obstructed. This lens relies on circulated lymphatic fluid to bring it nourishment and remove debris. Tension, however, compresses the lens, causing constriction of the lymph channels. When these channels are continually obstructed, the lens becomes malnourished, losing moisture and resilience, gradually drying and hardening. At the same time, debris within the lens accumulates. This debris accumulation, coupled with lens dryness, appears as an opacity or clouding of the lens, which we call a cataract.

Tension within the eye does not always result in a cataract, but it certainly contributes to eyestrain, an aching sensation felt around the eyes. In modern work environments, tension and eyestrain often go hand in hand and contribute to each other. Overuse of the eyes for reading and computer work necessarily creates strain, as eye muscles are forced into narrow movement. The tension comes from what might be called a self-imposed ocular paralysis.

Eyestrain and conjunctivitis, or pinkeye, also inhibit the use of the eyes. Conjunctivitis is the inflammation of the membrane that lines the eyelids. When this condition is present, the inner lids appear fiery red, instead of the usual medium pink. The whites of the eyes are often bloodshot, with the outer lids appearing swollen and reddened. Itchiness or a feeling of sand in the eye is a common sensation. If mucus or pus is present, a viral infection has caused the conjunctivitis. In our pollution-filled environment, though, conjunctivitis frequently stems from airborne allergens and irritants, and reactions to various chemical preservatives in foods and cosmetic chemicals used around the eyes.

Keeping Your Eyes Healthy

Because we rely so strongly on our eyes, we often forget that they are parts of an integrated body. Like other important organs, eyes have specific needs to keep them healthy. These needs include good neural flow, proper nutrition, and an elimination of accumulated waste. With some attention to diet and with proper eye exercise, the impairments and conditions of the eyes can often be corrected. Changes in sight routines, and some simple treatments, can return liveliness and glow to your overworked, tired, or sick eyes.

Diet

By far the most important nutritional need of eyes is vitamin A, which directly prevents night blindness. Taking the recommended daily allowance of vitamin A over a period of time will promote healing of most eye problems and illnesses.

In the balanced diet of a healthy person, a daily snack of one-quarter cup of raw, unsalted sunflower seeds provides the necessary vitamin A. This vision vitamin is also found in apricots, beet greens, broccoli, cantaloupe, carrots, cod liver oil, eggs, garlic, mustard greens, papayas, peaches, pumpkins, red peppers, spinach, sweet potatoes, Swiss chard, and yellow squash.

In the body, the liver stores vitamin A, utilizing it in the digestion of protein. To prevent an overburdening of the liver over tiem, take a beta-carotene complex. The liver converts beta-carotene into vitamin A, as needed. Beta-carotene supplements are available in dry form or suspended in an oil base. The dry form is not stored in the liver but is best for persons who cannot break down fats in digestion.

The average supplementation of vitamin A is 10,000 I.U. and needs to be accompanied by supplements of vitamins C and E, and the mineral zinc, for proper absorption. Take daily 3 g of vitamin C, 400 I.U. of vitamin E, and 50 mg of zinc. (Note: Pregnant women should never take more than 10,000 I.U. of vitamin A daily.)

An important dietary consideration for the sick eyes is elimination of certain foodstuffs from the diet, particularly nicotine, sugar, and caffeine. Especially damaging to vision is an ingested combination of all three, which can temporarily weaken the eyes and blur eyesight.

When eye problems are present, increase the vitamin and/or mineral supplementation, as follows:

Cataracts—Beta-carotene 25,000 I.U. to 50,000 I.U. daily (unless pregnant), until the cataracts begin to dissipate, which may take up to six months

Conjunctivitis—Beta-carotene up to 100,000 I.U. for one month, and 25,000 I.U. thereafter (unless pregnant); vitamin C up to 6 g.

Eyestrain—Beta-carotene up to 50,000 I.U. daily (unless pregnant); add vitamin B complex, 100 mg.

Eye Exercise

Like all muscled parts of the body, the eyes benefit tremendously from varied physical activity. Modern lifestyle at home and work causes us to maintain an unvarying routine of eye movement. We hold our eyes steady in a narrow range when we read, watch television, or work at a computer screen. To keep the eyes in good condition, some simple exercises and specialized rest reduce muscular stress around and within the eyeball, increase blood flow to the eyes, and help rejuvenate all ocular tissues.

At least once each hour, during intense eye activity, lightly flutter your eyes in continuous blinking, looking about you, moving only your eyes. As your eyes begin to feel less tense, squeeze them shut very tightly, then open them widely. Repeat the sequence of flutter-blinking, shutting, and opening twice more. This routine should be done at least three times each day, working up to a blinking sequence of 100 movements.

Perform the following maneuvers, in sets of six each, to strengthen the muscles around the eyes. With eyes open and head still, move your eyes as far to the left and right as you can. Then, move them up and down. Next, move them on an oblique from upper left to lower right, followed by an oblique from upper right to lower left. Finally, roll your eyes in circles to the right and then to the left. (Note: When your eyes are fatigued, be sure to perform these maneuvers more slowly.)

City dwellers experience an almost perpetual light stimulation to the eyes, even during sleep hours, from constantly shining streetlights and household night lights. Both the brain and the optic nerve need total darkness to obtain rest from constant stimulation. Although it is not necessary to sleep with an eye mask to block invading light, a fifteen-minute blackout session with the palms of the hands, as pioneered by Dr. William H. Bates in the early 1900s, gives the eyes an opportunity to refresh.

Sit with your elbows on a table and rub your hands briskly together. Next, cup your hands slightly, raising your eyebrows. Cover your eyes with your palms, resting the base of your palms on your cheekbones and crossing your fingers over each other on your forehead. Be careful not to apply pressure directly onto your eyes. Open your eyes once to make sure there is no light entering, and adjust your hands to block it. Close your eyes and remain in the darkness. To avoid staring into the dark, work with mental visualizations to keep your eyes from being active.

Over time, these new eye routines can yield improvements in both your general eye health and visual powers. Myopia, presbyopia, and astigmatism are likely to become less severe.

Herbal Treatments

Because we depend on our sense of sight, we need to respect the fact that the eyes are very delicate organs. Over-the-counter liquid solutions, including those for contact lens wearers, have strong chemicals, which can further irritate eyes even when they are supposed to maintain or heal them. When a pharmaceutical is necessary, never use it interchangeably on members of the family.

Treating the eyes with herbs and other naturally produced compounds has a long tradition. Some treatments have evolved through trial and error. However, certain herbs were chosen by an associative principle of herbology, called the "Law of Similars." This law suggests that if a part of a plant has an appearance similar to an observed part or excretion of the body, it will likely make an appropriate healing agent for that body part. A readily obvious example is the meat of a walnut, which after removal from the shell, looks very much like the two halves of the brain and is used accordingly to nourish it. With this law in mind, early herbalists noted that the lightly veined white petals of the eyebright flower looked very much like a bloodshot eye.

In fact, eyebright, *Euphrasia officinalis,* is the foremost eye remedy. It is high in vitamins A, B, C, D, and E, and in the minerals silicon, sulphur, and zinc—all of which are eye nutrients. Besides strengthening eye tissues, eyebright promotes the elasticity and resilience of nerves in and around the eyes. Taken as a tea, eyebright also detoxifies the liver, the storehouse for vitamin A. As a healing agent intermittently or over the longer term, eyebright is unparalleled in treating eyes.

Eyebright is a very delicate herbal and loses its potency through boiling. To make a tea, bring a cup of water to a boil, then remove it from the heat. Add a teaspoon or two of eyebright in bags or as loose tea, and steep the tea for up to nine minutes. After sipping one or two cups of tea over an hour, you will notice that your eyes feel much stronger and more relaxed.

Retain the teabags or the wet herbal mass to make an eye compress. The bags, or the wet herb placed in a white paper towel, can be applied directly over the eyes to rejuvenate the surrounding tissues. If you do not plan to use the bags or wet herb compresses immediately, place them inside a plastic bag and keep them in the refrigerator. Use them within the next five days.

Leftover eyebright tea can also be chilled and used later is an eyewash directly in the eye. Eyebright is very helpful for the conditions of blepharitis (an inflammation causing the eyes to itch and secrete fluids that crust the lids and lashes during sleep), bloodshot eyes, conjunctivitis, dry eyes, and itchy or tired eyes. A hot compress of eyebright is the best treatment for conjunctivitis.

Another fine herbal remedy is raspberry leaf tea. Also a delicate herb, raspberry leaf is infused the same way as eyebright and can also be used as a compress and eyewash. Raspberry leaf is good for healing bloodshot eyes, eyestrain, itchy or tired eyes, and sties. Again, a hot compress is best to relieve pain and bring the sty to head.

Pure aloe vera gel can be dropped directly into the eyes, reducing all types of burning and inflammation. Aloe vera is useful for treating the sting and the accompanying throbbing of eyes irritated from air pollutants, and for treating the inflammatory conditions of blepharitis and conjunctivitis.

Apiarists, or beekeepers, have tested the versatility of raw unrefined honey on a variety of health problems. Honey is high in vitamins C, D, E, and the B-complex, and is considered a natural antiseptic. For cataract healing, raw honey mixed with aloe vera, dropped into the eyes before sleep, will help dissipate cataracts over time. This same mixture cools and promotes the healing of eyelids inflamed with conjunctivitis.

Medical Assessments

Eyes are complex organs. However, a complete understanding the condition of this complex organ requires the help of a practitioner who specializes in eye health. Naturopathic approaches alone, however noninvasive, are not helpful in the case of complex disorders such as glaucoma or retinal degeneration. An examination by a qualified specialist, who can assess eye health, provides you with a wealth of valuable information.

In the allopathic medical community, three types of specialists deal with eyes. These are the optician, the optometrist, and the ophthalmologist. The optician is not qualified to assess eye health and is limited to filling prescriptions for eyeglasses and contact lenses. An optometrist can test the visual power of eyes and treat problems that do not require surgery. In some states, optometrists are permitted to prescribe certain medications. The ophthalmologist, however, is a medical eye specialist, trained to test the eyes, diagnose eye conditions, and prescribe corrective measures. Besides extensive knowledge of eye conditions, the ophthalmologist's knowledge will help you understand the intensity and duration of a condition and its effect on the eyes. Be aware that most ophthalmologists do not agree with herbal applications. Be sure to advise your ophthalmologist of any extra vitamin or mineral supplements your are taking, or herbal teas and washes you may be using to treat your eyes.

Considering how we rely on our eyes to help us maneuver through the day, good food and good practices go a long way toward improving our outlook on the world. Now that's beauty.

For Further Sutdy

The Eyes Have It: A self-help manual for better vision. Earlyne Chaney. Samuel Weiser, Inc., 1987.

Jude's Herbal Home Remedies. Jude Williams. Llewellyn Publications, 1997.

Prescription for Nutritional Healing, 3rd Edition. James Balch and Phyllis Balch. Avery Publishing Group, 2000.

Herbs for the Sweat Lodge

⇝ By Bernyce Barlow ⇜

Since so many folks are now using sweat lodges, sweat houses, and saunas for purification it seemed appropriate to compose an article on the proper use of the herbs in these instances. Sweating has been used universally for ages to clean out toxins in the body. Understanding the herbs best used in purification sweats will assist in maintaining good health and safety. Although the methods or structure of the facility that houses and captures the heat for a proper sweat differ from country to country, the process is generally very similar across cultures.

Setting up a Sweat Lodge

A sweat lodge or house is, in general, an enclosed structure often built from wood or sticks that will house a small group or individual for their sweat. It will be built to allow the heat to bring

on a profuse sweat in a person or persons in the hopes that illnesses, toxins, and infections will be eliminated through the process of sweating. Ancient healers sometimes sought this method to actually change the blood to treat certain conditions untreatable by any other method. It is also generally believed that when the body is clean, the mind and spirit are also cleared of any unwanted energy, therefore leaving the mind and spirit and body purified.

Traditionally, this process also uses a combination of herbs taken as internal teas, external tea washes, salves, and burnt herb smoke in order to aid in the purification and healing process. These herb remedies, many of which have been passed down through thousands of years of trial and error, will be addressed in this article. For many reasons, these remedies were kept secret through the centuries. One reason was a herbal healer was a profession, and to let folks know the secrets would likely mean a loss of a future job. Furthermore, for reasons of respect to the gods and goddesses who ruled over the herbs, ancient healers of the old ways took strict vows not to divulge their secret herbal combinations.

But times have changed. Herbal knowledge has made a comeback, and people have no qualms about using Mother Earth's healing plants to prevent illness and promote good health. It is actually very important to know the secrets of ancient healers, because using the wrong herbs or herbal combinations can actually cause more damage than anything else. Using the wrong herbs can actually bring on symptoms and conditions that were not a problem in the beginning of the healing process.

The herbs, teas, and external washes listed below are part of a solution that will prevent mistakes. These recipes have been used for thousands of years and have remained in the healers medicine bundle because they work. However, it is important to remember that individuals have unique chemical makeups, and what works for one person may not work for the next. Overall, though, these purification herbs have survived the test of time, trial, and error.

Using Herbs in the Sweat Lodge

As a rule, consistently throughout this article I am going to discuss the herbs that are used in Native American, Mexican, and Central American sweat lodges or sweat houses. Occasionally, there will be a herb that is known to another country or region that was adapted by the indigenous peoples into their healing methods. These adaptations have survived through a testing stage and will be included. Furthermore, I am going to divide this article into lodge materials, burnt herbs, internal teas, external tea washes, and salves. Burnt herbs are leaves and resins are placed on hot rocks to create an aroma useful in healing. Internal teas are sipped during the purification process, before the purification process begins, or after one exits the sweat lodge. External teas are used as a skin or eye wash either before, during, or after the sweat process. Salves are applied many hours before or directly after the sweat, but never during the sweat. This is in order to keep the pores of the skin from becoming blocked or clogged thereby preventing the perspiration from escaping.

It should also be mentioned that during the sweat process makeup, perfumes, aftershaves, sun block products, and the like should be removed from the skin. You should avoid sweating these products into your body as they can sting and irritate. Beforehand, be sure to remove all metal and plastic jewelry, as they can burn or melt in a hot lodge. Also remove your glasses or contact lenses before entering. Let your lodge leader know if you are taking any medication or other herbal remedies, and if you have any physical conditions like diabetes, high blood pressure or heart disease, pregnancy, skin conditions, asthma, or allergies to certain herbs. Before the lodge, fast for a day or eat very lightly. Large, heavy meals before a sweat can cause nausea.

Lodge Materials

The structure of the physical lodge can create a herb bath itself. That is, many lodges are built from herbs. For instance, willow is usually the tree chosen as a building material. Do not get creative when building a lodge by using what is available. Use willow— any type will do although some varieties are more flexible than others. Willow harvested in the spring right before a Full Moon is the most healing and flexible. Thank the willow for its sacrifice by leaving a small offering of tobacco. Do not remove the leaves; if you must remove the leaves, tuck them into the structure of the lodge dome. There is no use wasting precious medicine. Willow contains salicin, the natural precursor of acetylsalicylic acid, the active pain killer found in aspirin. The long branches of the willow are stretched, bent, and tied to make a hut or dome-shape where participants may sweat from the heat made from hot rocks placed in a indoor firepit pit within the lodge. The lodge is covered to capture the heat, but you should not cover the hut with plastic or any other material that may melt. As the willow is steamed in the process of the sweat, its natural healing properties become apparent in the way it helps to ease your aches and pains.

Burnt Herbs and Resins

Usually before entering a lodge, a participant will be smudged or given a smoke bath. Traditionally, this smoke bath is of burning sage. The leaves of the sage are bundled into a smudge stick or placed in an abalone shell, then set on fire. The fire is then fanned out to make a medicinal smoke. Avoid using metal containers for this process. Sage is used for its antibacterial properties and its histamine effects. One is considered clean after a sage smudge bath. It is also believed the sage will begin the purification process by cleaning up the energy field, often called an aura, that we carry with us. Different types of sage grow in various regions of our continent and Central America. All sage varieties are acceptable for this process. White sage is especially pleasing for its enchanting aroma.

Now that you are in the lodge, the lodge leader will begin to administer herbs on the hot rocks, allowing them to smoke then pour water on the rocks to create steam, creating something like a huge vaporizer. Often the water poured on the rocks has fresh-cut herbs soaking in it—sage, mugwort, and yerba mansa. The participants are given the wet herbs to hold up to their nose while water is being poured on the rocks. In this way, the steam will not burn the mucous membranes in the nose, and you will still gain from smelling the herbs. The lodge sessions are broken up into what is called rounds. Traditionally there are four rounds, with two to four herbs placed on the rocks in each round. Between rounds, the door covering is removed to clear the lodge and allow oxygen in. Participants should take this opportunity to wash themselves and stretch their legs.

The following is a list of herbs used on the rocks in the sweat lodge, and their individual healing properties.

Angelica—Two pinches of dried angelica can be used on the rocks for women's medicine and moontime conditions.

Cedar—Two or three pinches of cedar needles may be used on the rocks for purification. Both cedar and angelica are photosensitizing herbs which, when exposed to sunlight, can cause skin irritation or rash. When using either of these herbs in a sweat lodge, have participants wash with cool water between rounds, especially if the lodge is held during daylight hours.

Copal—Copal is another name for tree sap or resin. Used in very small amounts—a bead or two of the size of your fingernail—all copal is acceptable. Larger amounts will irritate the skin and make the eyes burn. Amber, dragon's blood, pinion, fir, cedar, and juniper resins work very well. If folks in the lodge complain their eyes are burning, have them place sliced cucumber cut into rounds over their eyes and back off the amount of resin you are using. This goes for burnt herbs, as well. Less is better in a lodge environment. Tree copals work on the nervous system and open up and cleanse chakra energy.

Juniper—Use two or three pinches of the needles or crushed berry powder. This is useful for urinary tract cleansing. As a smoke, the fatty oils of the juniper do not interfere with kidney or liver processing which must break down the juniper oils. This sometimes can cause damage to weak organs when taken as a tea. Juniper is also believed to ward off evil spirits.

Lavender—Three to five pinches of lavender flower smoke helps to soothe emotions, relax the body, and assist in healing depressed moods. Lavender is a very gentle herb.

Myrrh—Three to five pinches of the dried leaf of myrrh is useful for its antiseptic and astringent properties. Myrrh copal is also delightful.

Sweetgrass—Sweetgrass is often used outside of the lodge to brush any ashes off the rocks so the lodge does not get ash and unwanted wood smoke in it. It is usually braided with two or three inches of braid left loose to sweep with. Inside the lodge, sweetgrass is used to brush off debris from the outside firepit that the firetender may have missed while cleaning the rocks for the lodge. If the lodge leader accidentally puts too many herbs on the rocks, the sweetgrass makes a sweet-smelling whiskbroom.

Thyme—Three to five pinches of thyme is considered germicidal and antiseptic.

Turmeric—Two or three pinches of this spice is enough to increase bile secretion, helping the liver. Overuse of this herb is a big mistake. Turmeric has toxic oil constituents, but when burned the oils are reduced to manageable medicine. Don't use this herb if you have gallstones.

External Washes

An external wash is used in or out of the lodge to wash away perspiration and smoke residue, and to be absorbed into the body for medicinal affects. Loufa sponges are wonderful to use to cascade the wash over parts of the body, head, and hair.

In the lodge, a container is filled with the medicine wash made from herbs and spring water. Each participant must use their own sponge and medicine bowl, which the lodge leader can fill from the main container. This is to maintain good hygiene and prevent the spreading of skin conditions, germs, and mucus.

Do not use metal or plastic bowls to hold the medicine wash. Large gutted gourds or large wooden bowls are outstanding for this purpose. Smaller gourds that have been gutted can be used instead of loufa sponges. For additional magical healing energy, you can buy birdhouse gourd seeds and grow gourds for this purpose, and you can also grow the loufa sponges in your garden. I use the large gourds to pour water over the rocks, and I use large calabash gourds to hold the water. One nice thing about medicine washes is that if they are made correctly you can't overdo the process (unlike with the burnt herbs). I do suggest, however, that you keep the wash out of the eyes as much as possible. A little bit probably won't hurt your eyes, but for extra precaution close your eyes while you wash just like you do to keep soap and shampoo out when you shower.

External wash recipes vary but the one that seems to do the trick in the lodges is made as follows. Place two handfuls of specific dried leaves, roots, stems, or flowers (depending on what the recipe calls for) to simmer separately for ten minutes in a quart of spring water, then cool. If the wash calls for more than one herb, you can mix the washes together after making each separately. Unlike tea, leave the plants in the water. If you require a lot of wash then adjust your recipe accordingly.

My teachers are Native American, Mexican Indian (Yaqui), and Central American. When we gather and make teas we do not have modern kitchen measuring tools. That is why I often speak in terms of pinches and handfuls.

The following washes can be used in combination or by themselves to treat the specific ailment.

Arthritis—Use whole ginger root, whole licorice plant, oak, arnica, mugwort, castor, red or white willow, soy, nettles, and wild white poppy.

Arthritis and rheumatism—Make a castor pack by cutting a piece of flannel the size of the area you are covering. Soak it in castor oil, then place it over the body in the area you want to work on. This is very good for aches and pains or rheumatism and arthritis.

Bad complexion—Hawthorne, ginkgo, St. John's wort, calendula, buckwheat, peppers, corn silk, lemon, and rose hips. These plants are high in flavonoids and over time can improve capillary strength. Use the entire plant except the corn silk which you must separate from the stalk. Do not use the fruit or seeds of the pepper plant.

Acne—Goldenseal plant, especially the root.

Dry skin—Chamomile, fennel, rose geranium, lavender, palarosa, sandalwood, rosemary, jasmine, and rose. This wash encourages oil production. Use entire plant.

Oily skin—Sage, lemongrass, basil, eucalyptus, cedarwood, cypress, lemon, and yarrow. These plants normalize overactive oil glands. Heat from a sweat encourages oil production naturally, so those with oily skin should use these plants in washes to prevent more oil production or wash oil away after the sweat. Use entire plant.

Sun damage—Carrot plant, aloe, lavender, rosemary, and wild poppy. Use entire plant.

Internal Teas

With so may herbal tea recipes to choose from out there, I am not going to list many. Any good healing tea works in the lodge but I will list some very good teas that I favor for lodge work. To make internal teas for drinking during or after a sweat, place two teaspoons of the plant in six ounces of hot water. Drink up to three times during the sweat lodge process.

Arthritis—Arnica, willow, yucca. Use entire plant.

Cancer—Root of Raiz, root of tumba.

Stroke—Saffron, basil, mingui, olive tree.

Kidney and Liver—Milk thistle, nettle, Florida catsclaw.

Things to Think About

Sweat lodges are not cure-alls, but their benefit has been acknowledged for centuries. They do help prevent certain conditions, keep you healthy, and aid in the progress of getting well by removing toxins from the body and opening clogged pores. They provide soothing heat to conditions that respond to heat.

A good lodge leader understands the benefits and risks of using sweat lodges. Conditions like diabetes, low or high blood sugar, and migraines can be aggravated in a lodge. Contagious conditions like hepatitis should not be allowed into a lodge except under very strict conditions with a lodge intercessor that carries a medicine card. Pregnant women should not sweat at all. Neither should your pets. This is common sense. Children over the age of three can benefit from a lodge if the heat and herbs are minimal.

When folks begin to sweat in lodges their tolerance for the heat is usually very low, but after time this tolerance builds and more hot rocks can be added to the indoor pit. As the steam and heat eats up oxygen in a lodge, a good intercessor knows when the lodge door need to be opened for good health. No one should experience visions or headaches due to lack of oxygen.

After lodge, a good shower is necessary. Folks get hungry after a lodge as well, so a big dinner is often served. Serve food that replaces electrolytes and potassium lost during the sweat. Sport drinks also work well for this purpose.

There are many spiritual benefits to a good sweat as well, but that is a subject for another article. But when you think about it, the purification of the body leads to the mind and spirit even if spiritual ceremony is not employed during the lodge process.

So, for those who intend to use a sweat lodge for purification, remember safety first. Common sense and reliable herbs are the keys that make the experience empowering and healing. Leave your troubles and concerns outside the lodge and don't sweat the small stuff, because the big picture has to do with your connection to the elements of the earth, fire, water, and air. The green herb province will act as the bridge between you and the elements.

Herb Crafts

Enchanted Circles

⤜ By Ellen Dugan ⤛

Creating Magical Herb Wreaths

If you enjoy herbal magic and gardening, I, your very friendly neighborhood garden Witch, have some great projects for you to try during one of those dreary rainy days when the TV is on the fritz and your kids are driving you up the wall and well around the bend.

I am a gardener by trade. In fact, it is my hobby and my passion. Furthermore, as a Witch, a wife, and a working mother of three teenage children, I often absolutely rely on the simplest of nature's treasures for a bit of relaxation time, as well as a source of money-saving magical supplies.

If you want to tap into the simple magic of the herb garden, just follow the directions to make magical herbal wreaths to hang in your home on holidays and every day.

Magical Herbal Wreaths

Herbal wreaths are magical craft items that can be fun for everyone in the family. These "Enchanted Circles" may be used for a variety of purposes. They may serve as a gift for your favorite gardening buddy, or they may be imbued with a specific magical purpose—such as protection, love, or even prosperity.

Wreathmaking is actually an ancient practice. People made wreaths in the Middle Ages to celebrate the changing seasons and to mark the holidays. The circular shape of the wreaths, and their use of herbs or other plant matter, celebrates the circular cycle of life, growth, and death. Creating enchanted herbal wreaths is a fun and easy process from which you can learn something about the traditions of your magical forebears from a far-off and distant time.

Gathering Materials for the Wreath

There are three basic elements to wreath making. You need a base, some decorative materials—herbs, flowers, other plants—and a method to attach the decorative materials to the base. Making a wreath is not expensive nor difficult. You will likely have most of the necessary items on hand—especially if you grow your own herbs—or you can easily find them at your local arts and craft store.

Gathering and harvesting your plants is part of the cycle of gardening, and it mirrors the cycle of life. Personally, I enjoy the harvesting of the herbs and flowers for my wreathmaking as much as I enjoy the planting and the growing. Harvesting is just as important a part of the plant life-cycle as death is of the cycle of life itself.

To start, I frequently take a walk around my yard to see how I can use the bounty that the garden has to offer. These days, my garden has much to provide in terms of herbs and flowers, changing autumn leaves, acorns, pine cones, twigs, or fallen feathers. All of these items are very useful in making your magical wreaths.

Often a lazy hour spent outdoors yields more organic material than any trip to the store, though if you do go to the store be careful to choose items that feel right to you, that have some personal resonance, that remind you of someone or something, or that relate to the correspondence chart I've listed below.

When you begin to assemble the components for your own wreaths, you may care to refer to the correspondence chart, but again, don't ignore your own intuition. Let your instincts guide you as to what feels right, and what feels magical, to place on your wreath.

Before you actually harvest your herbs and flowers, consider these few gathering commonsense guidelines. They will help you avoid leaving a path of damage or harm behind you. They will also help you imbue your wreaths with as much magic power as possible.

> Use a sharp knife or garden scissors when gathering so you will not permanently damage any plant that had given its foliage to you.

> If you are on private property get permission before you begin collecting your natural materials.

> Do not dig up or cut wild flowers. Some of our native species are protected.

> Never take more than a fourth of the total plant, so it can recover after your harvest.

> Afterwards, you may wish to thank the plants by leaving a offering, such as a small gemstone or some natural plant fertilizer.

While you gather your plants, enchant or sing to them. This infuses the plants with the power of your magical purpose. I often make up spontaneous little charms that state my magical intent as I gather my herbs. (These charms rarely rhyme, and are not particularly poetic, so I won't subject you to them; you should feel free, however, to make up your own).

As for the singing, I have been known to sing whatever tune I think appropriate—from Loreena McKennitt to John Mellencamp, from Pavarotti to Paul McCartney. For instance, the song "It's a Lonely Old Night" just seemed appropriate while I was gathering the ingredients for a romance-enhancing spell. It seemed like the magical words of the song would add to the love magic I was trying to create. Who's to say—you never know...

There is the tradition of harvesting your herbs at certain cycles of the Moon or times of the day. Both are valid points and should be considered. To do this, you should consult an astrologer, or any astrological guidebook—such as Llewellyn's *Moon Sign Book*—for information on the best time to harvest certain plants according to time-honored astrological and gardening traditions.

The only word of caution I would give would be to try to avoid gathering your herbs late at night. That is to say, you don't want to be skulking around the yard at night with a flashlight if you can help it. Yes, working outside at night adds a certain mystique to the task, but in the end you cannot really see what you are doing in the dark, and accidents can happen. You don't want to nip a finger or take the wrong plant while you are out there—its not good karma.

If you are a clever Witch or magician, and you happen to have the light of the Full Moon to gather your herbs, then I say go for it! Otherwise, gathering is best left for the daylight hours.

Herbs gathered during a Full Moon (in the daytime) pack a powerful magical punch. However, if you are working for protection or to banish negativity, sickness, or other astral nasties, you should harvest during the waning Moon or, even better, during the New Moon. At the time of this three-day phase, take care to harvest in the morning or during the day. While the Moon is not visible because of the brighter light of the Sun, it is actually overhead for most of the daylight hours.

For wreaths that symbolize new beginnings—a new home, a new marriage, a new baby—you should harvest your herbs under the crescent Moon. A good time to work on this would be right at sundown, while the slim crescent Moon is visible in the western sky.

Finally, remember the ritual practice of not allowing your magical herbs to touch the ground while you are gathering them. Use a basket or a cloth bag to gather up your plants. When you are finished gathering, bring your treasures inside and get ready. It's time to make a magical wreath, Garden Witch style.

Making the Wreath

The following is a list of the basic supplies you will need to make your own personal magical wreath. Choose the right combination of:

A glue gun and glue sticks

Florist wire (20 gauge)

Floral picks

A base—such as a grapevine, straw, pine, or moss wreath

Dried or fresh herbs and flowers, seed pods, nuts, small twigs, and feathers

Ribbons in assorted widths and colors

Lay out the wreath first. Be sure to take your time and arrange things to your liking. Have fun, relax, and enjoy yourself. (And don't expect to be Martha Stewart on your first time out.)

It's much easier to shift pieces around before you glue them on than it is to pry them off afterwards. If you are incorporating twigs or viney things like bittersweet into the wreath, try to work them into the grapevine, for a more natural look.

When making a solid herbal wreath that has herbs covering the entire surface, use a straw wreath for a base. Begin by binding the herbs together with the florist wire into small clusters of equal size (they'll look like little bouquets), then wire a floral pick onto each bundle. Attach the herbs into the wreath with the floral pick. Begin with one bundle and then overlap the stems with the next bunch of herbs. Continue this until you have covered the entire base. Tuck the stems of the last bunch under the top of the first.

You may use different colors of ribbon to decorate your wreaths or to weave a pentagram inside the circle. Experiment with coordinating colors for certain needs and to align with the elements.

> Green ribbon—herbal magic, earth, winter
>
> Red ribbon—love, fire, summer
>
> Blue ribbon—intuition, water, autumn
>
> Yellow ribbon—creativity, air, spring

Elemental wreaths are a fun spin on magical wreaths. I made one for my daughter's room with a blue pentagram woven inside of a small grapevine wreath. Sea shells and miniature starfish adorn it, tapping into the magic of the ocean and the beach.

Use your imagination to add symbols that evoke the powers of the elements in your wreath. In this way, you can further call up the circular cycle of the year in your magic wreath enchantments.

Sample Wreaths

Ready to get started? Before I turn you loose, here are three seasonal wreath projects for you to try and get your creative juices flowing. These projects are meant to be a starting point—feel free to change them and add to them according to your own taste.

Lammas Wreath—Use a straw wreath for the base to evoke the summer. Decorate this wreath with sunflowers either dried or silk. Add stems of dried wheat, black feathers, or a small decorative silk blackbird, dried yellow yarrow, and bright orange or yellow marigolds. Purple ribbon looks great with these colors.

Harvest (Samhain) Wreath—Begin with a large grapevine wreath. Add dried yarrow, red cockscomb, and miniature ornamental corn. See if you can add a few miniature pumpkins or gourds. (Use the floral picks for the heavier items and glue them in securely.) Weave in bittersweet or rose hips and oak leaves. Embellish with a few gilded acorns. For Samhain I would weave a black or orange ribbon pentagram in the center of the wreath.

Yule Wreath—A live or artificial pine wreath as the base is traditional. Pine cones add texture and are easy to find. Add sprigs of fresh holly, dried rose hips, seed pods, nuts, and acorns. Small twigs painted white and then sprinkled with iridescent glitter are a sparkling addition. Tie on some bundles of cinnamon sticks for a prosperous new year.

It does not matter if you grow the herbs and flowers in your own yard and dry them yourself, find them while scavenging in the woods, or buy them at the craft store. You will enjoy creating your enchanted circles and keeping your eyes open for special natural treasures all year.

The Goddess is eternally bountiful. Walk gently, open your heart, and see what you find. Happy wreath making!

For Further Study

Magical Herbalism. Scott Cunningham. Llewellyn Publications, 1998.

The Magical Household. Scott Cunningham. Llewellyn Publications, 1999.

Easy Herbal Gifts in Thirty Minutes

❧ By K. D. Spitzer ❧

I t's easy and delightful to bring the garden into the kitchen. All it really takes is a good microwave or a food dehydrator, and some attention to detail, and you can preserve the summer's bounty to last the entire year. At the same time, you can use your herbal bounty to set up a small store of gifts ready to serve as stocking stuffers or bread and butter tokens.

Drying herbs or fruits in the microwave is a quick solution to a last minute need for proper herbal storage. To do this, it's important to use a microwavable paper towel or brown paper bag to hold the herbs—this is one time when recycled paper is just not suitable.

To start, heat the herbs in your microwave in thirty second intervals at half-power. You need to let the herbs cool each time as, in general, the

molecules will continue to vibrate or "cook" when the time is up. This way the herbs won't burn or over dry. Alos, be aware that the herbs on the outside edges of the paper towel will dry faster than the ones on the inside. Use approximately the same size herbs and stems in each batch.

Aromatic Lip Balm

Some store-bought lip balms actually dry your skin, thus creating a need for more balm. This herbal Aromatic Lip Balm is fragrant and soothing, and it moisturizes without leaving your lips flaking or peeling. It is also is inexpensive and simple to prepare.

Gather your supplies ahead of time, and the actual preparation will go very quickly—less than thirty minutes from start to cleanup. Start by getting a small container, such as a plastic tube or small tin. Such containers are easy to acquire.

Many grocery stores carry a line of natural products suitable for using here, and in general finding oils locally is simpler now than it used to be. Some oils are better moisturizers than others, so use the best you can afford. Good herb stores sell a cosmetic grade beeswax, but wax from a local apiary will be fine, though a little more golden in color.

The recipe makes about three ounces of balm, and if you use essential oils you can make several flavors quickly. On the other hand, using herbs from your garden really empowers the product. It's a little more time-consuming, but if you do the project in two parts, it's very manageable. Choose the version that suits your needs.

Dedicate a wooden spoon to this job, and use a small stainless steel pot for best results. I often infuse the oils with herbs in my simmering potpourri container. It holds about one cup, the heat of the candle is enough to warm the oil without setting it to boil, and it doesn't need to be watched so carefully. However, it does take longer; figure a couple hours.

I suggest you make the recipe once, as it is given, to see if you like the thickness of the balm. Adding more beeswax will thicken the balm; adding less wax will soften it. In general, you should add or subtract the amount of beeswax in very tiny increments.

Understand that after you have done this once, you are going to do it again. This project is fun.

5   tbsp almond oil, apricot kernel oil, jojoba oil,
        or a good quality vegetable oil

2   vitamin E capsules

1½   tbsp shaved beeswax or beeswax beads

1   tsp honey

10   drops essential oil (see notes below)

Warm the oil over very low heat or use a double boiler. Puncture the vitamin E capsules, and squirt the contents into the oil. Add the beeswax and melt. Remove from heat, and stir in the honey. Stir occasionally as the mixture cools. Add the essential oil before the wax cools and sets up. Stir well and pour into the containers of your choice.

Note: Peppermint or spearmint oil is a good choice for essential oil; use tea tree oil if you spend a lot of time outdoors skiing or boating. Fruit flavors like orange, lemon, or lime are pleasing to teenagers. Try to obtain natural essential oils rather than synthetic oils.

Variation: To use fresh herbs, use a double boiler for the almond oil, or place the pan on very low heat. Add two tablespoons of dried herbs to the oil, or four or five tablespoons of chopped fresh herbs, and let the mixture warm gently for thirty minutes. Strain the herbs through cheesecloth before continuing with the recipe. (Note: You can do this part one evening while you're cleaning up the kitchen; let the herbs and oil sit overnight and continue with the project on the following day.)

Bee balm leaves will lend a mild mint flavor to you lip balm; anise hyssop will give a licorice taste, and lemon verbena gives a hint of lemon. Plantain and chickweed are a soothing combo; comfrey is also a good choice, although not for children. Chamomile and sage, calendula, or lavender flower petals will lend color or mild flavor.

Flea Collars

Flea collars will earn you big points with a friend who is crazy about her animals. Depending upon your level of skill and commitment to the project, a flea collar can be put together quite easily during an evening of television, or in short bursts over several nights.

The simplest kind of flea collar requires grosgrain ribbon, Velcro circles, and a strong fabric glue. Buy double the length of ribbon you need to to go around the animal's neck. The ribbon should be one-inch wide for a small animal, one-and-a-half to two inches wide for a larger animal.

Choose a ribbon material that suits the personality of the animal. A big macho dog will need a quiet plaid, while a fluffy cat might prefer a jeweled collar. The latter is simple enough to make. Buy a package of rhinestones at a craft store, and a small squeeze bottle in a complementary color of dimensional fabric paint.

Decide where to position the jewels on the ribbon and carefully apply a small dot of paint at each of these points. Gently push a jewel into the dot so that paint oozes around the edge of each jewel. Let the jewels dry thoroughly before proceeding further.

If you sew, anchor the Velcro tabs by machine stitching one circle to each end of the ribbon. Be advised: You need to put the hook part of the Velcro on the inside of the ribbon and the felt part on the outside. When the collar is complete, the two Velcro pads will secure it invisibly on the animal's neck.

Sew the two ribbons together, stuff with the herbs, and secure the ends.

If you don't have a sewing machine, you'll need to secure the Velcro to the ribbon using a whipstitch around the edges. One Velcro tab goes on the inside ribbon and one on the outside. Carefully run a bead of glue along the edges of one ribbon and press the other ribbon into it, matching the edges. When dry, stuff with the herbs and secure the ends.

If you sew, you can bring a jauntier approach to the project using a large cotton red and white bandana. Fold the neckerchief in half diagonally from corner to corner. Allow five inches at each end to tie around the animal's neck. Then at a right angle to the fold and five inches from one end, stitch three-quarter inch; turn the cloth. Stitching parallel to the fold, sew to within five inches from the other end. Stuff with flea repellent herbs. Sew across the stuffing to secure it.

This leaves a good size triangle of cloth to accessorize as well as to protect your animal.

Blend together a potpourri of flea repellent herbs.

½   cup pennyroyal
¼   cup tansy leaves
¼   cup flea bane

Flea bane and tansy can be wildcrafted in August from plants harvested in wastelands or open fields. Dry in a dehydrator or in a microwave. Crumble these herbs to a very fine powder before adding to pennyroyal.

Bouquet Garni

Mixing your own herbs for a Bouquet Garni can offer a quick solution to seasoning your own soups and stews. It also makes a simple and attractive gift for someone you care for.

You need 100-percent cotton cheesecloth and 100-percent cotton kitchen string to make the herb bundles. You also need a piece of ten-inch grosgrain ribbon or lamp wicking. Cut the cheesecloth into four-inch squares.

For each square you need the following dried herbs.

1	crumbled bay leaf
1	tsp crumbled rosemary leaves
1	tsp common thyme or lemon thyme
1	tbsp crumbled sweet marjoram
1	tbsp crumbled celery leaves
1	tbsp crumbled Italian flat parsley leaves

Place the herbs on the cotton cheesecloth. Form it into the shape of a little hobo bag by tying up the corners and securing with the cotton twine.

Celery leaves can be cut from the tops of celery stalks. Purchase flat Italian parsley or harvest it from the garden. The flavor of Italian parsley is far superior to the curly. See page 203 for directions for drying herbs.

You will also need ten small red chili peppers.

Tack the bundles of herbs to the ribbon or lamp wicking alternately with the hot peppers. The cheesecloth can be secured with a single stitch through the top of the bag. Secure the pepper by sewing across the stem.

Bay Rum

Bay Rum is a famous classic men's aftershave that is very simple to make. This can be done with essential oils but I think using the spices themselves yields a better end result. Use attractive bottles to package the aftershave for gift giving. Start this project before Thanksgiving.

1	pint jar
	Handful bay leaves
2	cinnamon sticks
2	tbsp allspice berries
8 to 10	whole cloves

¼	cup dried orange peel
3	vitamin E capsules
	Dark rum

A pint canning jar is fine as a stock bottle. Pack it about half full with fresh bay leaves. Break up the cinnamon sticks and put on top of bay leaves. Crack or grind the allspice berries and add to mixture, along with the whole cloves. Also add the dried orange peel. Break open the vitamin E capsules and squirt into the herbs. Cover with dark rum, and add enough so that it rises about an inch or so above the surface of the herbs. It needs to sit in a warm place for four weeks. Shake occasionally. Strain and bottle.

If you don't have fresh bay leaves, used dried. However, you'll need to add several drops of bay laurel essential oil to strengthen the scent after straining the lotion.

If you use corked bottles, you can easily add a special touch. Wrap the bottle top and cork with a small amount of raffia. Melt an ounce or two of beeswax in a pan of water. Dip the top of the bottle into the melted wax repeatedly until it coats the cork to your satisfaction. (The wax is easy to clean up. Just wait until it hardens and lift from the surface of the water.) Tie or glue a label to the bottle.

For Further Study

The Complete Book of Incense, Oils, & Brews. Scott Cunningham. Llewellyn Publications, 1999.

Suppliers

Companion Plants

7247 North Coolville Ridge Road
Athens, OH 45701
(740) 592-4643
www.frognet.net/companion_plants/

Seeds and Plants

J. Crow Company
P.O. Box 172
New Ipswich, NH 03071
(800) 878-1965

Dried Herbs and Essential Oils

Featherfew Herbs
9 North Main St.
Farmington, NH 03835
(603) 755-2177

Bottles, Vials, and Containers

Sunburst Bottles
5710 Auburn Blvd. Suite 7
Sacramento, CA 95841
(916) 348-5576

Lavender Lane
6715 Donerail Drive
Sacramento, CA 95842
(916) 334-4400

Herbal Potpourri

❧ By Penny Kelly ❧

You arrive home from work late one November afternoon, and when you step inside the door you are enveloped by clouds of stale air bearing the essence of wet dog, old gym shoes, and burnt toast. Your children conveniently don't notice the smell—after all, they are the ones who let in the dog, dropped their gym shoes at the door, and burned the toast while waiting for you to arrive and make dinner for them. But *you* definitely do notice.

Taking one last deep breath, you enter silently, wondering if the house will need to be fumigated before you can ever draw a deep relaxing breath again…

If this has happened to you, perhaps you have not discovered potpourri. With the magical scent

of herbs, there is no reason for any home, basement, garage, or office to smell sour, flat, or stale. Your house can smell like a little corner of heaven just by using a few simple herbs and flowers gathered over the summer. More elegant or mysterious effects can be had by adding spices, or even essentials oils, to change the entire atmosphere of your home—and eventually your inner self—by simply becoming aware of the power of smell to affect mood, perception, health, your environment, attitudes, and behaviors.

The Tradition of Potpourri

In the French tradition, a potpourri was the name given to a stew. Literally, it means "rotten pot," or an odd assortment of meats and spices. In time, a potpourri came to mean an eclectic assortment.

In America, the term has come to mean specifically a mixture of dried flowers and spices used to perfume a room—and therefore is not "rotten" at all. The flowers chosen for potpourri mixes are usually highly aromatic, yet they don't have to be. With the use of an essential oil and a fixative, a nicely sized, shaped, or colored flower can be used to make an attractive potpourri that smells heavenly. Sometimes leaves and flowers are chosen simply because they dry out nicely without collapsing or losing color.

Every plant produces its own characteristic oils. Some plants produce a very large amount of oil, such as corn or safflower oils. Most herbs and flowers, however, produce only miniscule amounts of oil. These oils, which are generally known as essential oils, are then extracted and used for a variety of purposes.

Once dry, flowers are mixed with a fixative and stored in an airtight container out of the reach of daylight. Light has a tendency to react with plant oils and causes the oils to become rancid and lose their effectiveness and scent. In the event of this happening to your oils, you will realize perhaps "rotten" is not so far off after all.

An Abortive Attempt

My first experience with potpourri was mostly accidental and a dubious success at best. Early in my herb-growing years, I brought home several plants labeled "horsemint" thinking they were a new kind of mint. I put them in the vegetable garden with my other herbs, and they grew beautifully— producing a number of lilac-colored flowers. Since I didn't know anything about horsemint, and didn't have many herbal reference books at that point, I just watched it to see what would happen.

In time, I tried making a mint tea from the leaves, but it did not taste like mint at all. In fact, I quickly decided that I did not like the taste of horsemint at all. The flowers, while beautiful and numerous, also did not have a very pleasant scent.

Not knowing what to do with this plant—its leaves and flowers seemingly unappealing— and unwilling to just give up or ignore it I picked and dried the flowers, thinking maybe I could do something useful with them later. After they were dry, for some reason, I put the flowers in a decorative can that had once held Christmas cookies, and I left them in the pantry for later experimentation.

Gradually the can was pushed to the back of the pantry shelves, and about two years later I found it. Having forgotten what was in the can, I opened it up and to my amazement, there were the dried flowers, still in perfect condition. Their scent seemed to have intensified during the time in the can. Though I unfortunately still disliked the scent, I found it interesting and surprising that it could be so strong after such a long time. And for some reason, I started to wonder if maybe I could treat the flowers as a potpourri—a practice that I had discovered accidentally in the time that the can was stashed away and left untouched in my closet.

Thus bolstered, I put the can in the middle of the kitchen table with the cover off, and it wasn't long before my husband came in, turned up his nose, and said rudely, "What is that smell?"

"It's potpourri," I said, "do you like it?"

"It's awful," he replied and left the room. I was discouraged, but for some reason kept on.

My daughter came in shortly afterward, and she, too, protested the smell even more bluntly than my husband had. I gave up trying to convince myself that I could stand the scent of this flower and had to throw them out.

And that was my first experience with potpourri. It was not until quite some time later that I came across a herbal reference to horsemint. I found that it wasn't a mint at all; rather, it was part of the *Monarda* family *(Monarda punctata)* whose leaves were taken for digestive problems.

This whole experience, though, constituted my first (semi) successful attempt at drying flowers and using them as potpourri. It was too bad I started with something that I couldn't stand the smell of, but the result of this experiment ultimately was to trigger my curiosity as to how those flowers had kept such an amazing amount of scent in that dark can in the pantry.

Understanding the Mechanics of Potpourri

Since the horsemint fiasco, I have done no small bit of investigation into plants, oils, and smells. I had always thought flowers smelled pretty because they were flowers—a circular line of thinking if there ever was one—but in time I learned there was more to it than that. Whereas it had never occurred to me to wonder what was in the flower that made it have a scent, I was not surprised when I learned the answer. It was oil!

Research has shown that essential oils contain the highest levels of oxygenating molecules of any substance known to man. Translation: These molecules readily combine with oxygen, and therefore are quickly carried through the air into our olifactory, or scent-sensing, passages in the nasal canal.

Essential oils also contain minerals and act as catalysts in the body. They are made up of oxygen and amino acids, and their function is to carry nutrients into the human body and the brain. Their unique abilities are partly due to the presence of the sesquiterpins in the oils. Sesquiterpins have the ability to cross the blood-brain barrier and directly nurture and oxygenize the cells of the brain. They carry ozone and negative ions, both of which create an environment that bacteria and viruses cannot live in.

Information recorded on ancient papyri show that essential oils were the first medicine of man, even prior to herbs. These oils were the first antioxidants. Because of the amount of oxygen they carry, essential oils create an environment in which the cell membranes of the body become more permeable. When the human body is deficient in oxygen, the pH level of the cell changes, and cell walls thicken. It becomes difficult to get nutrients into the cell. Plant oils not only carry much needed oxygen to the body's cells, they deliver nutrients into and push toxins and other waste matter out of the cells. The overall result is an increase in antibodies, endorphins, neuro-transmitters, and an overall and magical sense of well-being and better health.

Essential oils are the catalyzing agents in all vegetables, herbs, plants, and flowers. When you collect these gifts of Mother Nature all summer, dry them carefully to preserve their natural oils, and release these oils in midwinter in a potpourri. Not only will you get a pleasant scent, you will also tap into a bit of the healing power that these oils are known for.

These concepts, of course, are the basis of all aromatherapy in the past and today. If you have wondered how the people of ancient times, especially the Egyptians, healed themselves without drugs, now you know. The answer is through the use of essential oils.

Simple, Handy Potpourri Scents You Can Make on Your Stove

Making a potpourri is a fairly simple process that gives you plenty of opportunity to experiment and be creative. Over the years, I have seen all sorts of exotic recipes for mixing herbs, flowers, spices, and essential oils. And I have tried quite a few. Some of them were wonderful, but I have always kept a deep appreciation for the simplest and handiest recipes that make use of the most readily available materials. After all, nothing is more discouraging to me than to read a recipe for something and discover that I have never heard of half the ingredients it calls for.

As I, like many of you, am overworked and undervacationed these days, I much prefer to try and find ways to make my extracurricular tasks as simple as possible. In recipes, this means I seek the easy-to-follow ones that make use of items that are likely to be on hand.

Simple Tip

Here's a simple tip to start: If you don't know a parsley plant from a potato plant, and have never given a thought to plucking posies or drying leaves, you can still create a subtle potpourri effect by putting a small pan with two to four cups of water in it on the kitchen stove or on the woodstove. If you're using the kitchen stove, turn the burner on low and then add the peel of an entire orange along with one teaspoon of nutmeg. Sit down and eat the orange you just took the peeling from while you wait for the water to warm up and the scent to fill the room.

If you want a deeper scent and have a few herbs on hand, add a tablespoon of basil or lemon balm. For a variation on this theme, slice an apple into the pan and add one teaspoon of powdered cinnamon (or one cinnamon stick) and one tablespoon of cinnamon basil.

One of my favorite scents for this is a rather unusual potpourri combination—onion and celery. For reasons that may have only to do with the way I am made, I love the scent of these two kitchen staples. The onion is surprisingly modified and sweetened when mixed with celery, and the overall effect is homey and comfortable. People walk in and say, "What's cooking? It smells good." They are surprised and sometimes somewhat disappointed when I say, "It's just my potpourri—onions and celery."

Potpourri Pots and Containers

A few years ago when my daughter left home for her own apartment, she left behind a small electric potpourri pot. She hardly ever used it, but as fate will have it, I fell in love with it and have been using it ever since.

The little electric pot holds a good quantity of flowers and leaves, enough to fill the entire house with a wondrous scent. The only problem with electric pots is that, if you do not take care, you can walk away and leave them plugged in. A day or two later you will end up with a foul, burned mass of leaves in the bottom of the pot that smells awful and is terribly difficult to clean up.

I have a couple of potpourri pots that use a candle to heat a small amount of water in a ceramic dish suspended above the candle. I use these, too, carrying them to places where electric plugs are few or inconvenient to get to. These have the advantage of turning themselves off when the candle goes out, but the candles have to be purchased and repurchased after each use, which is a small but significant expense in the long run. Inevitably, the biggest problem with this type of pot ends up being that you will discover you are out of candles when you are most in the mood to use it. Also, the smaller candle-based pots do not hold much in the way of flowers or leaves or peelings, though they are an excellent size for using essential oils and spices.

Besides the kinds of potpourri pots that use water and heat to dispense plant fragrances, I have a half-dozen decorative metal cans of varying sizes that I keep dried flowers in for very long periods of time. When I want the aroma and presence of a particular kind of herb or flower, I simply open the can for a short time and let the scent fill the air. I keep my favorites scents—typically lavender flowers, Thai basil, cinnamon basil, rosemary leaves, lilac flowers, and marjoram—in these convenient little cans.

I have also made a couple of potpourri dispensers using small Mason jars with a lid and ring. With a nail I poke one single hole in the lid, and fill the jar with pine needles and cones, or perhaps lavender and baby's breath, or maybe marjoram and rosemary. Then I put the lid on tight, tie a pretty ribbon around the neck of the jar, and set it on a table where the Sun will pass by for a few hours on winter days. When the Sun begins to hit the jar, it warms up. The herbs inside also get warm and begin to release their oils into the air. The single hole in the top allows some of the scent to move into the room in a very slow and subtle way. When the Sun moves away from the jar, the oils that have not yet escaped remain inside, waiting for the Sun to come by the next day.

Although most of the literature I have read discourages putting potpourri or any kind of oil in the Sun because sunlight causes the scent to dissipate quickly, I have found that the use of the jar with limited air exchange will continue to give off a light scent of whatever is in it for two to three weeks.

Of course, all kinds of pretty baskets and candy dishes can be used to hold an assortment of scents, and you can vary these to match your décor or the season. Once you have decided on the kind of container, all you need is to make a few potpourri mixes.

Potpourri Mix Recipes

Mixes are really quite easy to make because there are few rules. The only thing you really need to know is that sometimes you'll need a fixative, especially if you intend to keep your flowers and herbs in the open in a dish or basket.

Fixatives aren't quite as important if you're going to put your mix in water in a potpourri pot right away. But if you want to make a large batch of something and store part of it, a fixative will help keep the plant oils, or the essential oils you add to the mixture, from evaporating.

The most commonly used fixatives are orris root and benzoin, and both can usually be purchased from your local craft center. *Rodale's Illustrated Encyclopedia of Herbs* suggests using about one tablespoon of fixative per quart of flowers and herbs, but a friend of mind who is famous for her exquisite potpourri mixtures uses at least twice, and occasionally four times, this amount. She also adds a few drops of essential oil which she matches to the natural scent of the flowers and herbs that make up most of the mix and ends up with the fragrance of heaven in a dish.

You can achieve the same by experimenting with some of the following recipes.

Piney Potpourri

To makes a good room deodorizer, mix the following ingredients and use in one of the potpourri methods mentioned above.

1   cup rosemary

1   cup pine geranium

1   cup dried cranberries

1   cup tiny pine cones

1   cup lady's bedstraw

2   tbsp sandalwood

2   drops pine essential oil

Flowery Potpourri

A mixture of these herbs will freshen you on hot summer days.

1   cup rose petals

1   cup lavender

1   cup baby's breath

1   cup carnation

2   tbsp orrisroot

2   drops rose or lavender essential oil

Spicy Potpourri

This mixture is great for fall days.

1   cup Thai basil

1   cup thyme

1   cup sage

1   cup clove

1   cup cedar shavings

1   tsp powdered cinnamon

2   tbsp orrisroot

Baby's Nursery

This herb mixture is a delightful way to soothe both mother and infant.

1   cup violets
1   cup rose petals
1   cup baby's breath
1   cup lavender
1   tbsp orrisroot
1   drop violet essential oil

Healing Potpourri

This mixture works well in the sickroom or anytime you're under the weather.

1   cup lavender
1   cup dried lemon peel
1   cup frankincense
1   cup sandalwood
1   cup thyme
2   drops lavender or sandalwood essential oil

Everyday Potpourri

This mixture adds a wonderful overtone to any space, any time.

1   cup lemon balm
1   cup basil (lemon or sweet)
1   cup dried orange peel
1   cup spearmint
1   tsp nutmeg

Winter Holiday Potpourri

These herbs make the Christmas holidays especially fragrant.

1   cup pine or spruce needles
1   cup rosemary
1   cup bayberry

1   cup dried orange peel

1   cup dried cranberries or cherries

2   drops bayberry essential oil

1   drop pine essential oil

Spring and Summer Holiday Potpourri

Establish an Easter tradition with this combination of fresh scents.

1   cup magnolia petals

1   cup lily of the valley

1   cup violet or lavender flowers

1   cup lemon verbena

2   tbsp orrisroot

2   drops lily of the valley or lavender essential oil

These are only a few of the dozens of interesting potpourri mixtures that are possible using the many flowers and herbs that are available each growing season. You should feel free to experiment with your own combinations. Be sure to write down your favorite, and put them in your recipe file so you don't forget them. And be sure to try using dried flowers or leaves that just look interesting and don't have any particular scent—you can always add scent with essential oils.

In the end, your potpourri-scented home will become a place that invites relaxation every time you open the door.

Art in the Herbal Garden

By Roslyn Reid

T he use of art in gardens stretches back through the mists of time. One has only to think of the Hanging Gardens of Babylon—a garden that itself was considered an artwork—to see the how far back into antiquity this practice goes. Garden art brings into focus the aesthetic contrast between natural plants and created objects, highlighting the intrinsic beauty of both.

If we were being philosophical, we could say that "art" and "nature" are two ends of a continuum: One is totally artificial, the deliberate act of the hand of a human; and the other has no human involvement at all—though the word "garden" normally implies a little artfulness in the selection, layout, and planting of all parts of a garden. Still, a garden's intrinsic power comes from beyond the hand of humans.

Philosophies of Aesthetics

In aesthetics, two very different principles are often brought together. This juxtaposition of "opposites" can create a dynamic tension between extremes which brings out the attributes of both extremes more clearly. For instance, a monumental stone bench—or ornamental tub or planter—is set off by low-growing flowers around it, and by the tall trees behind it. By doing this, plants that might be overlooked in a purely natural setting are seen more clearly as a contrast when art is present. Furthermore, this contrast is between an object made by a person, and object made by nature, and this further serves to highlight the beneficial relationship between people and nature.

How one should balance art and nature is of course a matter of taste. Traditionally, there are "formal" gardens with massive stone walls, marble angels, mosaic walkways, and plants carefully selected not just for species but for exact shape, size, and condition. In this case, one might almost say that every detail is filtered through an artistic sensibility (though Mother Nature may debate this). On the other hand, there are gardens where the gardener has more fully let nature guide every decision—where the only "art" in view may be such "found art" objects as a pretty stone or piece of driftwood.

Strangely enough, in modern times the use of art in gardens seems to have dwindled. There are not as many examples today of this practice as there once was. Still, enclaves of art gardens can occasionally be found, often in unexpected places, by the determined seeker. While there is art in every garden, and while there are countless shelves of books about plants and gardening, the topic of including garden art along with your plants is not so commonly discussed. I hope this article gives you some new thoughts about using art in your garden planning.

What Is Garden Art?

We tend to think of art as something displayed on a walls indoors, possibly in a gallery, and having absolutely no connection to nature. Some gardens, meanwhile, are as "natural" as possible, consisting solely of plants that grow, by virtue of natural laws, in a more or less ordered arrangement. So the question is: What distinguishes art from other structures and objects intended for use in the garden?

Many garden items are intended for primarily functional purposes, such as storing equipment or providing people with shelter from the rain. Like other kinds of art, garden art usually serves decorative or inspirational purposes. However, I would point out, there can be a crossover. For example, although customarily constructed to be practical, benches can be designed to appear as works of art as well—as can planters, pathways, shelters, walls, potting sheds, and so on. All it takes is a bit of creative imagination, and you can bring the best of both worlds—art and functionality—into your garden.

Generally speaking, the word "art" designates an item that is one of a kind, and not mass-produced. Much garden art might best be considered quasi-art because it is usually not handmade, but mass-produced and then customized by its owner into a somewhat unique object.

Some may think of garden art as a collection of grandiose sculptures or monuments—the spectacular sixty-acre Sheldon Memorial Art Gallery and Sculpture Garden at the University of Nebraska in Lincoln is a good example, as are any number of public or university art gardens. But garden art might also be as simple as a pile of rocks. Sculpture in fact can be fashioned from almost anything which will stand up to the weather—concrete, fiberglass, metal, and so on. Even wood or other items that are found right in the garden can serve as material from which to fashion artistic works.

The Uses of Garden Art

What purposes might served by putting art in the garden? Let's examine a few examples in the hopes that we may gain a better sense of the purpose and basis for this practice.

Decoration

Hex Signs: A well-known example of decorative as well as functional "garden art" in the United States is the Pennsylvania Dutch hex sign, used by the Amish in southeastern Pennsylvania. Although no one knows the exact origin of this kind of sign, they are believed to be more than one hundred years old.

There are many theories about why the Amish have painted these symbols on their barns and other structures for so long. Some say hex signs are purely decorative, others think they are used for protection, and still others believe they are some kind of land ownership statement (much like cattle brands in the western United States). Many people ascribe magical powers to them, possibly because they are called "hex" signs—though the word actually is a reference to the fact that the signs are six-sided—and possibly out of a general sense of discomfort with a mysterious or unknown people.

Whatever their original purpose, hex signs have become very popular all across the country, both indoors and out. Furthermore, these charming icons are not particularly difficult to create. In chapter 13 of Scott Cunningham and David Harrington's book *Spell Crafts* (Llewellyn, 1999), the authors give directions on how to fashion one of these symbols for your own garden. There are quite a few ideas, designs, and correspondences to use for hex signs, as well as lists of needed materials, in this book—making it quite easy to create a hex sign for whatever purpose, magical or not, you might have in mind.

Just to give a few examples, if you wish to have a productive garden, you might use the color green (for fertility) with an eight-pointed star (a symbol of abundance) on your hex sign.

Some symbols are even simpler—raindrops can indicate a desire for rain; a Sun can indicate a desire for some sunshine. At the end of the chapter, Cunningham and Harrington even thoughtfully include a spell you can use to magically charge your finished product.

Fountains: The use of water in the form of streams, gullies, and, more to the point, fountains is a very common item of garden art. Versatile as well as charming, a fountain can be created out of many different materials in many different shapes. It could also contain figurines or be structured in several layers, giving it an even greater artistic effect. However, keep in mind that in order to place a fountain in your garden, a nearby source of both power and water is necessary.

Gazing Ball: Probably the most popular crossover garden art—that is to say, a form of decorative art used by people of all religions—is the Witch ball, also commonly known as a gazing ball. This is a clear or colored glass ball of any size, usually mirrored, that is mounted on a pedestal to reflect the garden around it. According to some, this object came to be called a Witch ball because it was used as a protective device to reflect the evil eye back at the giver.

Although gazing balls considerably predate the early Victorians in England, Witch balls were popularized by them. And since Victoriana is still very popular, this is probably why the globes seem fairly ubiquitous today. Making bases for them can be quite easy—suggestions range from overturned clay pots to carved PVC pipe, to old car springs, or a collection of wine bottles lashed together (this last suggestion would be particularly appropriate for gardens of the followers of Dionysus). Amber K gives further historical information about Witch balls in her article on them in Llewellyn's *2000 Magical Almanac*, titled "Witch Balls."

Religion and Inspiration

One of the most common use of garden sculpture by Pagans is for religious or ritual purpose. We're all familiar with the backyard statue of the Virgin Mary; but these days, similar Pagan-themed icons are turning up in many backyards, front yards, and gardens. Outdoor art of this sort can mark, for Pagans, a transition-type portal in the garden, or can be used to designate sacred space.

Examples of Pagan garden art may include a figure of a Sun god or fairies to help the garden grow. In fact, these kinds of "helping" figurines are not confined to use by Pagans—one can find them whimsically displayed in many gardens belonging to people of other faiths. Still, Pagans in general tend to be more knowledgeable about the tradition, history, and practical use of such items.

The Campanellis, Pauline and Dan, give instructions for creating a "sanctuary garden" using Pagan artwork in the "April" section of their book, *Wheel of the Year* (Llewellyn, 2000). They begin with suggestions for choosing the appropriate site, size, and plantings for the sanctuary—even including a layout for a working circle, and various ideas about how to arrange simple stones as garden art.

On the other hand, if you wish to be a bit fancier and go beyond simple stones, you can find extensive instructions on how to consecrate a statue in an article, titled "How to Consecrate a Statue," by Ann Moura (Aoumiel) in Llewellyn's *2000 Magical Almanac*. For this ritual, the author even includes a list of the herbs which you might have in your garden to enhance the magic of the art.

However, for even more ambitious Pagans, as well as people of other faiths, who have enough room, *Wheel of the Year* also mentions the use of mazes or labyrinths in a Pagan spiritual practice. (A labyrinth differs from a maze in that a maze is intended to be a puzzle from which to escape, while a labyrinth is intended as a spiritual journey, and as such it can be exited at any time.) According to the Campanellis, the magic of labyrinths gave rise to the spiral dance so popular in today's covens.

One of the most famous labyrinths on the East Coast belongs to the Fellowship in Prayer, a non-denominational spiritual organization in Princeton, New Jersey. Their labyrinth is constructed of white "goose egg" stones and red cedar mulch, and was placed on the site of their former meditation garden. In the center of the labyrinth are four tree trunks for use as benches, though there is also room for one to stand or lie down there. Workshops on techniques for constructing labyrinths for your garden can be found all over the country at retreat centers and other spiritual organizations.

Related to labyrinths and mazes is the latest idea for outdoor art—a medicine wheel. This is a Native American tradition, in which you start with a collection of stones and place them in a circular pattern. A cross is then constructed inside the circle to mark the four directions. The resulting quartered circle is then used ceremonially.

There are many different uses for medicine wheels—astrology, ritual, meditation, and so on. Some of the wheels are simple, and some are complex. The alignment of each wheel will be different according to its location and the influence of local tradition. The materials may vary for each medicine wheel, but the form, as described above, is basically the same in each case. For further historical data on medicine wheels, see Bernyce Barlow's article in Llewellyn's *2000 Magical Almanac* titled "Medicine Wheels and Astro-logical Sites."

If you would like more ideas and instructions on how to create your own outdoor sacred space or labyrinth, as well as a look at what others have done, I can also recommend Dan and Paula Campanelli's book *Circles, Groves & Sanctuaries* (Llewellyn,

1993). The second half of this book is dedicated to "Outdoor Magickal Spaces," and it includes many rituals that you can use to accompany or to tap into the magical energy of these kinds of sites.

Education and Commemoration

Another popular use of garden art is for educational or commemorative purposes. One need only think of markers beside garden plants which impart information about the flower or tree you are viewing, or plaques which dedicate a garden or part of a garden to someone's memory.

However, "educational" outdoor art doesn't stop there. A rather unusual example of it can be seen in the recent movie, *The Blair Witch Project*. In one scene, the filmmakers hung twig sculptures from trees in the woods to suggest a terrifying presence lurking there. A recent trend that is growing quite a bit in popularity is trail art. These items are similar to the informative plaques in a garden; though not all trail art is educational, some of it is used for purely decorative purposes.

The Rails-to-Trails Conservancy (www.railtrails.org) is an organization which has undertaken a project to place trail art on some of the many trails it has built all around the country on abandoned railroad tracks.

Impress the World

Lastly, some people place art in their gardens out of a need to erect monuments to themselves. A good example of this ego-centric art can be found at the gardens at San Simeon in California, an art garden built by the rich and very self-important William Randolph Hearst. Fortunately, many of these conceits, including San Simeon, eventually are opened to the public where they can be enjoyed by everyone.

Art Garden Materials

Naturally, any material intended for use in garden art must be durable—although some people prefer the ethereal nature of created objects. However, where art is concerned, my personal opinion is that we are better served in our everyday lives by the old saying "Life is short and art is long." So let's look at some durable materials that can be used in the creation of garden art.

The first and foremost—and ubiquitous—material found in art of the garden variety is concrete. Think of those little concrete figurines that are seen everywhere. Additionally, concrete is popular in large garden sculptures.

A very versatile material, concrete can be dyed, painted, textured, or even embedded with smaller articles at the time of casting. The only big drawback is that the use of concrete re-quires some kind of mixer and a mold—and expertise in using both. Plus, creating any sculpture bigger than a breadbox is likely to be daunting if you are only one person.

Fortunately, concrete works well for smaller objects, such as the popular garden gnome. These figures look best when they are "life-sized"—about the size of a small child. Some folks like to place plantings around them—low-growing plants like hen-and-chickens are a good choice. Or you can use a low-growing juniper to partially obscure the figure and add an air of mystery. For larger items, obscuring part of it with some creeping ivy is a time-tested trick. If the sculpture has crevices, herbs and flowers may be planted in them for a "natural" effect.

Unfortunately, at their time of purchase or making many concrete figures appear far too new for some peoples' tastes. One way to impart the appearance of antiquity is to plant moss on the figures. This is very easy—first, find some lichens or moss in the woods. (These are also available from some garden catalogs.) After you have gathered enough of this material to your liking, spread maple syrup or yogurt on your concrete figurine, then place the moss and lichens on top of the stuff. Spray these areas with a mister every day to keep them moist. In a week or so, the moss and lichens will take root permanently on the statue. Another way to make your garden figurines look old is to sponge-paint them—instructions for this can be found in craft books or on many home improvement websites; it is a very easy process to learn.

Metal is another common and easily obtained material used for garden art. Lead, bronze, even iron and steel are popular for outdoor sculptures, although according to the Campanellis some more traditional modern-day Pagan groups ban the use of iron in circle. This is for the metal's ancient association with banishing Witches, rather than for any actual effects it might have on Pagans. Generally, metal is used by sculptors who don't mind the welding or bending involved. Metal sculptures can be long-lasting and sometimes even kinetic—built to move in the wind. A good example of this would be metal wind chimes, whirligigs, and weather vanes.

Many sculptors like to work with found objects, such as metal parts from cars. In addition to being cheap, or even free, such items are durable and quite weather-resistant. Whimsical items such as dinosaurs and birds can emerge under the hand of a sculptor skilled in the use of such materials. Furthermore, these items can be painted any color to make a whimsical and magical piece of art.

Although quite durable, fiberglass is not commonly found as a material used for garden art. Fiberglass lends itself to making large quantities of identical items quite cheaply; but it can be a nasty medium for the individual sculptor to work in.

Wood is a popular artistic medium because it is easy to work with and is available almost everywhere in one shape or another. In fact, driftwood, a popular garden addition, has the advantage of already having been carved by the Goddess. However, as anyone who has a deck knows, wood is not durable for outdoor use unless a protective coating such as polyurethane is applied to it. Though if you're one of those people that prefer the "weathered" look, then you probably won't mind.

Two popular as well as elegant materials used for garden art are stone and marble. Both of these require much time and dedication to convert into a work of art, however. And should you decide to buy them already sculpted into a figurine, they are likely to be quite expensive.

Clay and pottery are commonly seen in garden art; and if you have a kiln or even a very hot oven, you can make your own artwork from these materials. There is no lack of such items in garden centers, although the larger pieces can be heavy and difficult to move. The early Freemasons placed large pottery jars in strategic corners in both gardens and rooms, in order to reflect sound back at someone standing in just the right spot.

One of the more unusual ideas for garden art is topiary. This is the practice of sculpting trees or shrubs into various shapes such as dragons or spirals. Botanical gardens can be a good place to view topiary, and courses in topiary are held in some night schools and garden centers. Topiary figures received wide exposure for being used as one of the instrumental elements to help set the chilling tone of Stephen King's popular book, *The Shining*.

Another uncommon form of garden art is the Japanese raked-sand river. This is a stretch of sand, contained in a low box, which is intended to duplicate an actual river. The sand is raked into lines which resemble waves in water, and items such as rocks can be placed into the "river" to produce "eddies" by raking the sand around them.

Placing Garden Art

Now that we've decided what materials to use for our garden art, we now need to decide where to place it in the garden. There are several approaches to landscape and garden design, but the most important consideration is the location of the garden. The design of the garden is determined by the lay of the land, the path of the Sun (or Moon), and the surrounding vegetation, structures, or natural formations. Scale is also a consideration—for instance, one would not place a large sculpture on a hill where it might tumble over and crush a visitor.

Another consideration for positioning is the purpose of the artwork. If your garden art is intended to help create a sacred space for outdoor ritual, you probably will not want to put it in a section of the garden which could easily be viewed by the public. Also, you need to leave enough clear space in the area to accommodate your circle of participants and whatever movement is customary for your rituals.

For those in colder climates, there is the issue of whether you want your gardens to look good year-round. Garden art can be placed with the intention of complementing a tree or shrub that erupts into blazing color in the fall, or flowers in the spring. It is often difficult to position art that will look good year-round.

One design technique that is growing in popularity is the practice of feng shui, the ancient Chinese art of placing objects in locations where they harmonize with natural forces. Feng shui divides any space into eight different sectors and assigns subjects to each sector. The major sectors and subjects are as follows.

North—Career

Northeast—Knowledge

East—Family and health

Southeast—Wealth

South—Fame and rank

Southwest—Marriage

West—Children

Northwest—Helpful people

A good book on feng shui, such as *Feng Shui* by Derek Walters (Simon & Schuster, 1988), is essential for your various design planning projects.

In addition to the major correspondences listed above, there are minor correspondences for each sector—for instance, a body part. Therefore, feng shui garden design can be planned along many different themes. For example, north is the "ear" sector, so the north section of the garden would be a harmonious spot—in more ways than one—in which to place wind chimes. South is the "eye" sector, so the garden art in this sector could be positioned at eye level or be very eye-catching through the use of color, shape, size, and so on. For this, an outdoor painting or sculpture of the Eye of Horus would be perfect.

West is the "mouth" sector of the garden, making it a logical place for edibles such as fruit trees or berry bushes. Artistic garden benches can be placed here to encourage visitors to relax and have a seat while munching on the landscaping. And east is the sector of the "foot," a good area to experiment with plant spirit figurines underneath bushes or with different types of walkways.

In the feng shui system, the sectors also correspond with certain colors. As well as being the sector of water, north corresponds with the color black, so a black fountain or pool (or even gazing ball) would be decorative as well as useful for scrying here. Conversely, the southern sector corresponds to both red and fire, making it a good place for an outdoor fireplace or incense burner.

East is blue or green, making topiary art a good choice for this sector. And the west sector corresponds to white along with metal, making it an appropriate place for chrome or nickel sculptures or wind chimes.

As you can see, careful planning is called for whenever you incorporate art into a garden. You might even consider consulting a landscape architect if your garden is complicated enough. And best of all—unlike plantings, if you don't like the location of your outdoor art, you can usually move it.

Websites Featuring Garden Art

http://www.garden-art.com. This is the Garden Art Gallery, featuring several artists and exhibits.

http://www.users.hughestech.net/chemungtech/ctlawnart.html. This is Chemung Tech's Lawn Art site—mostly unusual and bizarre items.

http://www.virginialandscapes.org/Articles/ornaments.html. The site of a nonprofit organization in Virginia that contains information on designing a garden using art.

http://www.familygardening.com/structures.html. A helpful article on the use of garden sculptures and ornaments.

http://www.sculpture.org/Outdoor.html. Lots of links to sites where you can view sculpture parks and gardens for pleasure and ideas.

For Further Study

Circles, Groves, & Sanctuaries. Dan and Pauline Campanelli. Llewellyn Publications, 1992.

Llewellyn's Magical Almanac, 1990–2002. Llewellyn Publications, 1989–2001.

Spell Crafts. Scott Cunningham and David Harrington. Llewellyn Publications, 1993.

Wheel of the Year. Dan and Pauline Campanelli. Llewellyn Publications, 1999.

Herb History, Myth, and Magic

Poison Ivy

⇜ By Robert M. Place ⇝

T he first herb that I learned to identify as a boy was poison ivy. We were at the lake where we usually went to swim in the summer. Without warning, my father pulled me over to a tree and pointed to the dark-green, broad-leaved vine surrounding the trunk.

"Be sure you stay away from that plant," he commanded me gently, "it's poison ivy."

That year in school, my teacher continued my education. She hung a large picture of the poison ivy plant on the bulletin board, and she said: "Look for the group of three shiny red leaves. When you see this, make sure you do not touch it. Now, what are you going to look for class?"

"The three shiny red leaves," we chanted together in answer to her question. "The three shiny red leaves."

The True Story of Poison Ivy

In reality, the three leaves of poison ivy are leaflets—or three parts of one leaf—and they are not always shiny. Some varieties of the plant are dull or hairy. The new growth of most poison ivy varieties has a reddish tinge in the spring, while the mature leaves are deep green, and they turn red in the fall.

Poison ivy may grow as a vine or a bush, and sometimes its leaflets are lobed or toothed. Its native habitat is in the eastern and midwestern parts of the United States, in eastern Canada, Mexico, and parts of eastern Asia. It has also been introduced to Europe and South America.

In the United States, west of the Rockies, we find it only in sandy beaches, but in the Northeast its bushy lobed relative called poison oak is prolific. In the past, experts disagreed as to whether or not these are separate species or varieties. Today, most agree that they are separate species. However, hybrid combinations of the two exist in the areas where their ranges merge.

Along with poison sumac, poison ivy and poison oak are three related members of the sumac family that contain the chemical urushiol, a poisonous irritant that can cause itchy skin rashes that can erupt in pustules.

First Contact with Poison Ivy

Growing up in the suburbs of New Jersey, I spent most of my summer roaming the forest on the crest of the hill behind our house. In spite of my father's instruction and the half-accurate information I was given in school, I learned more about this vine the hard way—by touching it. From this contact, I developed long red welts on my arms and side which after a day or two erupted in blisters containing a watery secretion. These pustules itched intensely.

At that time, in the late 1950s, people believed that the poisoning was systemic, and my parents, like every good parent at that time, instructed me not to scratch the rash, and especially not to break the blisters. It was believed that the fluid in these pustules was contagious, that it had the power to spread the irritation to other parts of body and even to other people. Not being able to scratch the itch was the worst part of the affliction. My only relief was to cover the rash with calamine lotion, an ointment containing zinc oxide and ferric oxide. This stopped the itch but I still had to wait two weeks for it to clear up.

At that time, "Poison Ivy" was the name of a hit rhythm-and-blues song performed by the Coasters. Wherever I went, I would hear the Coasters' lead singer, Carl Gardner, singing in my tiny transistor radio: "You're gonna need an ocean of calamine lotion… She'll really do you in, if you let her under your skin." Even the songs of the time reinforced the belief that the poison ivy infection was systemic.

It was not until the 1980s, when I was in my thirties, that I found out that this was not true. My wife, Rose Ann, is a dedicated natural gardener, and she has found through the years that combating poison ivy with natural weapons is not an easy task.

Still, Rose Ann persists in keeping poison ivy out of her garden because of a lifelong fear of the invader. Her fear stems from her first encounter when she was ten years old. She had been walking past the woods near her house and noticed some men burning leaves. In her innocence, she thought nothing of it as the smoke drifted over her. However, the next morning she had trouble seeing through the swollen slits of her eyes.

This swelling was accompanied by red itchy rashes over her face and arms. Her parents rushed her to their doctor, who confirmed that she had a case of poison ivy. Unlike my mother, her parents preferred to use a natural treatment. They made a mixture of vinegar and baking soda and covered the welts with the thick gelatinous substance. The vinegar smelled strong, and as the baking soda began to dry, it would flake off onto the furniture and the floor. But the worst part for her was not the smell or the mess, it was the fear of breaking the blisters and spreading the infection.

Many years later, Rose Ann was relieved to learn the results of a scientific study of the nature of poison ivy. According to the study, the scientists had discovered that poison ivy irritation was not systemic. The rash is only caused by an allergic reaction to the poison, urushiol. The blisters it causes only contain a harmless watery secretion.

How Poison Ivy Acts

Urushiol is contained in the sap found in every part of the poison ivy plant. To come in contact with it there must be a break in the surface that allows the sap to emerge. If one was careful and touched the plant without breaking it, urushiol would not emerge and no rash would result. However, if one is highly sensitive to the poison, the amount released by insects biting the leaves may be enough to cause a reaction.

Urushiol from poison ivy can also stick to your clothes, shoes, or dog, and hang out for a year or longer waiting to come in contact with your unsuspecting skin. Further, as my wife found out, urushiol particles can become airborne when the plant is burned.

Another common belief in my youth was that the poison ivy sap is hard to wash off oneself. It was generally recommended that one should wash with brown laundry soap after a walk in the woods. A friend of mine even recommended washing with kerosene after an irritation is noticed. The truth is that urushiol begins to penetrate the skin within minutes. If it is washed off before then—even merely with water—no rash will occur. After it begins to penetrate, though, the sooner it is washed off the less severe the reaction will be.

Rubbing alcohol can remove urushiol from the skin even after it has begun to penetrate, but kerosene is too strong and may further damage the skin. Soap, including brown laundry soap, is useless, and may even spread the oil. A shower with plenty of water will wash it away, but if the urushiol has already penetrated the skin, it may be too late to stop the rash. If you did contact the poison, don't forget to wash your clothes, shoes, and dog.

Urushiol reacts quicker on certain parts of the body where the skin is thinner. The rash may take a few days longer to show up on the tougher areas. This, combined with re-infection from secondary sources, is likely what convinced people that the rash was spreading.

Every Plant Has Its Purpose

In 1680, the philosopher, Thomas Brown, wrote: "Nature does nothing in vain."

These words have been called the only undisputed axiom in philosophy. However, if this axiom is really true, then we must ask: "What exactly was nature thinking when she created poison ivy?"

I began to find the answer to this question in the 1970s when I was teaching grammar school in a small town on the New Jersey shore. In the spring, I took some students on a field trip to Sandy Hook State Park, a section of the shore that forms a peninsula jutting north toward New York. It separates the Raritan Bay from the Atlantic Ocean.

Here, the beach is preserved in its natural state. One afternoon, the students and I were enjoying a guided nature walk through the sand dunes. Our guide, a park ranger, cautioned us to take care not to step on the poison ivy shrubs. However, unlike my father and teachers in days of old, his concern was for the plant.

The ranger informed us that poison ivy was the most important plant in this protected environment. Poison ivy is hardy enough to establish itself on the wind-swept beach, where most plants would be unable to grow. With its broad leaves, poison ivy catches the blowing sand and slowly helps to build up the sand dunes. The dunes in turn create a protected environment for the rest of the indigenous shrubs, which in turn provide food for the wild life.

Furthermore, not satisfied with simply creating the dunes, poison ivy continues its work by holding the dune together and preventing erosion with its roots. In fact, the ranger pointed out, the entire ecological environment is balanced by virtue of the creative and protective efforts of this one plant. On that walk, all at once I began to develop a profound new respect for this great childhood adversary.

Today, I live on the edge of a forest in the Hudson River Valley in New York State. Poison ivy has become part of my natural environment.

Unlike those who view it as a pest, I have developed a tolerant attitude toward the plant. Poison ivy is the warrior of the forest. Similar to how it acts along the shore, poison ivy grows at the edge of the forest, in fields and along paths. Its function is to claim new land, and protect it from human or animal invasion until trees can establish themselves and secure the area.

In fact, the first trees on this land are often other members of the sumac family. So what we perceive as a pest is really the forest's way of furthering and protecting itself, and bringing balance to an area.

Scientists have found poison ivy fossils in the United States that are 40 million years old. It is an established part of the ecosystem providing important food and shelter for wildlife. Bears, deer, rabbits, and mice eat the leaves and stems. Flickers, woodpeckers, and other birds eat its white berries. In fact, poison ivy berries in the winter reach out above the snow and are one of the few foods available in that season.

In turn, the birds do the plant the favor of spreading its seeds, especially under trees and telephone poles.

In the end, poison ivy is saying to us, "I have clamed this land for the forest, therefore do not try to uproot me or I will violently defend myself."

This is why its poison only comes out when the plant is broken. It is aggressive in its choice of location, but defensive in its use of its poison.

A Sacred Plant

The first Western writer to describe poison ivy was the explorer Captain John Smith. Writing in 1624 about the plants he observed in Virginia and New England, he mentions one called "the poysoned weed." He compares it to English ivy, and in mentioning its effects on humans declares that it is unduly feared because the rash that it causes.

Other early names for "the weed" included "poison creeper," "poison vine," "picry," and the curiously alchemical name, "Mercury."

Long before the first European settlers arrived, however, the Native Americans were well aware of this herb. Lists of herbs used by the first Americans to treat the poison ivy rash include peppergrass, horse nettle, wild lettuce, yellow giant hyssop, lady's thumb, Labrador tea, and jewelweed. All of these cures were passed on to the seafaring newcomers, but the native peoples also used poison ivy as a herb in itself. Native people in all of North America use poison ivy leaves to treat warts and similar afflictions; they used them in a poison potion for tipping arrows, and made baskets and spits for cooking meat from its stems. Modern scientists now seem to be catching up these ancient naturalists and are now experimenting with poison ivy as a ingredient in a possible cure for cancer.

Author William T. Gillis, in his article "Poison Ivy and Its Kin," which appeared in *Arnoldia*, the magazine of the Arnold Arboretum in Massachusetts, speculates that the Native Americans may have also used this herb—particularly the berries—in religious ritual. One startling bit of evidence is the fact the oldest surviving specimen of an actual plant are poison ivy seeds found in a medicine pouch dating from the thirteenth century uncovered at Mesa Verde, Colorado.

Obviously, that the seeds are included in a magic pouch is recognition of the spiritual power of the plant. Perhaps this ancient medicine man was making use of the warrior power of the plant—a power that is viewed rather as a nuisance by our modern culture.

While contemplating these sacred seeds, I am reminded of a quotation from *The Great Mother: An analysis of an archetype* by Erich Neumann (Pantheon Books, 1963). While explaining that poisons are universally governed by the Moon and the Mother Goddess, he states:

> The character of spiritual transformation is most evident in connection with intoxicants, poison, and medicine. The feeling that he is transformed when he imbibes them is one of the deepest experiences of man—sickness and poisoning, drunkenness and cure, are psychic processes that all mankind relates to an invisible spiritual principle.

Herbs that poison as well as cure are gifts of the Mother Goddess, and poison ivy can viewed as be both. Poisoning and curing both show the power of a plant.

Often in our modern world, we hear doubts expressed about the power of herbs to heal. Yet, we are not complete skeptics, because no one will deny the power of certain mushrooms to kill, or the power of poppies to addict us, or the power of poison ivy to make us itch.

When I first became involved in herbal healing, my father expressed disbelief in the effectiveness of herbs. Yet, it was he who first taught me of the power of plants when he taught me to identify poison ivy.

Some Practical Advice about Poison Ivy

The best way not to be infected by poison ivy is to not touch it, and definitely do not burn it. The worst thing one can do is the break the stems or leaves of poison ivy, crush the berries, or try to uproot it by hand. All of these activities will release large amounts of urushiol, and you will get a rash despite your best efforts to avoid it.

If your job or inclination require you to walk through poison ivy, you can protect yourself by rubbing IvyBlock ® on your skin before the contact. This barrier cream contains bentoquatam (quaternium 18 betonite) as an active ingredient. Urushiol will bond with this chemical instead of you skin. Studies have shown it to be 68 percent effective in preventing the rash, and if a rash does occur it is less severe.

After being exposed to poison ivy one can wash the urushiol away within two to eight hours by rubbing the skin vigorously with Tecnu ®, an over-the-counter product containing mineral spirits. Afterward you must rinse with plenty of water. My wife and friends use Tecnu regularly, and they testify to its effectiveness.

If you still have managed to develop a rash from contact with poison ivy, then I recommend the herb jewelweed. This herb grows from three to five feet in height, and has light green toothed leaves on a yellowish waxy stem and distinctive yellow or orange flowers. The flowers are about one inch long and shaped like a curved cone with a fluted edge—they look like an illustration from a nineteenth century fairy book. Jewelweed grows in moist places often very close to poison ivy. It is usually recommended to cover the poison-ivy rash with the sap from the jewelweed stem, but jewelweed sap does not always flow. In some cases, I have made a tea from the leaves and stems of jewelweed, and covered the infected area with gauze soaked in this tea. I found that this stopped the itching, dried up the pustules, and cured the rash in half the usual time.

Medical science will not verify the effectiveness of this remedy, but Native Americans have used it for centuries and it continues to be the most recommended herbal cure for poison ivy rash.

For Further Study

Nature's Revenge: The secrets of poison ivy, poison oak, and poison sumac and their remedies. Susan Carol Hauser. Lyons & Burford, 1996.

Midsummer Herb Magic

⋙ By Anna Franklin ⋘

As the Midsummer Sun reaches the point of greatest power and light, it imbues herbs with various special magical and healing properties.

Midsummer is the most potent time for gathering herbs, especially Sun-colored flower varieties such as St. John's wort. Anything round and rayed, such as the rose and the daisy, suggests the Sun itself. Other plants acquire strange properties at this time. An elder cut on Midsummer Eve, for example, will bleed real blood, and fern seeds can confer the gift of invisibility if gathered at midnight in the summer.

For centuries, a belief in the magical powers of herbs at Midsummer was common throughout Europe and the Middle East. At one time, the common custom was to hang plants up all over on St. John's Eve. In 1598, the historian John Stow wrote of the sight on such a day in London:

> Every man's door was shaded with green birch, fennel, St. John's wort, orpin, white lilies, and the like, ornamented with garlands of beautiful flowers. They had also lamps of glass with oil burning in them all night; and some of them hung out branches of iron, curiously wrought, containing hundreds of lamps lighted at once, which made a splendid appearance.

Witches generally believe that plants gathered at the time of the Summer Solstice are endowed with particularly distinct magical characteristics.

After all, summer is a fertile time of year when flowers bloom in abundance. In the Western mystery tradition, it is counted as the time when the opening flower is fertilized, and when the god impregnates the goddess. For the Welsh, summer was sacred to the goddess Blodeuwedd, the Flower Bride, created by magic from nine types of flowers to marry the god Lleu Llaw Gyffes. The Celts made floral sacrifices at Midsummer—the tradition of placing flowers on the largest stone on the farm carried this custom in Britain well into the nineteenth century. At this time, too, protective plants such as St. John's wort, rue, orpine, trefoil, rowan and red thread, vervain, and fennel were hung above the door and cattle stalls.

Gathering Herbs for Magic

If you gather your own herbal ingredients to use in magic spells and in incense, you will have to be certain that they were gathered in a reverent and magically empowered manner. When you come to mix the potion, cast the spell, or blend the incense you will remember the atmosphere of the meadow, riverbank, or garden where you picked the herbs. You will remember the day and the season and the enchanted feelings you had at the time.

Make sure the herbs you collect are not growing near a busy road, as they will be polluted. Do not use iron or steel to cut them, as it drains their life force, and don't let the herbs touch the ground after they've been picked as this has the same effect. You should always ask permission of the plant before you harvest it, and state clearly why you want its gifts—what purpose you have in mind. If you don't think you've had a reply, or are not sure, leave the plant alone. Also, only take a little of any one plant, and don't strip it bare. This will ensure that the plant will live on after you move on. Place the plant matter you have harvested in a clean paper, plastic, or fabric bag, and carry it carefully to the place you have set aside for your magical workings.

What nature provides is seasonal, and gathering ingredients can be a magical lesson in itself—attuning you to the turning of the year and teaching you about herb craft. In general, it is helpful to gather produce on a dry day, as any dampness will have a tendency to create mildew.

Drying Herbs

Any fresh herbs can be dried. To do this, pick your herbs and tie them together in small bunches. Hang them in the kitchen or in a well-ventilated shed to dry. As soon as they are dried out, they should be crumbled into jars and stored in a dark place. They might look decorative hanging in your house or pantry, but they will soon become dusty and begin to deteriorate if they hang too long.

Summer Solstice Herbs

The following herbs all take on special meaning during the Summer Solstice.

Angelica (*Angelica* spp.)

Angelica is a member of the parsley family and is probably a native plant of Europe. There are about thirty varieties of Angelica in all.

Angelica is invested with the power of the Sun and light, and the ability to cast off darkness and negativity. Use this plant in incense for Midsummer to celebrate the healing power of fire and the Sun to overcome winter, decay, and negativity. Angelica was used in medieval Europe to deter evil spirits—especially at Midsummer when they were thought to roam freely. Angelica is an important ingredient in incense of healing, protection, cleansing, exorcism, and purification.

Angelica Lustral Water

For a recipe to tap into the natural powers of angelica, infuse two heads of angelica flowers in a cup of hot water. Strain the water from the flowers, being careful to use no metal implements or containers. The resulting infusion can be used to purify the aura, the temple or other sacred space, your magical tools, and your home and work place. Sprinkle it about your person, add some to your bath, or use a sprig of rosemary to sprinkle it about the temple or home.

Chamomile (*Anthemis nobilis, Matricaria chamomilla*)

Chamomile is native to Europe, North Africa, and temperate Asia. It is sacred to the Sun and Sun gods including the Egyptian Ra, the Celtic Cernunnos, and the Norse Baldur. Chamomile connects with the Sun god's power of healing, regeneration, and protection. It may be used in incense with these intentions or added to herbal talismans to boost them with the Sun god's power. Chamomile is one of the sacred herbs of Midsummer and may used in the incense, or simply thrown onto the festival fire as an offering.

Dill *(Anethum graveolens)*

Dill is an aromatic upright annual herb native to the eastern Mediterranean, India, Iran, Russia, and western Asia. It was known as one of the St. John's Eve herbs, and was valued as a protection against witchcraft. Use dill as an incense to clear your mind and strengthen your personal focus. It can be added to incense for protection and for cleansing a sacred space. To Witches, dill is a sacred herb of Midsummer, and it can be used in the incense, cast on the bonfire, or placed in the ritual cup.

Elder *(Sambucus nigra)*

Elder is the name of a group of thirty species of small trees that grow in the temperate areas of the Northern Hemisphere. It is said that where the elder grows, the Goddess is not far away.

The elder has several stations throughout the year, and its character changes at each. The sweet blossom can be collected in June to make a good fixative for herbal incenses. The leaves should be gathered on Midsummer morning to add to healing incense. Add the blossom to Coamhain incense to invoke dryads and fairies. A love charm can be made by putting the flowers into a tankard of ale to be shared by a man and woman. They will then be married within the year.

Fennel *(Foeniculum vulgare)*

Fennel was held in high esteem by the Romans and was one of the nine sacred herbs of the Anglo-Saxons. During the Middle Ages, fennel was hung over the door on Midsummer's Eve to keep away evil spirits. It is one of the Witch's sacred aromatic herbs of Midsummer used as incense or thrown on the bonfire. In fact, fennel has a long association with the Sun and fire. In Greek mythology, the titan Prometheus used a hollow fennel stem to steal fire from the Sun and bring it to humankind. Greek islanders still carry lighted coals around in the pith of giant fennel.

Fern

Fern is the common name for any spore-producing plant of the phylum *Polypodiophyta*. It is associated with Sun gods and goddesses, as well as with gods and goddesses of the dawn such as Daphne. It is also sacred to the Great Goddess and the sky gods of thunder, lightning, and Midsummer. At the turning of Midsummer and midwinter, ferns allow access into the otherworld so we may contact its inhabitants—the Sidhe and the Wildfolk. Ferns were sacred to the Baltic Sun goddess Saule who appeared on the horizon at Midsummer wreathed in apple blossoms and red fern blossoms. You can use fern in incenses at Midsummer to protect your household and yourself for any and all divination purposes.

Gorse (Ulex eurpaeus)

Furze, or gorse, is native to Europe and is widely cultivated. The Sun and the element of fire rule it. Use gorse to invoke Jupiter, Onniona, spring goddesses, Sun gods, and Thor. Gorse was long burned at Midsummer, its blazing branches were placed round the herd to bring health to the cows and good luck for the rest of the year. In some parts of the British Isles, the Midsummer fire was lit with a branch of gorse.

Lavender *(Lavendula officinalis)*

Lavender is the name given to twenty-eight species of the genus *Lavandula* native to the Mediterranean region. Use lavender in incenses for the planet Mercury, the element of air, and to invoke the deities Cernunnos, Circe, Hecate, Medea, Saturn, and serpent goddesses. Lavender purifies, heals, and cleanses. Add it to incense for calm meditation and peace and harmony in the home. Also bring lavender to help calm difficult discussions and meetings, and add it to your Midsummer incense.

If you want to tap into some of the more strange magical properties of lavender, go to a natural or wild place such as a fairy mound or other spot known to be haunted by the fairy folk. Carry with you a sprig of lavender and inhale the scent. An old charm says that this will help you to see the little people.

Marigold *(Calendula officinalis)*

Marigold is a hardy annual herb native to central and southern Europe and Asia. Use it in incense dedicated to the Sun, the element of fire, the star sign of Leo, and to invoke Sun gods. Marigold is a herb of healing and protection, and can also be added to incenses for prophetic dreams, love, divination, and to consecrate divinatory tools such as crystal balls.

The name of this plant comes from the term "calends," or in Latin *kalendae*, the word for the first day of each month and the origin of our word "calendar." In ancient Rome, calendula was said to be in bloom on each "calend" throughout the year. The specific name "officinalis" shows also that this plant was included on the official list of herbal medicines. In ancient Egypt, calendula was used as a rejuvenating herb, while the Persians and Greeks used it for cooking, and the Hindus to decorate their altars and temples.

At Midsummer, garlands of marigold flowers hung on doors to prevent evil from entering. Marigold petals were also scattered on the floor under the bed to offer protection to sleepers. Marigolds planted on graves bless the departed souls. This is a good time of year to remember those who have gone from this life into the realms we call the Summerland.

Oak *(Quercus robur)*

There are more than 600 species of oak, all of which grow naturally only in the Northern Hemisphere. The primary power plant of the Summer Solstice is the oak. In ogham, the Irish alphabet of the fourth and fifth centuries, the oak is *duir*. This word means "door" in Gaelic. The word for door and oak, and perhaps Druid, come from the same root in many European languages. The oak flowers at Midsummer and marks the door opening on one side to the waxing and on the other side to the waning year. Oak was the most sacred tree of the Druids, and stood for an axis mundi—the doorway to knowledge. Oak wood constituted the sacred fires of Midsummer. The flowers and wood are used at Coamhain.

Rosemary *(Rosemarinus officinalis)*

Ruled by the Sun and the element of fire, rosemary is a hardy perennial native to the Mediterranean region. It helps the mind and the memory, so use it in incense designed to help you concentrate or meditate. Use also for healing, marriage, births, funerals, and memorial services, for protection and to dispel negativity and evil, to keep a lover faithful, for love spells, and for spells designed to help you retain your youth. The fairy folk are particularly fond of rosemary, and the incense tends to attract them.

A piece of rosemary wood cut on Midsummer morning is said to preserve youthful looks.

St. John's Wort *(Hypericum perforatum)*

St. John's wort is a hardy perennial herb native to Europe and western Asia. It is one of the many herbs that gain special powers at Midsummer, when it should be collected for magical purposes. The golden flowers are associated with the Sun and the flames of the Midsummer fires. The Irish called it *beathnua* (life-renewer), and the Welsh called it *dail y fendigaid* (the blessed one's leaf).

Medieval herbalists considered St. John's wort the golden herb which "shines like the Sun in the darkness" on St. John's Eve. It is a protective and countermagic herb. The botanical name *hypericum* comes from the Greek; it means "to protect." This refers to the belief that the plant could make evil spirits disappear. Furthermore, St. John's wort was called *Fuga*

Daemonum (flight of demons) because it repels evil spirits. It was believed to possess the quality of protecting the wearer against all manner of evil.

Country folk often picked bunches of the herb and hung them in byres and stables to frighten evil spirits and keep the devil away. It was tossed onto the *baal* or hearth fires and allowed to burn to protect the home against lightning and storms. St. John's wort gathered at noon on Midsummer Day was reputed to be effective against several illnesses. It was also believed that the dew collected from the plant on Midsummer morning would preserve the eyes from disease, while the roots gathered at midnight on St. John's Eve would drive the devil and evil sorcerers away.

The Sun, the element of fire, and the sign of Leo rule St. John's wort. The herb is sacred to Sun gods, particularly Baldur, and can be used in incenses to cleanse the working area, working tools, or person. It repels negativity and can be used in purification and exorcism.

Vervain *(Verbena officinalis)*

Vervain is a hardy herbaceous perennial native to Britain, Europe, North Africa, and west Asia. Vervain is sacred to Cerridwen, a shape-shifter who has aspects as a cat goddess, a Moon goddess, the harvest mother, and a crone or white sow. Vervain is one of the sacred herbs of Midsummer. It will cleanse and purify and will raise vibrations. It is sacred to poets and singers, heightens the consciousness, and intensifies clairvoyant powers. Use vervain to invoke the deities Aphrodite, Aradia, Cerridwen, Diana, Horus, Isis, Jupiter, Mars, Ra, Thor, Venus, and Zeus.

For magical purposes vervain should be gathered at the Summer Solstice. Gather enough for one year. Any vervain that has been left over from last year's gathering should be cast onto the Midsummer bonfire.

Yarrow *(Achillea millefolium)*

Yarrow, native to the whole of Europe, is a hardy herbaceous perennial. It is sacred to the Horned God and to the male principle. Yarrow tea may be used when working on aspects of masculinity and for connection with the god. It may be used throughout the cycle of the wheel in incenses to invoke the god. Yarrow is one of the sacred herbs of Midsummer, assigned to St. John, and should be gathered for magical purposes or for extra healing power at the solstice. It can be used in the incense or thrown onto the bonfire as an offering. Yarrow incense can be used to promote divination and clairvoyance.

Yarrow Spell to Ensure Love

On Midsummer morning cut nine heads of yarrow, saying:

> *I cut thee yarrow, that love may grow.*

Take the yarrow home and bind the stems together with a green ribbon. Hang the charm above the bed that you share with your lover, and this will ensure lasting love.

Sacred Herbs of Vodou, Santería, and Candomble

☙ By Scott D. Appell ❧

I n the summer of 1975, during a break from my graduate studies in horticulture and botany at Ohio State University, I visited Haiti. I was twenty-one years old.

Although the popular epithet "Le Perle des Antilles" (The Pearl of the Antilles) reflects Haiti's tropical splendor, horticultural and botanical wonders, and turquoise oceans, it is actually one of the poorest countries in the New World, and I was rather completely unprepared for all that I was to encounter there.

The Riches and Poverty of Haiti

Regularly during my stay, I traversed Haiti's two largest cities—Port-au-Prince, the capital city, and Petionville—via *tap-tap*, which is a Creole term for the psychedelic public mini-buses common in the country. I

was astonished with the cultural and classist dichotomy of this half-island country—the other portion, as you know, comprises the Dominican Republic.

The crushingly poor populace begged for coins or peddled Sun-baked, unidentifiable foodstuffs, rags, and trinkets as they negotiated glorious coconut palm-lined avenues, and streets lined with magnificent orange-flowered flamboyant trees—all amid fabulous gingerbread-covered Victorian-style public buildings and hotels, and cleanly whitewashed government offices. Daily, my nose was assaulted by the perfume of brine, sweat, manure, and garbage mixed with ocean salt and an ineffable tropical scent.

Scrawny dogs and chickens monopolized the thoroughfares, as emaciated *colporteurs* sold tourists desiccated anthrax-ridden goat and cow skins under the trees along the roadsides teaming with innumerable tropical flowers. Incorporeal whispers of "Blanc, blanc!" ("White, white!") shadowed my every move.

A now long-lost contact, employed by the *Departement a L'Interieur*, was kind enough to drive me around the impoverished countryside—an adventure that required special government-furnished passes. Cradling my 1973 copy of J. Hutchinson's *The Families of Flowering Plants*, a controversial taxonomic botanical opus of the time known for Hutchinson's new system of classifying plants based on their probable phylogeny, or early race history, I assimilated every aspect of the rural, agrarian life as we left Port-au-Prince to wind our way through the verdant mountainsides. I watched as we passed ubiquitous, well-scrubbed, Sun-bleached, white cotton clothing hanging on the lines, small herds of malnourished livestock, gaunt chickens and turkeys, and meager kitchen gardens in front of lean-to houses.

My escort and I enjoyed "botanizing" and discussing the various flora we encountered—both wild and cultivated, indigenous and alien.

I noticed a great many native African species, which was not unusual because Haiti's benign climate favored the growth of so many divergent pantropical plants and the heritage for many Haitians comes out of Africa. I recognized several plants species outright, and I was able to key out—or taxonomically identify a plant by a process of elimination using a written plant "key"—various unknown specimens. My work was sort of a scientifically based game of "Twenty Questions."

One of the non-Caribbean African plants that I noticed in particular was *Albizia lebbeck*, commonly called the siris tree, or lady's tongue tree. Although a common shade tree in Haiti—where, in Creole, it was liltingly called *tcha-tcha*—I knew something more about it. This tree is commonly used in African and Chinese medicine.

Mysterious Haitian Plant Species

Throughout my travels Haiti, I was surprised to encounter many surprising plants whose presence in the countryside soon began to take on a mysterious air. For instance, I found two species of datura *(Datura metel* and *Datura stramonium)* both in cultivated gardens and in roadside ditches. The former species, a large, night-blooming herbaceous plant which produces masses of huge white trumpet-shaped flowers, and which is now a popular garden ornamental in the United States, I knew to be an important medicinal and hallucinogenic part of the pharmacopeia of India and China. *Datura stramonium*, which we know familiarly as jimson weed, or thornapple, and which was evening-blooming and bore small pink beautifully scented flowers, was formulated into an hallucinogenic drink called *wysoccan* by native Algonquin peoples. I was certain of both of these identifications, as I was well familiar with the fact that when their flowers are pollinated both species of datura develop ovoid (egg-shaped) or globoide (globe-shaped) spiny fruiting capsules.

At one location along the route, my guide pointed to the barbed seed pods of the *Datura stramonium*, and instructed that the Haitian common name for the plant was *concombre zombi*—or, in other words, "the zombie's cucumber."

Daturas are lethally poisonous to man and beast alike, due to the properties of the tropane alkaloids—particularly scopolamine and hyoscyamine—that are found in it. In fact, these plants are related to the more well-known toxic herbs such as mandrake, deadly nightshade, and belladonna which belong to the plant family *Solanaceae*.

My only questions at the time were: Why was there so much of it growing in people's child-filled gardens or at accessible roadsides? And where exactly did the name "zombie's cucumber" come from? Of course, despite my studies, I didn't exactly live in a vacuum. I happened to know what zombies were; they were the walking dead. After all, like many people I loved the 1945 RKO cult film *I Walked With a Zombie*. But zombies were fictitious, weren't they?

It was all very mysterious and intriguing, but before I found any answers to my questions my summer break had come to an end, and I had to fly back to Columbus, Ohio. As I shopped for souvenir gifts at the Marche aux Fer (The Iron Market) in Port-au-Prince, and bargained for several primitive iron sculptures cut from the bottoms of rusty oil barrels, I was saddened that I had to leave, and I couldn't get rid of an odd gnawing feeling in the pit of my stomach. Something important was bound to happen if I only had time to stay on. Despite it all, I definitely felt that something portentous already had occurred, and that, somehow, my life had changed for good.

Ten Years Later

A decade passed. My studies were completed, I had joined the working world. Life had continued as it will.

In 1985, I happened to read a book by Harvard ethnobotanist Wade Davis. It was nonfictional masterpiece called *The Serpent and the Rainbow*. This book would transform my life all over again.

Dr. Davis had gone to Haiti to explore the world of zombification, as well as the plants integral to the Vodou religion. The hairs on the back of my neck stood on end as I devoured his opus; we had traversed the same roads, visited some of the same sites, and heard the same local names for plants—concombre zombi and tcha-tcha. But unlike my simple, inquisitive amblings, Dr. Davis' explorations of Vodou became life-threatening on several occasions, as he became close to secret societies and the dangerous drugs they made from local plants.

I was stunned. Through the pages of his book, Dr. Davis had answered my horticultural and botanical questions of ten years earlier, and he had inspired more of them.

About the same time, to further enthrall me, I discovered the innumerable nonfictional writings on the subject of Migene Gonzalez-Whippler (see bibliography at the end of this article), who researched Santería. In addition, I found publications by Maya Deren, a woman who made several ethnographic documentaries in Haiti, Alfred Metraux, and Zora Neale Hurston, among many others.

The pieces of a gigantic and cosmic botanical puzzle began to fit together for me. I knew I was on to something, and I had discovered my calling in life—ethnobotany, the study of plants of culinary, medicinal, and religious importance to global humanity, their communities, and their livestock. In time, I was seriously studying the use of plants for use as fodder, dye, fibers for clothing, and other household items such as paper, basketry, lumbers for building materials, and flora used for brewing and vintning.

Introduction to the New World African Religions: Vodou, Santería, and Candomble

Whenever I explain my fascination with Vodou, Santería, and Candomble to my colleagues, I use the following similes in order to make a simple introduction to them. (I hope the practitioners of these religions will please not take umbrage at my gross oversimplifications).

These religions are agrarian-based, pantheistic, and ani-mistic, and have very similar mythologies to those of ancient Greece and Rome. That is to say, there are multitudinous major and minor gods and goddesses in these religions; there is a ruler of the gods, a god of war, a goddess of love, a god of herbal healing, a set of twins, and so on.

Collectively, these deities are known in Vodou as *loa*, in Santería as *orishas*, and in Candomble as *orixas* (pronounced in the same way as orishas—with an "sh" sound). These deities are the supreme lords of the elements of nature, and they exercise direct influence on humans, whom they are capable of protect-ing or punishing. They have innumerable exploits, adventures and love affairs, and they may even change sexes. Their legends, known as *patakis* in Santería, are wonderfully exciting to read. However, the major difference between the New World-African religions and the beliefs of early Greece and Rome is that Vodou, Santería, and Candomble are living, vital theologies—practiced by an estimated one hundred million people from all walks of life in the Americas today. And the mythologies of Greece and Rome are relegated to the classroom, and taught as historical beliefs from dead religions.

In order to understand Vodou, Santería, and Candomble, we must go to western Africa to uncover the beginnings of these three similar, but distinctly different, religions, and to uncover subsequently the sacred herbs they utilize. Sadly, this article permits only the merest and most basic overview.

During the slave trade, thousands of Yoruba people from southwestern Nigeria, and the populations of neighboring provinces of Dahomey (Benin), and Togos were brought to the New World.

Catholic France brought slaves to her island outpost of Saint Domingue, which was later to become Haiti, while Catholic Portugal brought her bondaged to Brazil, and Spain brought hers to Cuba and Puerto Rico. In addition, other Caribbean islands such as Jamaica and Trinidad were populated with Yorubas abducted by the British and Dutch.

Whenever possible, even though it was strictly and expressly forbidden, the uprooted Yorubas took the necessities of life with them to the New World. In general, these constituted familiar agricultural products and sacred herbs, and of course their religion, Fon, which is still practiced in Nigeria today.

As slaves, the Yorubas were forced to partake of the religion of their captors or face the dire penalty of death. Subsequently, in order to survive, these stalwart Africans began to pray to their Fon deities under a veil of Christianity. In this way, they were able to keep their own faith alive. In this way, the people of Yoruba origin came to have a syncretized, or harmoniously blended with differing principles, religion made up of both Fon and Catholic beliefs. And consequently, at religious services both public and private, Fon and Christianity began to be practiced concurrently by these people as one new divergent doctrine.

The countries in which these New World-African religions were being practiced were isolated from one another—usually by vast expanses of water. As it is with any living biological organisms suddenly separated by enormous distances, independent evolution is inevitable; and so it was with this newly syncretized religious teaching.

In Cuba and Puerto Rico, Santería—which in Spanish means "the way of the saints"—developed along with its darkly negative counterpart Brujeria ("the way of the Witch"). At the same time in Brazil, Candomble—"the way of the saints" in Portuguese—evolved, along with its sister theologies, Macumba and Quimbanda. Meanwhile the Shango cult emerged in Trinidad, and a combination of African and South American Indian traditions combined in northeast Brazil to form the Xango religious tradition.

On the island nation of Haiti, only a few of the original African deities became popular, and because there were more tribes involved in the syncretic mixture—such as the Arada people—the resulting religion, Vodou, which is also spelled Vaudun or Vodoun, has only traces of Yoruba and Dahomey beliefs remaining. Furthermore, when practitioners of Vodou moved into the southern United States—namely Louisiana—Vodou itself transmuted into American Hoodoo, or Voodoo.

All these aforementioned theologies, and many more I have no room to mention, derived from the original West African Fon tradition, marking quite an amazing journey when you get down to thinking about it.

A Few Words About Vodou and Zombification

No writing concerning Haitian Vodou, no matter how basic and meager, can ignore the subject of zombies (which is spelled zombis in Creole) and the process by which they are made. Once again, though, here we only have space for the shallowest of overviews.

Zombies are people whose death has been duly recorded by medical authorities, whose burial has been attended by friends and family members, but who are discovered, sometimes years later, walking the streets in a mental state bordering on quiet derangement. To the collective population of Haiti, these people are the walking dead—their bodies have been removed from the tomb, and resuscitated by a *bokor* or *malfacteur*—holy evil doers or sorcerers—using a process no one really fully understands, or wants to.

However, to set the record straight, even though we are all well acquainted with the classic Hollywood horror-movie depictions of zombis, they are not the walking dead at all. Rather, zombis are not dead, nor have they ever been dead. However, they have appeared dead.

For the man or woman who is chosen as a victim—for they are indeed victimized—a state of profound paralysis is accomplished through zombification. This condition is characterized by absolute immobility, during which time the border between life and death is not at all ascertainable—even to trained physicians. There is absolutely no physical movement, the pupils do not dilate or constrict, there is no discernible pulse or heartbeat, and there is no reaction to pain. Unbelievably, the individual who has been zombified hears, sees, and feels everything that is happening to him or her, but is unable to react physically.

This condition is achieved by the use of a combination of animal and plant poisons. The zootoxin, or animal posion, is namely tetrodotoxin, a potent neurotoxin which stops the conduction of nerve signals, produced within the puffer fish, *Diodon hystrix*, and *Sphoeroides testudineus*. This substance is combined with the venom secreted by the skin of *Bufo marinus*, or giant cane toad.

The phytotoxin, or plant poison, includes that of the tcha tcha, or *Albizia lebbeck*, which may cause pulmonary edema, or an abnormal accumulation of liquid in the lungs. It is administered as a *coup poudre*, or magical powder, that is blown in the face, and aspirated by the individual. It can also be ingested. During this powder's manufacture, in order to avoid self-poisoning, the creator has his or her skin completely covered, and wears a kerchief to cover the face.

After pronounced deceased, the victim is buried in their local cemetery, and days later force-fed an antidotal paste derived from plant products which counteracts the effects of the initial poisoning. It is in this way that the zombi is resurrected, and disjointedly rises from the grave.

Ritual Herbs Integral to Vodou, Santería, and Candomble

The sacred herbs of Santería, Vodou, and Candomble are used principally as botanical sacrifices, hallowed remedies, or in specific ethnic recipes dedicated to each loa, orisha, or orixa. The various deities of all three theologies have particular favorites, and not surprisingly, given the original West African foundation of all three religions, there is some overlap.

For our purposes, though many people use the word in a much narrower sense, I will be using the word "herb" in its ethnobotanical connotation. That is, any plant of religious or medicinal significance is a herb, even though this may include foliage, fruit, flowers, trees, and shrubs.

To satisfy any of the New World-African traditions, botanicals can be purchased from ethnic neighborhood specialty shops—called *botanicas* in Spanish, or *casas de santos* in Portuguese. However, horticulturally clever practitioners can cultivate their own plants in gardens, windowboxes, or home greenhouses, or on windowsills, patios, rooftops, or terraces. I believe the process of growing herbs and subsequently using them ceremoniously, creates a far more empowering and satisfying experience. Remember, however, that each theology has specific guardians of the various flora who must be propitiated. Be forewarned; to neglect a plant's guardian while harvesting it is to invite dire consequences upon yourself. If you are an uninitiated practitioner, know that this is an integral procedure of very real religions.

Before you do begin growing, however, you should know something about the United States Department of Agriculture (USDA) Hardiness Zones. The USDA has set up an easy-to-follow guideline for potential outdoor growers of plants, which I refer to below.

The various categories, called Zones—which range from USDA Zone 1 to USDA Zone 11—reflect the annual winter temperature lows for a typical year in a specific geographical location within Canada, the United States, and points south. Basically, the larger the number of a USDA Zone, the warmer the winter clime.

For example, USDA Zone 1 is in midcentral Canada, and USDA Zone 11 lies in the Florida Keys, Hawaii, and the Caribbean.

USDA Zone 1:	Below -50°F
USDA Zone 2:	-50°F to -40°F
USDA Zone 3:	-40°F To -30°F
USDA Zone 4:	-30°F To -20°F
USDA Zone 5:	-20°F to -10°F
USDA Zone 6:	-10°F to 0°F
USDA Zone 7:	0°F to 10°F
USDA Zone 8:	10°F to 20°F
USDA Zone 9:	20°F to 30°F
USDA Zone 10:	30°F to 40°F
USDA Zone 11:	Above 40°F

Another alternative to growing is to peruse your local food markets or garden centers. Undeniably, unenlightened Americans are amazed to find that many of the fruits and vegetables they pick over in the grocery—the herbs they procure from their farmer's market and the landscape material they admire in garden centers—are often of major religious significance.

Examine the following information, and wonder at some of the familiar flora; I guarantee you will never regard plants the same way again. These are only a smattering of the extensive ethnobotanical inventories of the three religions.

Common Herbs of the Caribbean Religious Traditions

Basil *(Ocimum* spp.) (Family: *Lamiaceae)*

Spanish: *albahaca morada* or *basilica;* Portuguese: *alfavaca*

Basil is only second to the tomato as the leading kitchen staple grown by Americans. We culture this aromatic annual herb anywhere we can: in gardens, on patios, terraces, or window ledges, in windowboxes, and on windowsills. As many of us know, basil has an ancient medicinal, magical, and mythological history. Although the familiar sweet basil *(Ocimum basilicum)* is native to tropical Asia, there are more obscure species indigenous to Africa; namely *Ocimum americanum* from tropical Africa, and *O. gratissimum*, native to Tanzania. In African traditions, basil is not considered an edible flavor-enhancer, but rather is a sanctifying, altar-scouring, and medicinally hallowed herb.

Considered a sweet herb, as opposed to a bitter herb such as rue, albahaca morada is always associated with the goddess of the sea waters and the personification of maternity, Yemaya, who has been syncretized with Our Lady of Regla in Cuba.

On the other hand, practitioners of Afro-Brazilian religions consider basil sacred to the seven orixas—Obaluaie, Oxala, Oxossi, Iansa, Oxum, Xango, and Iroko. Obaluaie is actually the name of the youthful identity of Omulu, who in his adolescence was a virile warrior. Oxala, often syncretized with Jesus, is generally considered the father of the orixas, and represents the peacefulness of death. Oxossi is young and beautiful and rules over the forests and the hunt. Iansa controls the spirits of the dead, as well as being goddess of the winds and tempests. Oxum is the goddess of fresh waters, wealth, and beauty. She is goddess of the Oxum River in Nigeria. Xango is god of thunder, lightning, and justice. And most interesting of all is Iroko, who is often syncretized with Francis of Assisi. This is the god of the jurema, the white fig tree *(Ficus doliaria)*, who represents the changing seasons.

Basil is also an integral ingredient for several types of head washes and purification baths.

Mint *(Mentha* spp.) (Family: *Lamiaceae)*

Spanish: *menta*—mint; *yerba buena*—spearmint; Portuguese: *hortela-pimenta*—peppermint

The ancient Greeks and Romans appreciated the culinary attributes, pleasing fragrance, and insect- and vermin-repellent qualities of mint, which is native to Africa and Eurasia. One of the most beloved of the garden herbs, mint is hardy in USDA Zones 3 to 6, depending on the species, and may be used medicinally as a tonic, antispasmodic, calmative, antiseptic, and analgesic.

In Santería, spearmint, or *yerba buena*, is considered a sweet herb and is associated with the orisha Yemaya, goddess of the sea waters and maternity. Menta, also a sweet herb, is used in *despojos*, or special healing and empowering baths.

Hortella-pimenta is always associated with Oxala, considered the father of the orixas, and Chief of Planet Earth; he is often syncretized with Jesus Christ. Peppermint also decorates the altar of Exu, messenger of the gods who is saluted, appeased, and propitiated first, as only he may allow access to the other deities. Peppermint is incorporated into ritual bath mixtures because it counteracts negative fluids.

Lettuce *(Lactuca sativa)* (Family: *Compositae*)
Spanish: *lechuga*; Portuguese: *alface*

This well-known salad ingredient, a native of North Africa and Asia, has been cultivated for the dining table since 4500 BC in ancient Egypt. But lettuce did not appear in manuscripts until British botanist Gerade's *Herball* of 1597.

America's Shaker Christian fellowship utilize an extract pressed from heirloom lettuce varieties as a substitute for opium as a sleeping agent.

Lechuga is considered a sweet herb, and always associated with the orishas Yemaya and Oschun, who is syncretized with Nuestra Señora de La Caridad del Cobre, Our Lady of the Charity of Copper, the patroness of Cuba. Named in honor of the river of the same name that crosses the region of Oshogbo, in Nigeria, Oschun is the symbol of river waters, without which the planet would be barren.

Alface is associated with Candomble *eguns*, or the spirits of the dead, and Iansa, the renowned Goddess of the Fire Sword, the only deity formidable enough to handle the eguns. Iansa dominates the winds and lightning, and uses this power to control electrical equipment and machinery, create cooling breezes, and invoke cyclones and tornadoes. Lettuce tea is used as a calmative for insomnia, and aids in counteracting the uneasiness caused by visitations by the eguns. *Alface* is also an important constituent to the secret egun ceremonies.

Rue, or Herb of Grace *(Ruta graveolens)* (Family: *Rutaceae)*
Spanish: *ruda;* Portuguese: *arruda*

Rue has been cultivated for its medicinal properties for millennia, and remains an important component of modern herb gardens—usually to USDA Zone 5. Rue holds a place in biblical and Western magical herb gardens alike. It is grown for its vermifugic and insecticidal properties. Traditionally the most potent rue was that acquired by theft. This herb bears blue-green, bipinnate or tripinnate (feather-shaped) aromatic foliage held on woody stems. Although the taste is very bitter, rue finds its way into sandwiches, teas, and certain Mediterranean cuisines and liqueurs. Be aware, however: Many people suffer severe dermatological reactions upon contact with any part of the plant.

Practioners of Santería consider *ruda* to be sacred to the orisha Chango, one of the major deities of the pantheon, and god of fire, thunder, and lightning, who has been syncretized with Saint Barbara. Ruda is also holy to Aganyu, symbolized by the volcano and syncretized with Saint Christopher.

Arruda is used to represent and propitiate all the orixas in Candomble, and its medicinal attributes are well recognized. This plant is used as a vermifuge, calmative, emmenagogue, and antirheumatoid. Extruded juices are applied to open wounds to aid healing. It a considered a strong agent to ward off the evil eye. Rue is also believed to reduce envy, counteract black magic, and bestow the blessings of the orixas. It is burnt as a censing herb, as well.

Uncommon Herbs

Datura *(Datura stramonium)* (Family: *Solanaceae)*

Creole: *concombre zombi;* Portuguese: *figueira-do-diabo*

The best-known common name in the United States for this plant is jimson weed, which is an etymological corruption of Jamestown, the first permanent British settlement in America. Established on May 14, 1607, in Virginia, Jamestown was the first place in the New World this lethally toxic plant was encountered. Another common American epithet is thornapple.

Datura, hardy to USDA Zone 7, bear white to purple, evening-blooming, scented, and trumpet-shaped flowers which are followed by spiny seed capsules. The variety "Horn of Plenty" produce lilac-shaded flower, and spineless pods. All datura are indigenous to the Americas and have become naturalized all over Europe and Asia.

Interestingly, datura has worked itself into many ethnic materia medicas and pharmacopoeias, including the indigenous populations of North, Central, and South America. The foliage, fruiting capsules, and seeds of datura contain the largest amounts of tropane alkaloids. Small doses induce a hallucinogenic state in people. Slightly higher portions are fatal. An Old World species, *Datura metel,* is used extensively in Africa, India, and China.

Concombre zombi has a most amazing use within the confines of zombification. The paste force-fed to the paralyzed zombified victims in order to counteract the initial poisoning is actually a mashed mixture of the toxic *Datura stramonium,* mixed with sweet potato and sugar cane syrup. This is further evidence that the phytochemical configuration of the entire zombification process is utterly astonishing.

In Brazilian Candomble, *figueria-do-diablo,* or "The Devil's figs," are used in carefully measured doses in various magical remedies in order to counteract vomiting and swelling of the testicles.

Castor Bean *(Ricinus communis)*
(Family: *Euphorbiaceae)*

Spanish: *higuereta;* Portuguese: *mamona* or *carrapateira*

The castor bean is a popular annual ornamental plant. It is cultivated throughout the United States for its great stature and large palm-shaped, dark green-to-purple foliage. At six to ten feet in height, this plant makes a handsome and fast-growing temporary hedge or screen. It is native to West Africa and Old World tropics, and is hardy to USDA Zone 9. All plant parts, and particularly the attractive seeds, are lethally poisonous. Interestingly, the oil pressed from the seeds is used to make the familiar product castor oil. In Nigeria, the fermented seeds of the plant, known as *ogili* or *ogiri,* are added to soups and stews in many recipes.

In Santería, *higuereta* is considered sacred to the orisha Obatala, who is syncretized with Our Lady of Mercy, and who is known as King of the White Cloth for his habit of always dressing in immaculate white clothing. Obatala is also the father of mankind and the messenger of Olofi, who may be interpreted as God the Creator, or the process of creation. The plant is also incorporated into sacred remedies to aid headaches, diphtheria, and cancer.

The practioners of Candomble utilize *mamona* in ceremonies honoring the orixa Exu, who is often likened to Saint Peter, and who acts as the trickster opener of doors, the universal agent of magic, and the messenger of the gods.

Agricultural Herbs

Corn *(Zea mays)* (Family: *Gramineae)*

Creole: *grain* or *mais;* Spanish: *maiz;* Portuguese: *milho*

Corn is an agriculturally important New World grass developed in Central and South America around 3500 BC. The populace of Africa never saw corn until its introduction during the slave trade. However, Nigerians were well acquainted with sorghum *(Sorghum bicolor)*, sugar cane's African counterpart. I believe it is quite possible that corn took over the traditional ethnobotanical uses of sorghum within the context of the Fon religion.

In Haitian Vodou, yellow corn meal is the holiest medium with which to draw *veves*, or a symbolic design unique to each and every loa. Without a doubt, this is the most artistically impressive ceremonial factor of the theology. In general, veves are designs traced upon the ground of the peristyle, or the roofed, open-air, lean-to ceremonial area, or of the *oum'phor* or *hounfor*, or the Vodou temple, which may or may not include the peristyle, or or upon sacred foods and other offerings. These designs are rendered with impeccable precision and geometric accuracy with alternating colors from yellow and white wheat flour, brown rice flour, red brick powder, gray ashes, and pulverized leaves.

Cornmeal biscuits are often given as food offerings at these ritual. Initiates to the religion are given a restricted diet frequently including fat- and salt-free corn gruels. Cooked, salt-free corn dishes, always prepared by the men, are employed to honor the practioner's deceased African ancestors during the ceremony *manger-morts* or *Mange-les-morts*, which is celebrated each April 31.

Practioners of Santería employ corn and corn products as well to propitiate the orishas. Eleggua relishes toasted corn and corn meal balls with honey and palm oil. Babalu-Aye accepts corn and popcorn covered with palm oil. The favorite food of Chango is *amala*, a mixture of cornmeal and palm oil. Oshun favors a similar dish. The orisha Oya, identified with thunder-bolts, fire, and wind, welcomes rice with corn.

Corn is also included in food offerings by the devotees of Candomble. *Abado*, or toasted corn, is one of the favorite foods of Omulu, the god of disease and pestilence. Oxum, goddess of the sweet waters, adores *ado* or *adum*, toasted ground corn mixed with palm oil and honey. In addition, *axaxo*, or yellow corn meal mixed with coconut slices, and *canjica*, yellow or white corn cooked with salt, are popular oblations.

Banana *(Musa x paradiso)* (Family: *Musaseae*)

Creole: *figue-bananes;* Spanish: *guineo;* Portuguese: *bananeira*

The USDA reports that bananas are the most popular fruit in the United States. Although they are enjoyed in foods as diverse as exotic cocktails and baked goods, and prove integral to various Caribbean and Latin American cuisines, bananas are native to tropical Africa, India, and southeast Asia. The populace of western Africa, in fact, were well acquainted with the numerous attributes of the banana. They utilized the fruit, flowers, shoots, and leaves for food, fermented beverages, and building materials. Bananas can be cultivated outdoors in USDA Zones 8 to 11, depending on the species.

According to the accepted traditions of Vodou, the banana plant is sacred to the first *houn'gans*, or male Vodou priests, and to the original, most learned of the *mam'bos*, or female Vodou priestesses—in a parallel Adam and Eve myth. In fact, there is also a snake in the legend, the *bramine*, who enjoys touching and eating the *figue-bananes*. In addition, by virtue of the fact that the banana plant always increases in height and width, the banana symbolizes eternal life. Bananas caramelized in sugar is a favorite dish of Erzulie, a love goddess often syncretized with the Virgin Mary.

In Santería, bananas, as well as *plantanos*, or plantains—the unripened fruit of various *Musa* species—are the preferred fruit of various orishas, and they are proffered by devotees as propitiating offerings. Oggun, popularly syncretized with Saint Peter, represents work and all human effort, and as such he is the divine ironworker who toils eternally and indefatigably. He relishes seven plantains covered with palm oil. Yemaya, the goddess of the sea, and Oshun, ruler of river waters, both relish unblemished, perfectly ripe yellow bananas. Aganyu, who is most often syncretized with Saint Christopher, symbolizes all earth forces, particularly the center of the earth and volcanoes. In common belief, he savors nine green plantains covered with palm oil.

Practioners of Candomble revere the *bananeira*, or the banana plant, as a sacred tree of mystery and enchantment. Its foliage makes a practical and magical substitute for platters filled with sacred foods and botanicals. In addition, bananas and plantains themselves are incorporated into various cooked dishes, such as *oguede*, that are often designated as consecrated offerings. Bananas are held sacred by all the orixas.

Sugar Cane *(Saccharum officinalis)*
(Family: *Gramineae)*

French: *sucre de cane*; Spanish and Portuguese: *cana*

The species name, *offinalis*, reminds us that sugar cane was originally considered one of the "official" medicinally important plants. In fact, sugar cane remains an important constituent of the Chinese materia medica, where its juice is employed to promote expulsion of phlegm from bronchial passages, stimulate gastric activities, and treat wounds, ulcers, and boils. Sugar cane can be cultivated outdoors year round in USDA Zones 10 and 11; otherwise it is treated as an annual plant.

Haiti was formerly a vast producer of sugar cane, and it is not surprising that fermented cane juice—rum—is a favorite liquor of many of the loas, and that *clairin*, or white rum, is particularly popular. Erzulie, the goddess of love, has a penchant for pale and sugary drinks, and nearly all the loas enjoy Coca Cola. Plantains caramelized in sugar are accepted, too.

Refined sugar and sugar cane syrup, known as *melao de cana*, sweeten various food offerings to the orishas of Santería. *Eleggua* is very fond of sweets and candies of all sorts, especially caramels. The Divine Twins, the Ibeyi, who are syncretized with saints Cosme and Damian, enjoy cakes and cookies as well. Seven burnt coconut balls sprinkled with *melao de cana* is the favorite sacrificial food of Yemaya. Rum is an important libation for many of the orishas as well.

Brazilians believe that *cana* merits special attention because it was the first agricultural crop to be commercially produced on a grand scale in Brazil—awarding the Portuguese colonists vast fortunes. Therefore, this botanical is believed to attract sound providence. Disciples of Candomble equate sugar cane with the orixa Exu, and they prepare it in a specific fashion to place on his altars. The foliage and husks are burned as purification incenses. Sugar is incorporated into various sacrificial dishes, including *afura*, a rice cake made with sugar, and *alua*, a fermented corn or rice flour beverage enhanced with pineapple rind, ginger root, lime, and raw or white sugar.

Yam *(Dioscorea alata,* and other species) (Family: *Dioscoreaceae)*

Creole: *ignames* or *yam;* Spanish: *name;* Portuguese: *batete*

Yams are native to tropical Africa, and are an important source of carbohydrates for many indigenous peoples. Although similar in appearance, taste, and texture to sweet potatoes *(Ipomea batata)* from South America, yams are in fact botanically unrelated. They may be cultivated outdoors in USDA Zones 9 to 11.

Every autumn, practioners of Haitian Vodou celebrate the first fall harvest of *ignames* with a ceremony called the *manger-yam*. This yam-feast, which blesses the first tubers to be harvested, is practiced in exactly the same fashion as by the Fon of Dahomey and Togo in Africa today.

This agrarian festival, which is practiced in all Vodou sanctuaries, is two days long. During first day, in the *coucher des ignames*, or the "putting-to-bed of the yams," the tubers are anthropomorphized into sacred characters and subsequently introduced to, and blessed by, the loas. During following day, in the *lever des ignames*, or the "rising of the yams," the mam'bo aligns the tubers that have slept under the eye of the gods and spirits on the ground, and makes propitiating sacrifices and prayers to them. Later on, the ignames are cut up and cooked with fish, and everyone present feasts themselves. The loa's share is buried in a hole dug in front of the altar. Yams are also placed on the altars of the loas as food offerings.

In Santería, cooked *names* find their way into various tidbits and dishes designed to please particular orishas. Oggun, the inexhaustible iron worker, enjoys roasted yams; as does Orunla, the champion of the *babalawos,* or high priests of Santería. The goddess Oya, who is syncretized with Nuestra Senora de Candelaria, or Our Lady of Candlemas, also accepts *names.* She is also guardian of the gates of death. The father of mankind, and peace and purity personified, Obatala, enjoys towering piles of peeled, white-fleshed names sprinkled with pure cocoa butter and *cacarilla,* or pulverized egg shells.

Brazilians also incorporate yams into various sacrificial dishes destined for the altars of their orixas, including *batete* (raw yams mixed with oil and salt), *bobo* (yams with pure bee honey), and *ipete* (cooked mashed yams seasoned with palm oil, onion, pepper, and ground shrimp).

Pumpkins *(Cucurbita maxima)*
Spanish: *calabaza, ayuama,* or *zapallo*

Watermelons *(Citrullus lanatus)*
Spanish: *sandia*

Gourds *(Lagenaria siceraria)*
Creole: *calbasse;* Spanish: *calabaza;* Portuguese: *cabaca*

Approximately 760 species comprise the family *Cucurbitaceae,* one of the most agriculturally important plant families. In addition to the pumpkins, watermelons, and gourds mentioned above, it includes such familiar produce as cucumbers, zucchini, melons, loofas, and squash. Watermelons and gourds are native to western and northern Africa, and are highly valued by the local populations as foodstuffs, containers, vessels, and musical instruments. Pumpkins, on the other hand, are indigenous to Central and South America, and are similarly prized by Native Americans.

Gourds are integral to Haitian Vodou. A practioner rarely communicates with the loa without first inviting them to eat something he or she knows they like. Ritual meals are cooked in accordance with traditional Haitian recipes, but the kind of dishes, the way of preparing them, and manner of serving them must follow exact rules. The proper way consists of serving in hollowed gourds a mixture of raw cut up ignames (yams), sweet potatoes, pumpkins, and other "winter vegetables." *Calbasse* are also used as ladles to dispense anointing blessed waters or botanical decoctions during the ritual *assiette de Guinee*, and as the *asson*, or sacred rattle.

Pumpkins and watermelons are also important to Santería. The goddess of the rivers, Oshun, loves pumpkins filled with honey and yellow-fleshed melons such as honey dew. Her *ebbos*, or ritual cleansings made in an effort to dispel evil and attract love, are frequently placed in hollowed-out pumpkins. Watermelons are the favorite food of Yemaya, goddess of the seas and maternity. *Sandias* are also consecrated constituents of *omiero*, a sacred healing and cleansing potion. These aid in remedying burns, dermatological problems, and whooping cough. Gourds are used as sacred rattles, vessels, and ladles.

The music dedicated to Candomble is often accompanied by the *cabaca*, a dried gourd rattle. In other sects, it may be called a *xaque-xaque*, *ague*, or *afoxe*. Dried gourds may also be halved, painted, and used as receptacles for food presented to the orixas.

Trees and Shrubs

Coconut *(Cocos nucifera)* (Family: *Arecaceae*)
Spanish and Portuguese: *coco*

Originally from the South Pacific, the coconut is widely grown throughout the pantropics for its oil and fruit which is used fresh, dried, desiccated, and as cream. It factors in a wide range of byproducts including thatching, matting, stuffing, ropes, fiber, and charcoal. It provides edible flowers, as well as sugar, vinegar, and palm wine. Scorched roots furnish a coffee substitute, and young seed shoots are eaten raw. The coconut palm is hardy to USDA Zones 10 and 11.

In Santería, the coconut is used in all the major ceremonies, and some of the best-known spells are prepared with this fruit. Coconut meat performs one of the most important divinatory systems in Santería, the Darle Coco al Santo, or "give coconut to the saint" ceremony, performed by the santero or santera—male or female priest. Any of the orishas or the eggun—spirits of the dead—may be contacted to answer specific questions during this ceremony.

To start, the shell of the coconut must be broken with a hard object, such as a hammer, metal mallet, or iron weight, on a table or sturdy shelf—never on the floor. The shelled and hulled meat, which as we all know is white on one side and brown on the other, is broken into four pieces. Basically, the four pieces are tossed on the floor, and as they fall, they will either present the brown side or the white side upward. It is the numbers of light or brown sides up that is interpreted. Coconuts also find their way onto altars as food offerings to the orishas. Eleggua, who is syncretized with Saint Anthony of Padua, and who is the opener of doors and messenger of the gods, accepts coconuts, as does Orunla, the symbol of wisdom. Babalu-Aye, who is syncretized with Saint Lazarus and perceived as the personification of all epidemics, debilitating diseases, leprosy, dermatitis, and AIDS, prefers green (unripe) coconuts.

Coconuts also are incorporated into food offerings in Brazilian Candomble. *Mungunza* is a dish of dried white corn kernels boiled in milk and coconut milk, and *ratapa* is a dish that mixes purees of fish and shrimp boiled in coconut milk, palm oil, and malagueta peppers.

Siris Tree, or Lady's Whisper Tree (*Albizia lebbeck*)
(Family: *Mimosaceae*)

Creole: *tcha tcha*

This massive, fast-growing tree is indigenous to the Old World tropics, ranging from West Africa through Asia, southeastward to Australia. Attaining a height of fifty feet in cultivation, the siris tree is only hardy to USDA Zones 10 and 11. It ultimately develops a broad-spreading crown atop a short thick trunk. Planted throughout the New World tropics, the Caribbean and the Antilles, it is a popular shade tree. The leaves are dark-green and bipinnate, or double feather-shaped, and are shed each year for a brief period during spring. The extremely fragrant flowers are greenish-yellow globes, about two inches in diameter, which appear during the brief dormancy period. They are followed by flattened seed pods—reminiscent of such familiar plants as locust trees and wisterias to which they are related. The dried pods rattle in the breeze—hence the common name of lady's whisper.

Known in Creole as *tcha tcha*—possibly an onomonopoetic allusion to the sound the dried seed pods make—the ground bark and seed pods, which contain saponins and sapotoxins, are integral to the manufacture of the *coup poudre* of the Vodou zombification process. I have seen bunches of the dried pods sold in New York City botanicas.

Brazilian Cherry (*Eugenia fragrans* and *E. uniflora*)
(Family: *Myrtaceae*)

Creole: *bois-dine*; Portuguese: *pitanga* or *pitangueira*

Brazilian cherries are native to most of eastern Brazil, French Guiana, and neighboring Surinam—hence the alternative common name of Surinam cherry. Eugenias, named after Prince Eugene of Savoy, 1663–1736, a lover of botany, are cultivated in frost-free USDA Zones 10 and 11 for their glossy, dark-green, aromatic foliage, small fragrant white blossoms, and deliciously acid-sweet, dark-red-to-almost-black fruit. Brazilian cherries become small shrubby trees that grow up to twenty feet high, and their resilient, flexible wood is often used by indigenous peoples to make bows.

In Brazilian Candomble, the *pitangueira* is used in ceremony as an homage to the orixa Oxossi, Lord of the Forests and King of the Hunt. Because Oxossi is also a dreamer, idealist, and lover of all things, this handsome orixa is considered the patron of the arts. Eugenias are used in *abos*—ritual purification baths given to a neophyte at the time of initiation—head washes, environmental cleansings, and evocative incenses. The plant is also used a vermifugic tea.

During the passages of initiation in Haitian Vodou, the novitiates are given a strictly enforced salt-free diet, as well as a purifying beverage containing the juice of *bois-dine*, the Brazilian cherry.

I have an unsubstantiated pet theory about the use of the Brazilian cherry in New World-African religions. One species, *Eugenia coronata*, is native to tropical West Africa, and I believe, that in all likelihood, this is the plant included in the founding of the Fon tradition; the New World species have been incorporated as a new, but somehow familiar, substitute.

Sources of Eclectic Herb Plants and Seeds

J. L. Hudson, Seedsman
Star Route 2, Box 337
La Honda, CA 94020
Catalog: $1

The Banana Tree, Inc.
715 Northhampton St.
Easton, PA 18042
(610) 253-9589
Catalog: $3

Well-Sweep Herb Farm
317 Mt. Bethel Road
Port Murray, NJ 07865
(908) 852-5390
Catalog: $2

Taylor's Herb Gardens
1535 Lone Oak Road
Vista, CA 92084
(619) 727-3485
Catalog: $3

For Further Study

Mama Lola: A Vodou priestess in Brooklyn. Karen McCarthy Brown. University of California Press, 1991.

Sacred Arts of Haitian Vodou. Donald J. Cosentino, Editor. UCLA Fowler Museum of Cultural History, 1995.

Santería: African Religion in Latin America. Migene González-Whippler. Original Publications, 1992.

Santería Experience: A journey into the miraculous. Migene González-Whippler. Llewellyn Publications, 1992.

Santería: The religion, faith, rites, magic. Migene González-Whippler. Llewellyn Publications, 1994.

Sarava! Afro-Brazilian Magick. Carol L. Dow. Llewellyn Publications, 1997.

Secrets of Voodoo. Milo Rigaud. Translated by Robert B. Cross. City Lights Books, 1985.

The Serpent and the Rainbow. Wade Davis. Simon and Schuster, 1985.

Spirits of the Night: The vaudun gods of Haiti. Selden Rodman and Carole Cleaver. Spring Publications, 1992.

Voodoo in Haiti. Alfred Métraux. Translated by Hugo Charteris. Schocken Books, 1972.

Plants of the Gods: Their sacred, healing, and hallucinogenic powers. Richard Evans Schultes and Albert Hofmann. Healing Arts Press, 1992.

Filmography

The following feature length films portray aspects of Vodou, Santería, or Candomble. The quality of representation runs the spectrum from ridiculously silly to sublimely accurate. Parental discretion is advised. Actual subject area is given for each film.

Angel Heart
Director: Alan Parker
Starring: Mickey Rourke, Robert De Niro, Lisa Bonet
Produced by: Caroloco Entertainment, USA, 1987
Subject: Vodou

The Believers
Director: John Schlesinger
Starring: Martin Sheen
Produced by: Orion Pictures, USA, 1987
Subject: Santería and Brujeria

Black Orpheus (Orfeo Negro)
Director: Marcel Camus
Starring: Breno Mello, Marpessa Dawn
Produced by: Dispat Films, Italy/France/Brazil, 1959
Subject: Candomble

I Walked with a Zombie
Director: Jacques Tourneur
Starring: James Ellison, Frances Dee
Produced by: RKO Radio Pictures, USA, 1943
Subject: Vodou

Mambo Kings
Director: Arne Glimcher
Starring: Armand Assante, Antonio Banderas
Produced by: Alcor Films; Warner Bros., USA, 1992
Subject: Santería

Midnight in the Garden of Good and Evil
Director: Clint Eastwood
Starring: John Cusack, Kevin Spacey
Produced by: Silver Pictures, Warner Bros.,USA, 1997
Subject: Hoodoo

The Serpent and the Rainbow
Director: Wes Craven
Starring: Bill Pullman, Cathy Tyson
Produced by: Universal Pictures, USA, 1988
Subject: Vodou

White Zombie
Director: Victor Halperin
Starring: Bela Legosi
Produced by: Halperin Productions, USA, 1932
Subject: Vodou

Ethnographic Documentaries

The following nonfictional short film is superb and worth tracking down.

Divine Horsemen: The Living Gods of Haiti
Director: Maya Deren
Produced by: Mystic Fire Video, USA, 1953
Subject: Vodou

Sage Advice

✐ By Elizabeth Barrette ✐

How can a man grow old, who has sage in his garden?

Chinese proverb

T hroughout history, and in many cultures over the world, sage has long reigned as the king of herbs.

It thrives across a wide range of habitats, and is very easy to grow. Even novice gardeners can usually succeed in growing and cultivating it. It comes in many varieties, and lends itself to countless uses.

In fact, it is so popular that when people hear the word "herb," one of the first thoughts that leaps to mind is sage. Truly, something about this special plant has a firm hold on our collective attention. We find references to it in the oldest herbals and garden plans. We extol its virtues in songs, plays, paintings, and other great works. If you grow just one herb, it should be this one—you can do almost anything with it.

Let's take a closer look at the story of sage, shall we?

Exotic-Yet-Commonplace Sage

Although the term "sage" can refer to several related plants of the genus *Salvia*, most properly it refers to the specific species *Salvia officinalis*—often called garden sage. (The misnamed "sagebrush" does not belong to this genus at all, but rather to *Artemisia*.)

Sage originates from the Mediterranean and North Africa. The common form of sage appears as a large bushy plant that generally grows two to three feet tall. Sage can spread horizontally for several feet as well, but does not tend to run the way mint does. It has square woody stems that are covered with a light down. Sage usually blooms during June, and takes on shades of mauve-blue, though its tiny flowers can be white, pink, or indigo. Its oval gray-green leaves grow in opposite pairs and reach about two inches in length. The leaves generally have a distinctive nubbly texture, and contain a rather intensely aromatic oil which easily rubs off on your fingers when you touch the leaves.

Several cultivars of sage offer more exotic features. The lemon-and-lime colored leaves of gold-variegated sage yield a milder flavor than garden sage. So, too, do the leaves of tricolor sage, which has the added feature suggested by its name—green leaves with beautiful pink and white margins.

Magically, the gold-variegated sage holds some undertones of solar energy. Purple sage displays a rich burgundy color and makes a tea especially good for soothing sore throats. Variegated purple sage has leaves with green, purple, pink, or cream blotches, and a strong, robust flavor. The purple varieties are in fact excellent for magical applications. Meanwhile, prostrate sage features a sprawling growth habit and balsamic fragrance. Holt's mammoth sage grows rapidly to a huge size, ideal for harvesting large quantities of the herb.

Cultivating Sage

Even if you have a brown thumb and can't grow anything else, you will likely be able to grow sage. Most varieties of sage are hardy, though some varieties such as tricolor sage require winter protection, while others like garden sage grow well into USDA Hardiness Zone 4 (well up into Canada—see page 269 for more details). Sage is a species that requires full Sun and light, and dry alkaline soil with good drainage. It is not a heavy feeder though—in fact, if the soil is too rich, you'll get lots of luxurious foliage with very meager fragrance and flavor. Bees love this plant, and honey from its flowers has a wonderfully robust musky-nutty taste.

Sage grows well either from seed or from cuttings. Plant the seedlings about two feet apart, and water them carefully until they are established. Harvest lightly the first year. Prune mature sage plants regularly to keep them bushy, and replace old woody plants every few years. They like marjoram, rosemary, thyme, germander, or lavender as a companion plant; but they don't get along well with onions or chives.

With its fragrant foliage and blue-to-white flowers, sage also makes an ideal addition to a "moonlight" garden—that is, one designed with plants that look and smell their best at night—or a "potpourri" garden—one designed with plants that release scent when petted. Finally, folklore offers a couple of odd admonitions regarding sage. You should never plant it in your own garden but should ask a stranger to do so for you, and you should never give it a bed of its own but should plant it with some other herb.

Harvesting and Storing Sage

Some of the details here depend on the use you have intended for your sage, as this is a wonderfully useful plant with many diverse applications in everything from cooking to casting spells.

In general, you should harvest sage by snipping or plucking the leaves just before the flowers appear, although you can get a second or even third harvest from mature plants later in the season. After harvesting, spread the leaves on paper or cheese-cloth, out of direct sunlight, so they can dry slowly. When dry, store them in an airtight glass jar. Some recipes call for fresh sage leaves to produce a jelly or sauce with a long shelf life, so for those you should skip the drying stage and just pick the leaves at the last minute.

Timing is important. For culinary purposes, you typically get the strongest flavor in your sage by picking the leaves in mid-morning after the dew has dried and the aromatic oils are at their strongest. For magical purposes, though, you might prefer to harvest at noon—for peak solar energy—or at midnight to tap into peak lunar energy. You should definitely pay attention to the Moon's phase, and harvest during a waxing Moon for spells of abundance or health, and during a waning Moon for spells of banishing or protection. (Check the handy Moon tables in the back of this almanac for lunar signs and phases.)

If you work frequently with astrology, you might also want to harvest in accord with various planetary motions that have significance to you.

The History of Sage

The use of sage dates back to antiquity. It was commonly used as a means of flavoring and preserving food, maintaining health, empowering spells, and even conducting trade. Therefore, sage has always been an extremely popular garden plant. Maps and other records of old monastery gardens typically show a generous selection of sage, such as the Plan of St. Gall, drawn in 820 AD. Some herb books offer complete "blueprints" of many period gardens, should you wish to recreate one. About the same time, Walahfrid Strabo, who lived in 807–840 AD, wrote the poem "Hortulus," or "The Little Garden," in which he described the work of the gardener, the characteristics of various plants, the ways of growing and cultivating the plants, and the plants' eventual use. And of course this early gardening master included a good description of one of his favorite plants, sage. Later on, Albertus Magnus listed it as one of the essential components of a pleasure garden in his "On Vegetables and Plants," written circa 1260 AD.

People from lands as far away as Italy and China believed that sage could convey longevity to one who used it. In fact, this is where sage got its genus name—*Salvia*, from the Latin "salvere," which means "salvation or cure." The Romans considered sage a sacred herb and gathered it from the wild with great ceremony. First, they would make sacrifices of wine and bread; then, dressed in a white robe, the barefooted harvester would then pick the leaves. Various customs forbade anyone to cut sage with an iron blade. This herb also played an important role in the tea trade, as the people in China would trade their best green tea for sage at a ratio of three or four to one.

When England colonized America, along with the human colonists came a number of botanical colonists—that is, plants from the Old World that would serve to sustain the settlers in the New World. During this period, people favored a "kitchen garden," planted right outside the door which included herbs, flowers, and vegetables all together. For the settlers, sage was a favorite along with other common herbs such as thyme and mint. This interest continued through the American Revolution; Thomas Jefferson's 1,000-foot kitchen garden featured twenty-six different herbs, including sage.

Magical Uses

You can use sage in a wide range of spells, rituals, charms, and other applications. According to tradition, the primary magical properties of sage include protection, longevity and immortality, prosperity, wisdom, and the granting of wishes. Its gender is masculine, its planet Jupiter, and its element air. Sage also counts among the sacred herbs used for the Samhain and Mabon.

Most of the lore regarding longevity and immortality states that you should eat sage every day to improve your lifespan expectancy. Sage uplifts your spirits and prevents every-day challenges from wearing you down. Carry it to cultivate wisdom or to shield against the "evil eye." In general, it absorbs bad luck and other negativity, banishing tension and disruptive influences or energies. Use the leaves in spells to enhance your health and intelligence, or to settle your finances. For wishes, write your desired goal on a leaf of sage and sleep with it under your pillow for three nights—if you dream of your wish, then it will likely be granted.

One of the best and most popular magical uses of this herb is for smudging to purify a person, place, or object. To do this, simply waft the smoke over whatever you want to purify. Or you can also purify by adding the crushed leaves to a ritual bath. Sage is used similarly for blessings, prayers, and dedications. You can burn sage loose on charcoal, or tie it tightly into wands which smoulder after being lit and blown out. Sage mixes well with other smudges such as cedar or sweetgrass. Some varieties yield a richer or milder smoke, so sample several to see which you prefer.

Many people like to leave sage as an offering to deities, totem spirits, fairies, or other entities. For this purpose, some practitioners often mix it with other offering herbs such as tobacco, mistletoe, or vervain. Still others prefer to use sage by itself. You can also add sage to the ritual chalice of water, wine, or juice that you use in ceremonies. I find that the multicolored cultivars of sage work best as offerings, because the mixed colors represent a blending of different worlds. Historically, sage comprises one of several ingredients used to make "Black Cat" powder, which was once used for hexing. Today, however, sage appears almost exclusively as an offering or focus for totemic work or divine supplication involving feline patrons.

A Simple Wisdom Charm

For a charm to bring wisdom to you, you'll need nine fresh sage leaves, a felt-tip pen, a small piece of Aida cloth, a piece of tissue paper, a tapestry needle, and embroidery floss in a contrasting color. For the cloth and floss, choose colors suitable to your goal: blue, purple, or silver-gray. Cut a rectangle of Aida cloth measuring about three inches by one-and-a-half inches. Near one end, embroider a symbol of wisdom, such as the rune Uruz or the owl-eyes of Athena. Then fold the cloth in half so that the short ends meet. Carefully sew up the sides to make a nice little pouch.

Next, take the leaves of sage and write the word "wisdom" on each one with your felt pen. Hold them in your hands, breathing in their scent. Center yourself, and invoke your favorite deities of wisdom to help you in this task. You may want to sing a verse like this:

> *Lady of the mind's eye,*
> *Open my inner sight*
> *That I may clearly see*
> *Which path I face is right.*

Take a few minutes to meditate on the virtue you seek before you continue with the spell.

Now wrap the leaves in the tissue (to keep crumbs from sifting out through the cloth) and stuff them into the pouch. Sew the top of the pouch closed. Allow it to dry for a few days in a warm, dry place. This makes a convenient way to carry sage without getting crumbled leaves in your pocket. You can modify the details to create a charm for any of this versatile herb's other properties, too.

Arts and Crafts

Although not as flashy as yarrow or lavender, sage does have a number of handy applications in the area of arts and crafts. Overall, sage dries beautifully. Garden sage retains an excellent gray-green color when it is dried; purple sage holds a subtle and rich burgundy color when dry, though the others varieties vary in how well they dry.

Sprigs of dried sage are useful as a nice addition to herbal wreaths, baskets, and preserved bouquets. Sage also makes a fine cut herb for fresh bouquets, tussie-mussies, and similar projects. Sage, which is a fairly hardy plant, grows well as a seedling in a living wreath. This involves planting herbs in a ring of wet sphagnum moss. Prostrate sage, with its gracefully drooping habit, works especially well in this project.

For all of these applications, you might want to keep in mind the romantic "flower language" in which sage unsurprisingly sends a message of long life and wisdom.

Aside from craft projects, there are a couple of other, more practical, uses for sage. Because of its inherent insect-repelling properties, sage is a good choice for potpourri sachets intended for placement in drawers or trunks. Tucked among your clothes, sage imparts a subtle fragrance while protecting from any sort of magical damage. Industrially speaking, dyers use this herb to produce several different colors used in textile manufacture—including buff yellow (with an alum mordant), deep yellow (with chrome), or green-gray (with iron).

Sage's Health-Giving Properties

Many herbs have a history of medicinal usage, but not all of them stand up to scientific investigation. However, sage has proven effective in a number of ways. First, it aids in the digestion of fatty meats. For centuries, in fact, this well-known feature has encouraged chefs to make use of the herb in many recipes. Furthermore, sage helps relieve diarrhea, and it helps settle the stomach.

A tea brewed from the leaves of common sage serves as an antiseptic blood and nerve tonic; it also works as an astringent agent for the body to dry up breast milk, night sweats, mucus congestion, and so on. Purple sage yields a tea that soothes sore throats and other mouth irritations—try it with sage honey added for an extra treat. Sage also contains hormone precursors useful for treating menopause and irregular menstruation; a compress of sage soothes hot flashes and relieves fluid retention. For that reason, pregnant women should avoid large doses of this herb.

Herbalists often use sage as an ingredient in salves or bath powders for its astringent and antiseptic properties. In aftershave lotion, sage soothes and stimulates the skin, particularly when it is combined with lavender. Women can get a similar effect with sage facial steams or afterbath splashes. In shampoo or herbal rinses, it conditions and darkens silver hair. But be careful: Once use is discontinued, your hair can take on a slight greenish tint.

Historically, hunters often slept with bundles of sage tucked into each armpit. The herb would help suppress perspiration, absorb human odors, and generally impart a subtle leafy fragrance to the skin. Hunters would also chew the leaves to whiten their teeth and freshen their breath. In all, these properties of sage made it much easier for the hunters to sneak up on their keen-nosed prey.

Sage also yields a powerful essential oil. This is not something easily made at home, but you can find it readily through aromatherapy sources. Diluted in a carrier such as almond oil or cocoa butter, this oil soothes sore muscles and pain from arthritis or rheumatism. It also makes a good insect repellent; mix four or five drops of sage essential oil with eight ounces of water, and spray on plants or surfaces to deter aphids, moths, and flies.

The Culinary Uses of Sage

Countless recipes call for the use of sage in specific quantities and combinations, but you don't really need them if you want to experiment with this herb in the kitchen. Sage works just fine in some very simple applications, though always use the herb sparingly to avoid having its strong flavor dominate a dish.

To start, try throwing one or two bruised leaves of sage into a pot of stew. Add tender young leaves sparingly to salads. Press leaves onto the outside of a roast, or stuff them into the body cavity of poultry before cooking. Deep-fry sprigs of sage as a garnish for meats of all kinds. Mince fresh leaves and add them to the breading for fried chicken or pork chops. Cut branches of sage to lie under shish kabobs or Cornish hens while grilling them. To make herbal butter, simply chop a leaf into a small bowl, add a couple tablespoons of butter, and microwave to melt.

Of course, sage also stands out in more complex applications. You can find suitable recipes in any cookbook, or in some herbal guides that feature a cooking section. Popular recipes with sage include meat pies, omelets, savory cheese crusts or dips, soups, marinades, and stuffings. Aside from the herb itself, sage vinegar is also a favored ingredient in a number of upscale recipes.

Because of its antibacterial properties, sage makes a very good natural preservative for food. The herb's most common applications as a preservative include use with condiments, poultry, fish, and other meats—especially sausage. Actually, a combination of sage and rosemary works better than either herb alone. Distilled extracts of these herbs provide odorless, tasteless antioxidants which extend the shelf life of foods like soy oil and potato chips.

Sage has served us long and well since at least the dawn of agriculture, and probably before then. It flavors our food, soothes our ailments, and delights our noses. In the garden, it forgives a fair amount of inept treatment to grow and thrive for years. Magically, sage helps to protect us, and it encourages personal growth.

Sage comes in more different colors and forms than we know what to do with. It is an herb that offers something for everyone. Invite it into your life and see what it has to say to you.

For Further Study

The Complete Book of Herbs. Lesley Bremness. Viking
    Studio Books, 1988.
    This is an excellent general guide with full-color photos,
    some garden plans, lots of crafts, and yummy recipes.

Cunningham's Encyclopedia of Magical Herbs. Scott Cunning-
    ham. Llewellyn Publications, 1991.
    This is the best herbal reference for magical and spiri-
    tual applications.

A Druid's Herbal for the Sacred Earth Year. Ellen Evert
    Hopman. Destiny Books, 1995.
    This is another good magical and medicinal guide with
    a strong Celtic emphasis.

Herbs: The visual guide to more than 700 herb species from around the world. Lesley Bremness. Dorling Kindersley Publishing, 1994.
This is a good identification guide, with attention paid to the various features and uses of each plant.

Mother Nature's Herbal. Judy Griffin, Ph.D. Llewellyn Publications, 1997.
Only a few color plates, but this book offers a lot of recipes, both culinary and medicinal.

Rodale's Illustrated Encyclopedia of Herbs. Claire Kowalchik and William H. Hylton, editors. Rodale Press, 1987.
This book includes extensive information on each herb, its growth requirements, and various uses; it also has lots of general data on garden styles, crafts, cooking, and so on. Good pen-and-ink illustrations with plenty of color photos, too.

Eye of Satan

≫ By Eileen Holland ≪

Caution: Eye of Satan seeds are the most poisonous seeds on the planet. Eating just one can kill a human or an animal. Ingesting them causes severe stomach problems with vomiting and diarrhea, followed by collapse, then death. Keep Eye of Satan out of the reach of children, who may think it is candy. Keep it away from pets as well.

E ye of Satan is just one of the many names for a powerfully magical, and rather dangerous, seed. While the name is meant to evoke the potency of its toxicity, the plant is not evil. In fact, whenever someone asks me what they can bring me from Egypt, Eye of Satan is usually what I request.

I first encountered Eye of Satan while I was living in Egypt. I had just moved there and could not yet speak much Arabic. My husband, who is Egyptian, took me to a spice vendor so that I could stock our kitchen with local flavors. The spice vendor's stall was a Witch's delight, a riot of interesting colors, textures, and aromas. I remember in particular a small man's tiny kiosk that was entirely crammed with rows of exotic spices and herbs carefully arrayed in hanging bunches or displayed in jars.

Some unusual items immediately caught my eye. I pointed, asked what each one was, and my husband translated. Hand of Maryam. Blood of the Brother. Eye of Satan. The vendor was eyeing me strangely by then, because I had inquired about his magical plants. My husband, embarrassed and uncomfortable, hustled me away.

Islamic fundamentalists were killing foreigners regularly in Egypt at that time, in false hope of igniting an Islamic revolution. We lived in a small city in the Nile Delta, where I was the only American for many miles around. I was easily recognizable as a foreigner because of my fair skin and red hair. My husband rightly feared that the spectacle of me at market, tyring to buy magical plants and giving the appearance of knowing what to do with them, might provoke a lynching by the local superstitious townspeople, or draw a fundamentalist hit squad to our doors.

From then on, my husband visited the spice shops on his own. But I could not forget the jar full of red seeds that I had seen, and I asked him to bring me some.

When he did bring them, the seeds in the bag were freshly harvested. They were brilliant red with bright blue "eyes," so brightly colored that I couldn't believe they were natural. I planted some in pots of earth on our balcony, and to my surprise they all sprouted. These were indeed seeds, not beads. Egypt being Egypt, hungry birds quickly ate the sprouts.

I began experimenting with the seeds, to discover their magical uses. It would have been simpler, of course, to have my husband to ask someone about this, but nothing in Egypt is ever simple. Getting a straight answer about anything from an Egyptian is a frustrating puzzle to a straightforward American. This this is especially true when discussion turns to anything having to do with the occult.

Egypt's Magical History

Egypt's magical history is much longer than its Islamic one, so folk magic and high magic both thrive despite being forbidden according to Islam. Still, most modern Egyptians, including my husband, are very uncomfortable speaking about anything magical. I was on my own so far as Eye of Satan was concerned.

The bright blue of the "eye" of the seeds was the exact color of blue traditionally used in the Middle East for averting the evil eye. The symbol of the eye has also long been used in the Middle East for protection. Its origins come from the Eye of Horus, the ancient *wadjet* amulets, and the eye painted on the palm of the bright blue Hand of Fatimah amulets found nearly everywhere in Egypt today.

These seeds, which turned out to be Eye of Satan, have long been used for warding off the evil eye. I began using it as a charm, and found it to be more powerful than garlic for protection against evil. Though a major Egyptian religious leader sent emissaries with a letter for me, no one who wished me harm turned up at our apartment or at the family farm where we spent weekends.

My first experiments with the seeds went like this: Egyptian stoves usually have a tiny burner in addition to the usual ones, intended for preparing small pots of Turkish coffee. I heated the burner one night, turned it off, then put two of the Eye of Satan seeds on it. They immediately began to smoke—whitish smoke that, while not exactly aromatic, did smell somehow "Witchy" and narcotic.

My husband and I sat in the room outside the kitchen, where we usually sat after dinner, and watched the burning seeds through the open doorway. Darkness fell but we did not turn the lights on. The seeds burned slowly, emitting thin smoke for a good long time. They glowed like two eyes in the darkness, and from this it was fairly easy to figure out that they were used for protection.

Learning more about the plant that produced the seeds became a small obsession with me. I was doing research for my grimoire in the library and botanical gardens of the local agricultural university at that time, but I could find nothing about this plant. One day, while touring the botanical garden with my husband and his friend, my attention was drawn by a plant growing up the fence that enclosed the garden's perimeter.

It was just a weed, not a botanical specimen labelled with its Latin name, but it captivated me. I knew, in the way that Witches often know things, that this leafy green vine was magical. I stopped and stared at it. My husband's friend confirmed what I suspected; this was the plant which produced Eye of Satan.

Eye of Satan Characteristics

The Eye of Satan plant does not look magical; it is just a bunch if big leaves composed of sword-shaped leaflets. But to me, somehow, it has a distinct magical feel.

At the botanical garden, I asked my husband's friend if he knew the plant's botanical name—he told me something like "Sinus tarabensifolia." As I was not as well acquainted then with the inner workings of Egyptian culture—as I later came to be— I did not know yet that it is culturally impossible for the average Egyptian man to admit that he does not know something.

In fact, his answer wasn't even close to the correct botanical name for the plant, and it set me off on the wrong track in my quest for learning more about it. It was not until years later, when I was back in the States and had access to the Internet, that I finally got my answers.

Names for Eye of Satan

The Eye of Satan has a particularly complicated linguistic heritage. Other names for Eye of Satan include rosary pea, rosary bean, precatory pea, precatory bean, prayer beads; jequirity, jequirity pea, bean, or seeds; Indian licorice, crab's eye, wild licorice, and lady bug seed. *Ain shaitan* (Eye of Satan) and *ain afreet* (Eye of the Ghost) are two of its Arabic names. Its Hindi plant names include *rati, gunga,* and *goonteh. Colorine, peronilla, jequerite,* and *ojo de cangrejo* are some of its Spanish names. *Chapelet* is a French name for Eye of Satan. And, after a long search, I managed to discover that *Abrus precatorius* is its actual botanical name.

The Botanical Characteristics of Eye of Satan

Eye of Satan is a twisting perennial vine of the pea family that grows wild in the tropics and subtropics. It can reach a height of up to ten feet, and can become an invasive weed in lush climates such as Florida. Its long green leaves are composed of alternate leaflets that grow outward from a central spine.

Eye of Satan blooms with clusters of small flowers that range in color from white to red to purple. It fruits with long brown pods that contain shiny red seeds. Each rounded seed is about one-eighth inch long, and has a small black spot on it. (The bright blue spots that I saw on Egyptian seeds darkened and became black with time.) There is one variety of Eye of Satan that produces white seeds. It is only the seeds that are used magically.

The Magical Properties of Eye of Satan

Eye of Satan is the most powerfully protective herb that I have ever encountered. It acts specifically against the evil eye, breaks hexes and curses, and averts incubi and succubi. In Egypt, it is added to loose incense mixtures, burned over charcoal.

Eye of Satan can be carried as a charm, used in spells, added to mojo bags, or simply kept in a bowl on the altar or beside the bed. To keep evil away it can be grown outside the house, or sprinkled in a circle around the outside of the home. For protection while driving, scatter some of the seeds in the trunk and engine of your car. For safe journeys, put some seeds in the bottom of each suitcase.

In Afro-Caribbean magical traditions, Eye of Satan is considered a powerful charm for attracting good luck, love, and money. It is sold in botanicás for love spells, and is found in manufactured luck and money charms sold in Mexico and South America.

Other Uses

In the past, the seeds of Eye of Satan, which weigh about one carat, have been used as a measure for gold and precious stones. They got some of their names because Christians once used them to make rosaries. The seeds are still sometimes strung like beads to make bracelets and necklaces, but great care must be taken when wearing them because they are so toxic.

The root has been used as a substitute for true licorice, but this is inadvisable because it is poisonous.

Eye of Satan is a host plant for caterpillars of the ceraunus blue butterfly, but in general the seeds are a deadly poison to animals. Any animal who eats the seeds should be rushed immediately to a veterinarian.

High John, Low John, & Chewing John

By Eileen Holland

Three roots called High John, Low John, and Chewing John are traditional herbs of African-American folk magic, justifiably famous for their ability to get the mojo working.

High John

The full name of the root High John is High John the Conquerer Root. It is also called hi-john, conqueror root, mojo hand, jalap, bindweed, jalup root, jalap bindweed, and turpeth. Its botanical names, *Ipomoea jalapa* and *Ipomea purga*, refer to Xalapa, Mexico, and to the old medicinal use of the root as a drastic purge.

Jalap is a wild climbing vine of the morning glory family that is native to South America, tropical North America, and Mexico. It has twining stems and blooms with red flowers.

The tuberous roots are hard, woody, dark brown, and have a plesant smell before they have dried. The root is the only part of the plant that is used magically.

High John the Conqueror was a trickster of African-American legend, the son of an African king who wound up as a slave in America. John may have been enslaved, but he never lost his pride. He played the fool but he was nobody's fool, and he constantly outsmarted white people. High John the Conqueror became a surrogate for rebellion. If something got damaged or went missing, slaves would say that High John was up to his tricks.

Earth, Saturn, and Mars are all High John's planets. Fire is its element, and its gender is male. It corresponds to the zodiac sign Gemini, and is sacred to High John the Conqueror and all trickster gods. High John is a powerful magical herb used for strength, mastery, victory, power, inner power, increase, overcoming difficulties, Trickster-energy, solving problems, winning in court, finding a job, love spells, money spells, divination, happiness, good health, better business, ending depression, eliminating confusion, luck in gambling, and manual dexterity in games of chance. High John has the powers of protection and attraction, and it protects against black magic. It breaks up hexes and destroys them. High John can attract love, luck, lust, prosperity, prestige, spiritual blessings, and success. Along with St. John's wort, High John is even said to confer invincibility.

A High John root boosts the power of any spell or charm that it is added to. The root is usually carried as a charm, or added to mojo bags. I put one in my briefcase when I go to court, and keep one in the bag where I store my Blue Justice Powder. It is widely believed that regularly dressing the root with magical oils increases its power. To attract money, the root is typically dressed with mint oil or a money oil, and carried in a green flannel mojo bag. It can also be wrapped in bills and carried in the pocket as a money charm. High John roots are used in male sex magic for attraction, and for success with women. A man carries a High John root below his waist to enhance his sexual prowess.

High John roots are used to make High John the Conqueror Oil, a hoodoo staple for which there are many different recipes. Bayberry, patchouli, bergamot, and vetiver essential oils are all traditional ingredients. The High John root is usually placed in the master bottle, to empower the oil. It is used for anointing (especially the arms and hands prior to gambling), and for dressing candles. High John Oil overcomes obstacles to victory or success, removes negative conditions, and gets you chosen over your competition. It is said to be helpful when you have to enter a situation you feel unsure of, or uneasy about. Some Christian magicians say the 23rd Psalm when using High John Oil. High John roots can be used to empower other magical oils by placing one in the master bottle.

Powdered, High John can be added to incense mixtures and to magical powders, baths, and floor washes. A fresh root can be placed in a bag and shattered with a hammer, then ground in a spice mill, but once a root has dried it is very difficult to break up. The floor wash is used on floors, doorways, and windowsills, especially those made of wood, to scrub away negativity and render people who enter the home powerless to harm its residents. High John the Conqueror floor wash is said to bring power, strength, and victory to a home or business where it is used.

High John incense can be burned for divination, good luck, attaining goals, banishing negativity, and to help solve difficult problems. It is reputed to be an aphrodisiac.

Caution: Do not ingest High John because it is a cathartic purge, an overly powerful laxative.

Low John

Low John is also called trillium, southern John, Low John the Conqueror, wake robin, white wake robin, snow trillium, great white trillium, birth root, and beth root. *Trillium grandiflorum* is its botanical name.

Low John is a perennial plant with dense whorls of dark green leaves. It loves shade, thrives on rich and moist soil, and is usually found in woods. Great white trillium tends to provide ground cover because its roots creep and spread underground. Native to eastern North America, Low John blooms in spring with a single spectacular white flower that may fade to a pinkish color. The fruit is a blackish berry that appears in the autumn. The only part of the plant used magically is the root.

Pluto and Venus are Low John's planets. Its gender is female, and water is its element. In the old language of flowers, Low John indicated "Ardor." The root is carried or added to mojo bags as a charm for love, prosperity, good luck, and help in family matters. It can also be used in love spells and money spells. Rub your body with Low John to attract love. Use High John and Low John together to request help from the universe with whatever crosses or concerns you.

Chewing John

Chewing John is galangal, an aromatic root once used like ginger as a spice. Other names for it include galangal root, galang, galingal, galingale, greater galanga, Little John to Chew, African juju powder, China root, India root, catarrh root, East Indian catarrh root, colic root, gargaut, maraba, kaempferia, and kampferia galanga. *Khalanjan* is its name in Arabic, and the word "galingal" was derived from this. Its botanical names are *Alpinia galanga* and *Alpinia officinalis.*

Galangal is a grassland plant of the ginger family, native to tropical Asia. It has long, narrow leaves and grows from four to six feet in height. Its white flowers have deep red veins. The aromatic root is dark red and resembles ginger. The root is the only part of the plant used magically.

Chewing John got its name because hoodoo practitioners would chew a piece of it in court, then spit the juice where the judge would walk through it in order to influence the outcome of a trial. It corresponds to the planets Mars and Pluto, and to the element of fire. Its gender is male and it is sacred to Vulcan. Galangal increases the power of any spell it is added to. It is used for psychic protection, lust, exorcism, health, money spells, psychic power, success and favor in court, psychic awareness, good luck, consecration, and work on the astral plane.

Powdered, Chewing John is used as incense and added to sprinkling powders and floor washes. Galangal powder is a charm for health, protection, good luck, and developing your psychic potential. It is sprinkled around the home or on the bed-sheets for sex magic and to increase desire.

Galangal is added to incense mixtures for uncrossing and jinx breaking because it breaks hexes and curses and sends negative spells back to their makers. It is a traditional ingredient in abramelin incense, used in guardian angel rituals.

Medically, galangal is a stimulant and a mild hallucinogen, once used to treat gas, nausea, and upset stomach. It can be used in poultices to draw boils. A decoction of its leaves can be added to the bath for energy. The powder was once used as a medicinal snuff to break up congestion.

Like ginger, galangal can be used in cooking as a spice or condiment. It is used to make ginger beer and liqueur. The essential oil of galangal is used in perfumery.

The
Quarters and
Signs of the
Moon and
Moon
Tables

The Quarters and Signs
of the Moon

Everyone has seen the Moon wax and wane through a period of approximately twenty-nine-and-a-half days. This circuit from New Moon to Full Moon and back again is called the lunation cycle. The cycle is divided into parts, called quarters or phases. There are several methods by which this can be done, and the system used in the *Herbal Almanac* may not correspond to those used in other almanacs.

The Quarters

First Quarter

The first quarter begins at the New Moon, when the Sun and Moon are in the same place, or conjunct. (This means that the Sun and Moon are in the same degree of the same sign.) The Moon is not visible at first, since it rises at the same time as the Sun. The New Moon is the time of new beginnings, beginnings of projects that favor growth, externalization of activities, and the growth of ideas. The first quarter is the time of germination, emergence, beginnings, and outwardly directed activity.

Second Quarter

The second quarter begins halfway between the New Moon and the Full Moon, when the Sun and Moon are at right angles, or a 90-degree square to each other. This half Moon rises around noon and sets around midnight, so it can be seen in the western sky during the first half of the night. The second quarter is the time of growth and articulation of things that already exist.

Third Quarter

The third quarter begins at the Full Moon, when the Sun and Moon are opposite one another and the full light of the Sun can shine on the full sphere of the Moon. The round Moon can be seen rising in the east at sunset, and then rising a little later each evening. The Full Moon stands for illumination, fulfillment, culmination, completion, drawing inward, unrest, emotional expressions, and hasty actions leading to failure. The third quarter is a time of maturity, fruition, and the assumption of the full form of expression.

Fourth Quarter

The fourth quarter begins about halfway between the Full Moon and New Moon, when the Sun and Moon are again at 90 degrees, or square. This decreasing Moon rises at midnight, and can be seen in the east during the last half of the night, reaching the overhead position just about as the Sun rises. The fourth quarter is a time of disintegration, drawing back for reorganization and reflection.

The Signs

Moon in Aries

Moon in Aries is good for starting things, but lacking in staying power. Things occur rapidly, but also quickly pass.

Moon in Taurus

With Moon in Taurus, things begun during this sign last the longest and tend to increase in value. Things begun now become habitual and hard to alter.

Moon in Gemini

Moon in Gemini is an inconsistent position for the Moon, characterized by a lot of talk. Things begun now are easily changed by outside influences.

Moon in Cancer

Moon in Cancer stimulates emotional rapport between people. It pinpoints need, and supports growth and nurturance.

Moon in Leo

Moon in Leo accents showmanship, being seen, drama, recreation, and happy pursuits. It may be concerned with praise and subject to flattery.

Moon in Virgo

Moon in Virgo favors accomplishment of details and commands from higher up while discouraging independent thinking.

Moon in Libra

Moon in Libra increases self-awareness. It favors self-examination and interaction with others, but discourages spontaneous initiative.

Moon in Scorpio

Moon in Scorpio increases awareness of psychic power. It precipitates psychic crises and ends connections thoroughly.

Moon in Sagittarius

Moon in Sagittarius encourages expansionary flights of imagination and confidence in the flow of life.

Moon in Capricorn

Moon in Capricorn increases awareness of the need for structure, discipline, and organization. Institutional activities are favored.

Moon in Aquarius

Moon in Aquarius favors activities that are unique and individualistic, concern for humanitarian needs, society as a whole, and improvements that can be made.

Moon in Pisces

During Moon in Pisces, energy withdraws from the surface of life, hibernates within, secretly reorganizing and realigning.

January Moon Table

Date	Sign	Element	Nature	Phase
1 Tue.	Leo	Fire	Barren	3rd
2 Wed. 6:34 pm	Virgo	Earth	Barren	3rd
3 Thu.	Virgo	Earth	Barren	3rd
4 Fri. 8:23 pm	Libra	Air	Semi-fruitful	3rd
5 Sat.	Libra	Air	Semi-fruitful	4th 10:55 pm
6 Sun. 11:41 pm	Scorpio	Water	Fruitful	4th
7 Mon.	Scorpio	Water	Fruitful	4th
8 Tue.	Scorpio	Water	Fruitful	4th
9 Wed. 4:57 am	Sagittarius	Fire	Barren	4th
10 Thu.	Sagittarius	Fire	Barren	4th
11 Fri. 12:18 pm	Capricorn	Earth	Semi-fruitful	4th
12 Sat.	Capricorn	Earth	Semi-fruitful	4th
13 Sun. 9:41 pm	Aquarius	Air	Barren	New 8:29 am
14 Mon.	Aquarius	Air	Barren	1st
15 Tue.	Aquarius	Air	Barren	1st
16 Wed. 9:00 am	Pisces	Water	Fruitful	1st
17 Thu.	Pisces	Water	Fruitful	1st
18 Fri. 9:35 pm	Aries	Fire	Barren	1st
19 Sat.	Aries	Fire	Barren	1st
20 Sun.	Aries	Fire	Barren	1st
21 Mon. 9:47 am	Taurus	Earth	Semi-fruitful	2nd 12:47 pm
22 Tue.	Taurus	Earth	Semi-fruitful	2nd
23 Wed. 7:28 pm	Gemini	Air	Barren	2nd
24 Thu.	Gemini	Air	Barren	2nd
25 Fri.	Gemini	Air	Barren	2nd
26 Sat. 1:17 am	Cancer	Water	Fruitful	2nd
27 Sun.	Cancer	Water	Fruitful	2nd
28 Mon. 3:31 am	Leo	Fire	Barren	Full 5:50 pm
29 Tue.	Leo	Fire	Barren	3rd
30 Wed. 3:40 am	Virgo	Earth	Barren	3rd
31 Thu.	Virgo	Earth	Barren	3rd

February Moon Table

Date	Sign	Element	Nature	Phase
1 Fri. 3:44 am	Libra	Air	Semi-fruitful	3rd
2 Sat.	Libra	Air	Semi-fruitful	3rd
3 Sun. 5:35 am	Scorpio	Water	Fruitful	3rd
4 Mon.	Scorpio	Water	Fruitful	4th 8:33 am
5 Tue. 10:21 am	Sagittarius	Fire	Barren	4th
6 Wed.	Sagittarius	Fire	Barren	4th
7 Thu. 6:08 pm	Capricorn	Earth	Semi-fruitful	4th
8 Fri.	Capricorn	Earth	Semi-fruitful	4th
9 Sat.	Capricorn	Earth	Semi-fruitful	4th
10 Sun. 4:15 am	Aquarius	Air	Barren	4th
11 Mon.	Aquarius	Air	Barren	4th
12 Tue. 3:53 pm	Pisces	Water	Fruitful	New 2:41 am
13 Wed.	Pisces	Water	Fruitful	1st
14 Thu.	Pisces	Water	Fruitful	1st
15 Fri. 4:26 am	Aries	Fire	Barren	1st
16 Sat.	Aries	Fire	Barren	1st
17 Sun. 4:58 pm	Taurus	Earth	Semi-fruitful	1st
18 Mon.	Taurus	Earth	Semi-fruitful	1st
19 Tue.	Taurus	Earth	Semi-fruitful	1st
20 Wed. 3:50 am	Gemini	Air	Barren	2nd 7:02 am
21 Thu.	Gemini	Air	Barren	2nd
22 Fri. 11:16 am	Cancer	Water	Fruitful	2nd
23 Sat.	Cancer	Water	Fruitful	2nd
24 Sun. 2:36 pm	Leo	Fire	Barren	2nd
25 Mon.	Leo	Fire	Barren	2nd
26 Tue. 2:47 pm	Virgo	Earth	Barren	2nd
27 Wed.	Virgo	Earth	Barren	Full 4:17 am
28 Thu. 1:47 pm	Libra	Air	Semi-fruitful	3rd

March Moon Table

Date	Sign	Element	Nature	Phase
1 Fri.	Libra	Air	Semi-fruitful	3rd
2 Sat. 1:51 pm	Scorpio	Water	Fruitful	3rd
3 Sun.	Scorpio	Water	Fruitful	3rd
4 Mon. 4:55 pm	Sagittarius	Fire	Barren	3rd
5 Tue.	Sagittarius	Fire	Barren	4th 8:25 pm
6 Wed. 11:48 pm	Capricorn	Earth	Semi-fruitful	4th
7 Thu.	Capricorn	Earth	Semi-fruitful	4th
8 Fri.	Capricorn	Earth	Semi-fruitful	4th
9 Sat. 9:56 am	Aquarius	Air	Barren	4th
10 Sun.	Aquarius	Air	Barren	4th
11 Mon. 9:56 pm	Pisces	Water	Fruitful	4th
12 Tue.	Pisces	Water	Fruitful	4th
13 Wed.	Pisces	Water	Fruitful	New 9:03 pm
14 Thu. 10:34 am	Aries	Fire	Barren	1st
15 Fri.	Aries	Fire	Barren	1st
16 Sat. 11:01 pm	Taurus	Earth	Semi-fruitful	1st
17 Sun.	Taurus	Earth	Semi-fruitful	1st
18 Mon.	Taurus	Earth	Semi-fruitful	1st
19 Tue. 10:20 am	Gemini	Air	Barren	1st
20 Wed.	Gemini	Air	Barren	1st
21 Thu. 7:06 pm	Cancer	Water	Fruitful	2nd 9:28 pm
22 Fri.	Cancer	Water	Fruitful	2nd
23 Sat.	Cancer	Water	Fruitful	2nd
24 Sun. 12:12 am	Leo	Fire	Barren	2nd
25 Mon.	Leo	Fire	Barren	2nd
26 Tue. 1:44 am	Virgo	Earth	Barren	2nd
27 Wed.	Virgo	Earth	Barren	2nd
28 Thu. 1:04 am	Libra	Air	Semi-fruitful	Full 1:25 pm
29 Fri.	Libra	Air	Semi-fruitful	3rd
30 Sat. 12:21 am	Scorpio	Water	Fruitful	3rd
31 Sun.	Scorpio	Water	Fruitful	3rd

April Moon Table

Date	Sign	Element	Nature	Phase
1 Mon. 1:48 am	Sagittarius	Fire	Barren	3rd
2 Tue.	Sagittarius	Fire	Barren	3rd
3 Wed. 6:58 am	Capricorn	Earth	Semi-fruitful	3rd
4 Thu.	Capricorn	Earth	Semi-fruitful	4th 10:29 am
5 Fri. 4:07 pm	Aquarius	Air	Barren	4th
6 Sat.	Aquarius	Air	Barren	4th
7 Sun.	Aquarius	Air	Barren	4th
8 Mon. 3:57 am	Pisces	Water	Fruitful	4th
9 Tue.	Pisces	Water	Fruitful	4th
10 Wed. 4:40 pm	Aries	Fire	Barren	4th
11 Thu.	Aries	Fire	Barren	4th
12 Fri.	Aries	Fire	Barren	New 2:21 pm
13 Sat. 4:55 am	Taurus	Earth	Semi-fruitful	1st
14 Sun.	Taurus	Earth	Semi-fruitful	1st
15 Mon. 3:56 pm	Gemini	Air	Barren	1st
16 Tue.	Gemini	Air	Barren	1st
17 Wed.	Gemini	Air	Barren	1st
18 Thu. 1:01 am	Cancer	Water	Fruitful	1st
19 Fri.	Cancer	Water	Fruitful	1st
20 Sat. 7:20 am	Leo	Fire	Barren	2nd 7:48 am
21 Sun.	Leo	Fire	Barren	2nd
22 Mon. 10:35 am	Virgo	Earth	Barren	2nd
23 Tue.	Virgo	Earth	Barren	2nd
24 Wed. 11:22 am	Libra	Air	Semi-fruitful	2nd
25 Thu.	Libra	Air	Semi-fruitful	2nd
26 Fri. 11:15 am	Scorpio	Water	Fruitful	Full 10:00 pm
27 Sat.	Scorpio	Water	Fruitful	3rd
28 Sun. 12:13 pm	Sagittarius	Fire	Barren	3rd
29 Mon.	Sagittarius	Fire	Barren	3rd
30 Tue. 4:03 pm	Capricorn	Earth	Semi-fruitful	3rd

May Moon Table

Date	Sign	Element	Nature	Phase
1 Wed.	Capricorn	Earth	Semi-fruitful	3rd
2 Thu. 11:43 pm	Aquarius	Air	Barren	3rd
3 Fri.	Aquarius	Air	Barren	3rd
4 Sat.	Aquarius	Air	Barren	4th 2:16 am
5 Sun. 10:46 am	Pisces	Water	Fruitful	4th
6 Mon.	Pisces	Water	Fruitful	4th
7 Tue. 11:22 pm	Aries	Fire	Barren	4th
8 Wed.	Aries	Fire	Barren	4th
9 Thu.	Aries	Fire	Barren	4th
10 Fri. 11:32 am	Taurus	Earth	Semi-fruitful	4th
11 Sat.	Taurus	Earth	Semi-fruitful	4th
12 Sun. 10:04 pm	Gemini	Air	Barren	New 5:45 am
13 Mon.	Gemini	Air	Barren	1st
14 Tue.	Gemini	Air	Barren	1st
15 Wed. 6:33 am	Cancer	Water	Fruitful	1st
16 Thu.	Cancer	Water	Fruitful	1st
17 Fri. 12:52 pm	Leo	Fire	Barren	1st
18 Sat.	Leo	Fire	Barren	1st
19 Sun. 5:01 pm	Virgo	Earth	Barren	2nd 2:42 pm
20 Mon.	Virgo	Earth	Barren	2nd
21 Tue. 7:19 pm	Libra	Air	Semi-fruitful	2nd
22 Wed.	Libra	Air	Semi-fruitful	2nd
23 Thu. 8:38 pm	Scorpio	Water	Fruitful	2nd
24 Fri.	Scorpio	Water	Fruitful	2nd
25 Sat. 10:20 pm	Sagittarius	Fire	Barren	2nd
26 Sun.	Sagittarius	Fire	Barren	Full 6:51 am
27 Mon.	Sagittarius	Fire	Barren	3rd
28 Tue. 1:54 am	Capricorn	Earth	Semi-fruitful	3rd
29 Wed.	Capricorn	Earth	Semi-fruitful	3rd
30 Thu. 8:35 am	Aquarius	Air	Barren	3rd
31 Fri.	Aquarius	Air	Barren	3rd

June Moon Table

Date	Sign	Element	Nature	Phase
1 Sat. 6:37 pm	Pisces	Water	Fruitful	3rd
2 Sun.	Pisces	Water	Fruitful	4th 7:05 pm
3 Mon.	Pisces	Water	Fruitful	4th
4 Tue. 6:51 am	Aries	Fire	Barren	4th
5 Wed.	Aries	Fire	Barren	4th
6 Thu. 7:07 pm	Taurus	Earth	Semi-fruitful	4th
7 Fri.	Taurus	Earth	Semi-fruitful	4th
8 Sat.	Taurus	Earth	Semi-fruitful	4th
9 Sun. 5:29 am	Gemini	Air	Barren	4th
10 Mon.	Gemini	Air	Barren	New 6:46 pm
11 Tue. 1:15 pm	Cancer	Water	Fruitful	1st
12 Wed.	Cancer	Water	Fruitful	1st
13 Thu. 6:39 pm	Leo	Fire	Barren	1st
14 Fri.	Leo	Fire	Barren	1st
15 Sat. 10:23 pm	Virgo	Earth	Barren	1st
16 Sun.	Virgo	Earth	Barren	1st
17 Mon.	Virgo	Earth	Barren	2nd 7:29 pm
18 Tue. 1:11 am	Libra	Air	Semi-fruitful	2nd
19 Wed.	Libra	Air	Semi-fruitful	2nd
20 Thu. 3:42 am	Scorpio	Water	Fruitful	2nd
21 Fri.	Scorpio	Water	Fruitful	2nd
22 Sat. 6:42 am	Sagittarius	Fire	Barren	2nd
23 Sun.	Sagittarius	Fire	Barren	2nd
24 Mon. 11:01 am	Capricorn	Earth	Semi-fruitful	Full 4:42 pm
25 Tue.	Capricorn	Earth	Semi-fruitful	3rd
26 Wed. 5:36 pm	Aquarius	Air	Barren	3rd
27 Thu.	Aquarius	Air	Barren	3rd
28 Fri.	Aquarius	Air	Barren	3rd
29 Sat. 3:00 am	Pisces	Water	Fruitful	3rd
30 Sun.	Pisces	Water	Fruitful	3rd

July Moon Table

Date	Sign	Element	Nature	Phase
1 Mon. 2:49 pm	Aries	Fire	Barren	3rd
2 Tue.	Aries	Fire	Barren	4th 12:19 pm
3 Wed.	Aries	Fire	Barren	4th
4 Thu. 3:16 am	Taurus	Earth	Semi-fruitful	4th
5 Fri.	Taurus	Earth	Semi-fruitful	4th
6 Sat. 2:01 pm	Gemini	Air	Barren	4th
7 Sun.	Gemini	Air	Barren	4th
8 Mon. 9:36 pm	Cancer	Water	Fruitful	4th
9 Tue.	Cancer	Water	Fruitful	4th
10 Wed.	Cancer	Water	Fruitful	New 5:26 am
11 Thu. 2:08 am	Leo	Fire	Barren	1st
12 Fri.	Leo	Fire	Barren	1st
13 Sat. 4:41 am	Virgo	Earth	Barren	1st
14 Sun.	Virgo	Earth	Barren	1st
15 Mon. 6:39 am	Libra	Air	Semi-fruitful	1st
16 Tue.	Libra	Air	Semi-fruitful	2nd 11:47 pm
17 Wed. 9:13 am	Scorpio	Water	Fruitful	2nd
18 Thu.	Scorpio	Water	Fruitful	2nd
19 Fri. 1:02 pm	Sagittarius	Fire	Barren	2nd
20 Sat.	Sagittarius	Fire	Barren	2nd
21 Sun. 6:26 pm	Capricorn	Earth	Semi-fruitful	2nd
22 Mon.	Capricorn	Earth	Semi-fruitful	2nd
23 Tue.	Capricorn	Earth	Semi-fruitful	2nd
24 Wed. 1:40 am	Aquarius	Air	Barren	Full 4:07 am
25 Thu.	Aquarius	Air	Barren	3rd
26 Fri. 11:04 am	Pisces	Water	Fruitful	3rd
27 Sat.	Pisces	Water	Fruitful	3rd
28 Sun. 10:39 pm	Aries	Fire	Barren	3rd
29 Mon.	Aries	Fire	Barren	3rd
30 Tue.	Aries	Fire	Barren	3rd
31 Wed. 11:17 am	Taurus	Earth	Semi-fruitful	3rd

August Moon Table

Date	Sign	Element	Nature	Phase
1 Thu.	Taurus	Earth	Semi-fruitful	4th 5:22 am
2 Fri. 10:46 pm	Gemini	Air	Barren	4th
3 Sat.	Gemini	Air	Barren	4th
4 Sun.	Gemini	Air	Barren	4th
5 Mon. 7:02 am	Cancer	Water	Fruitful	4th
6 Tue.	Cancer	Water	Fruitful	4th
7 Wed. 11:27 am	Leo	Fire	Barren	4th
8 Thu.	Leo	Fire	Barren	New 2:15 pm
9 Fri. 1:03 pm	Virgo	Earth	Barren	1st
10 Sat.	Virgo	Earth	Barren	1st
11 Sun. 1:38 pm	Libra	Air	Semi-fruitful	1st
12 Mon.	Libra	Air	Semi-fruitful	1st
13 Tue. 3:01 pm	Scorpio	Water	Fruitful	1st
14 Wed.	Scorpio	Water	Fruitful	1st
15 Thu. 6:25 pm	Sagittarius	Fire	Barren	2nd 5:12 am
16 Fri.	Sagittarius	Fire	Barren	2nd
17 Sat.	Sagittarius	Fire	Barren	2nd
18 Sun. 12:15 am	Capricorn	Earth	Semi-fruitful	2nd
19 Mon.	Capricorn	Earth	Semi-fruitful	2nd
20 Tue. 8:16 am	Aquarius	Air	Barren	2nd
21 Wed.	Aquarius	Air	Barren	2nd
22 Thu. 6:11 pm	Pisces	Water	Fruitful	Full 5:29 pm
23 Fri.	Pisces	Water	Fruitful	3rd
24 Sat.	Pisces	Water	Fruitful	3rd
25 Sun. 5:48 am	Aries	Fire	Barren	3rd
26 Mon.	Aries	Fire	Barren	3rd
27 Tue. 6:32 pm	Taurus	Earth	Semi-fruitful	3rd
28 Wed.	Taurus	Earth	Semi-fruitful	3rd
29 Thu.	Taurus	Earth	Semi-fruitful	3rd
30 Fri. 6:45 am	Gemini	Air	Barren	4th 9:31 pm
31 Sat.	Gemini	Air	Barren	4th

September Moon Table

Date	Sign	Element	Nature	Phase
1 Sun.4:14 pm	Cancer	Water	Fruitful	4th
2 Mon.	Cancer	Water	Fruitful	4th
3 Tue. 9:36 pm	Leo	Fire	Barren	4th
4 Wed.	Leo	Fire	Barren	4th
5 Thu. 11:16 pm	Virgo	Earth	Barren	4th
6 Fri.	Virgo	Earth	Barren	New 10:10 pm
7 Sat. 10:57 pm	Libra	Air	Semi-fruitful	1st
8 Sun.	Libra	Air	Semi-fruitful	1st
9 Mon. 10:48 pm	Scorpio	Water	Fruitful	1st
10 Tue.	Scorpio	Water	Fruitful	1st
11 Wed.	Scorpio	Water	Fruitful	1st
12 Thu. 12:44 am	Sagittarius	Fire	Barren	1st
13 Fri.	Sagittarius	Fire	Barren	2nd 1:08 pm
14 Sat. 5:47 am	Capricorn	Earth	Semi-fruitful	2nd
15 Sun.	Capricorn	Earth	Semi-fruitful	2nd
16 Mon. 1:54 pm	Aquarius	Air	Barren	2nd
17 Tue.	Aquarius	Air	Barren	2nd
18 Wed.	Aquarius	Air	Barren	2nd
19 Thu. 12:18 am	Pisces	Water	Fruitful	2nd
20 Fri.	Pisces	Water	Fruitful	2nd
21 Sat. 12:11 pm	Aries	Fire	Barren	Full 8:59 am
22 Sun.	Aries	Fire	Barren	3rd
23 Mon.	Aries	Fire	Barren	3rd
24 Tue. 12:55 am	Taurus	Earth	Semi-fruitful	3rd
25 Wed.	Taurus	Earth	Semi-fruitful	3rd
26 Thu. 1:26 pm	Gemini	Air	Barren	3rd
27 Fri.	Gemini	Air	Barren	3rd
28 Sat.	Gemini	Air	Barren	3rd
29 Sun. 12:01 am	Cancer	Water	Fruitful	4th 12:03 pm
30 Mon.	Cancer	Water	Fruitful	4th

October Moon Table

Date	Sign	Element	Nature	Phase
1 Tue. 6:58 am	Leo	Fire	Barren	4th
2 Wed.	Leo	Fire	Barren	4th
3 Thu. 9:52 am	Virgo	Earth	Barren	4th
4 Fri.	Virgo	Earth	Barren	4th
5 Sat. 9:51 am	Libra	Air	Semi-fruitful	4th
6 Sun.	Libra	Air	Semi-fruitful	New 6:18 am
7 Mon. 8:57 am	Scorpio	Water	Fruitful	1st
8 Tue.	Scorpio	Water	Fruitful	1st
9 Wed. 9:21 am	Sagittarius	Fire	Barren	1st
10 Thu.	Sagittarius	Fire	Barren	1st
11 Fri. 12:45 pm	Capricorn	Earth	Semi-fruitful	1st
12 Sat.	Capricorn	Earth	Semi-fruitful	1st
13 Sun. 7:51 pm	Aquarius	Air	Barren	2nd 12:33 am
14 Mon.	Aquarius	Air	Barren	2nd
15 Tue.	Aquarius	Air	Barren	2nd
16 Wed. 6:07 am	Pisces	Water	Fruitful	2nd
17 Thu.	Pisces	Water	Fruitful	2nd
18 Fri. 6:13 pm	Aries	Fire	Barren	2nd
19 Sat.	Aries	Fire	Barren	2nd
20 Sun.	Aries	Fire	Barren	2nd
21 Mon. 6:57 am	Taurus	Earth	Semi-fruitful	Full 2:20 am
22 Tue.	Taurus	Earth	Semi-fruitful	3rd
23 Wed. 7:17 pm	Gemini	Air	Barren	3rd
24 Thu.	Gemini	Air	Barren	3rd
25 Fri.	Gemini	Air	Barren	3rd
26 Sat. 6:10 am	Cancer	Water	Fruitful	3rd
27 Sun.	Cancer	Water	Fruitful	3rd
28 Mon. 2:20 pm	Leo	Fire	Barren	3rd
29 Tue.	Leo	Fire	Barren	4th 12:28 am
30 Wed. 6:59 pm	Virgo	Earth	Barren	4th
31 Thu.	Virgo	Earth	Barren	4th

November Moon Table

Date	Sign	Element	Nature	Phase
1 Fri. 8:28 pm	Libra	Air	Semi-fruitful	4th
2 Sat.	Libra	Air	Semi-fruitful	4th
3 Sun. 8:10 pm	Scorpio	Water	Fruitful	4th
4 Mon.	Scorpio	Water	Fruitful	New 3:34 pm
5 Tue. 8:01 pm	Sagittarius	Fire	Barren	1st
6 Wed.	Sagittarius	Fire	Barren	1st
7 Thu. 9:59 pm	Capricorn	Earth	Semi-fruitful	1st
8 Fri.	Capricorn	Earth	Semi-fruitful	1st
9 Sat.	Capricorn	Earth	Semi-fruitful	1st
10 Sun. 3:27 am	Aquarius	Air	Barren	1st
11 Mon.	Aquarius	Air	Barren	2nd 3:52 pm
12 Tue. 12:42 pm	Pisces	Water	Fruitful	2nd
13 Wed.	Pisces	Water	Fruitful	2nd
14 Thu.	Pisces	Water	Fruitful	2nd
15 Fri. 12:38 am	Aries	Fire	Barren	2nd
16 Sat.	Aries	Fire	Barren	2nd
17 Sun. 1:23 pm	Taurus	Earth	Semi-fruitful	2nd
18 Mon.	Taurus	Earth	Semi-fruitful	2nd
19 Tue.	Taurus	Earth	Semi-fruitful	Full 8:34 pm
20 Wed. 1:25 am	Gemini	Air	Barren	3rd
21 Thu.	Gemini	Air	Barren	3rd
22 Fri. 11:48 am	Cancer	Water	Fruitful	3rd
23 Sat.	Cancer	Water	Fruitful	3rd
24 Sun. 8:00 pm	Leo	Fire	Barren	3rd
25 Mon.	Leo	Fire	Barren	3rd
26 Tue.	Leo	Fire	Barren	3rd
27 Wed. 1:42 am	Virgo	Earth	Barren	4th 10:46 am
28 Thu.	Virgo	Earth	Barren	4th
29 Fri. 4:54 am	Libra	Air	Semi-fruitful	4th
30 Sat.	Libra	Air	Semi-fruitful	4th

December Moon Table

Date	Sign	Element	Nature	Phase
1 Sun. 6:15 am	Scorpio	Water	Fruitful	4th
2 Mon.	Scorpio	Water	Fruitful	4th
3 Tue. 6:58 am	Sagittarius	Fire	Barren	4th
4 Wed.	Sagittarius	Fire	Barren	New 2:34 am
5 Thu. 8:39 am	Capricorn	Earth	Semi-fruitful	1st
6 Fri.	Capricorn	Earth	Semi-fruitful	1st
7 Sat. 12:54 pm	Aquarius	Air	Barren	1st
8 Sun.	Aquarius	Air	Barren	1st
9 Mon. 8:46 pm	Pisces	Water	Fruitful	1st
10 Tue.	Pisces	Water	Fruitful	1st
11 Wed.	Pisces	Water	Fruitful	2nd 10:49 am
12 Thu. 7:58 am	Aries	Fire	Barren	2nd
13 Fri.	Aries	Fire	Barren	2nd
14 Sat. 8:43 pm	Taurus	Earth	Semi-fruitful	2nd
15 Sun.	Taurus	Earth	Semi-fruitful	2nd
16 Mon.	Taurus	Earth	Semi-fruitful	2nd
17 Tue. 8:43 am	Gemini	Air	Barren	2nd
18 Wed.	Gemini	Air	Barren	2nd
19 Thu. 6:30 pm	Cancer	Water	Fruitful	Full 2:10 pm
20 Fri.	Cancer	Water	Fruitful	3rd
21 Sat.	Cancer	Water	Fruitful	3rd
22 Sun. 1:48 am	Leo	Fire	Barren	3rd
23 Mon.	Leo	Fire	Barren	3rd
24 Tue. 7:05 am	Virgo	Earth	Barren	3rd
25 Wed.	Virgo	Earth	Barren	3rd
26 Thu. 10:53 am	Libra	Air	Semi-fruitful	4th 7:31 pm
27 Fri.	Libra	Air	Semi-fruitful	4th
28 Sat. 1:41 pm	Scorpio	Water	Fruitful	4th
29 Sun.	Scorpio	Water	Fruitful	4th
30 Mon. 4:01 pm	Sagittarius	Fire	Barren	4th
31 Tue.	Sagittarius	Fire	Barren	4th

About the Authors

SCOTT APPELL is currently the director of education for the Horticultural Society of New York. He is a member of the publications committee of the Pennsylvania Horticultural Society and a board member of the American Violet Society. He is a contributing author to Smith & Hawken's *Book of Outdoor Gardening* and Rodale Press's *1001 Ingenious Gardening Ideas*, as well as botanical consultant for *Gardens by the Sea: Creating a Tropical Paradise*, published by The Garden Club of Palm Beach. He has written three books, *Pansies; Lilies;* and *Tulips*, all published by Friedman/Fairfax Publishers of New York. His latest work, *Orchids* (also published by Freidman/Fairfax) is slated for winter 2001. In addition, he is guest editor and writer for *Landscaping Indoors: Bringing the Outdoors Inside*, one of the *21st-Century Gardening* series of handbooks, published by the Brooklyn Botanical Garden, slated for winter 2001. He lives, writes, and teaches horticulture in New York City. His private horticultural consultation company is called The Green Man.

BERNYCE BARLOW is author of Llewellyn's *Sacred Sites of the West* and has been a contributer to the Llewellyn almanacs since 1995. She is a researcher, speaker, and leads sacred site seminars throughout the United States. She is best known for her magical tools of enlightment that come from the Acme Toy Company, and she swears that her cartoon totems are real!

ELIZABETH BARRETTE lives in central Illinois in a huge old Victorian farmhouse, where she enjoys landscaping and generally puttering with native plants. She has been studying

Pagan and related topics for many years, and currently works as managing editor for *PanGaia* magazine and editorial assistant for *SageWoman*. She is active as a freelance writer in the Pagan, speculative fiction, and gender studies fields. Her writing has appeared in *Circle Network News, LunaSol, PagaNet News, Terra Incognita,* and *Spicy Green Iguana.* For more info, her personal Website is at: http://www.worthlink.net/~ysabet/index.html.

CHANDRA MOIRA BEAL is a freelance writer in Austin, Texas. She lives with a magical house rabbit named Maia, and has authored hundreds of articles about everything from mermaids to law. Chandra also self-published *Splash Across Texas,* a guide to aquatic recreation in Texas.

DALLAS JENNIFER COBB is a mother, partner, lover, writer, and feminist. Recently escaped from the city, she builds her relationship with the earth by practicing organic gardening, gentle wildcrafting, and permaculture. She makes herbal-based natural body and health care products. Contact her at: gaias.garden@sympatico.ca.

MARY CZAP lives in Amherst, Massachusetts, and has written for several city newspapers in San Diego and Middletown, Connecticut. She has also written for *Healthy & Natural Journal.* She is a bookworm happily living with her husband Peter and a cat named Foo. When she grows up she wants to be a novelist.

ELLEN DUGAN, also known as the "Garden Witch," is a psychic-clairvoyant and has been a practicing Witch for over fifteen years. She and her husband raise their three magical teenagers and tend to their enchanted gardens in Missouri. Ellen received Master Gardener status in the spring of 2000. She is currently working on a "Garden Witchery" book.

MARGUERITE ELSBETH, also known as Senihele (Sparrowhawk), is a hereditary Sicilian strega, and is also proud of her Lenni Lenape (Delaware) Indian ancestry. She is a professional astrologer, tarot reader, and spiritual healer, specializing in crisis counseling, spiritual troubleshooting, and difficult relationship issues. Marguerite has published numerous articles in Llewellyn's annuals, is the author of *Crystal Medicine*, and coauthor of *The Grail Castle: Male Myths and Mysteries in the Celtic Tradition*, and *The Silver Wheel: Women's Myths and Mysteries in the Celtic Tradition*. She currently resides in the Southwest desert. Please visit her website at: www.practicalSPIRITkeeping.com.

ANNA FRANKLIN lives in a village in the English midlands. She trained initially as a photographer and artist, but was pushed in the mid-1980s to acknowledge her spiritual life. She then retrained as a therapist in reflexology and aromatherapy, herbalism, and healing. Today, Anna is the high priestess and founder of the Hearth of Arianhod, where she helps run training and teaching circles, discussion groups, and postal networks for distant members. She is also a third-degree Witch. Together with Sue Phillips and Amazon Riley, Anna runs the Holistic Healing Center. She has written for a number of Pagan magazines and has contributed to several books.

SARA GREER lives in Seattle with her husband. She began her fascination with herbs in the 1970s, upon discovering a herb tea blend named "Evening in Missoula." Eventually her interest expanded beyond teas, and she began to study herbs in earnest. She has been making herbal remedies for more than a decade.

EILEEN HOLLAND is the author of *The Wicca Handbook*, and webmaster of "Open, Sesame"—a popular witchcraft site located at: www.open-sesame.com. She is a Wiccan priestess, an ordained interfaith minister, and an initiate of an ancient Egyptian mystery tradition.

MINDY HOUSTON is a practicing Witch currently under second-degree training. She has an obsession for ancient cultures, myths, and history. Her enjoyments are talking with her animals, fairy and dragon folk, spending time with her niece, puzzles, dispensing herbal and magical advice, making her own herbal products, aromatherapy, reading, baking, meditation, and herbal teas.

PENNY KELLY is a naturopathic physician and health counselor for those with catastrophic illnesses. She and her family own and operate Lily Hill Farm and Learning Center, an organic farm with a small inn where people come to attend classes in developing intuition and getting well naturally. Penny is the author of several books, including *The Elves of Lily Hill Farm*, and has been a regular contributor to Llewellyn's *Moon Sign Book* since 1996. She lives and writes in Lawton, Michigan.

CAROLYN MOSS runs workshops on all aspects of growing and using herbs in Cheshire, England. She designs herb gardens and has a particular interest in dyeing, herb scents, and Native American herbs. A small flock of black Hebridean sheep graze Carrie's field, along with the children's ponies. They were acquired as part of a great interest, which started with the use of herbs, in local naturally raised food produce.

LEEDA ALLEYN PACOTTI is a naturopathic physician, specializing with health crises involving the subtle bodies. Returning to ancient traditions, she practicies with herbal and flower remedies and counsels in health astrology. She is currently pursuing groundbreaking research in dream language to diagnose health states, following the precepts and disciplines of ancient healers.

DIANA RAJCHEL OLSEN lives in southern Minnesota with her husband amidst a sanctuary for homeless plants. She is a third-degree priestess in Shadowmoon Coven, a founder of the Minnesota State University, Mankato Pagan organization, and the resident author of the webpage Medea's Chariot at: www.Nexus.MNIC.net/~rajchd. When not doing "Witchy" stuff, she works on her MFA in creative writing.

ROBERT M. PLACE is an internationally known visionary artist, and the designer, illustrator, and coauthor of *The Alchemical Tarot* and *The Angels' Tarot*. Robert is recognized as an expert on Western mysticism, the history of the tarot, and as a gifted teacher of divination. He has taught and lectured at the New York Open Center, the Omega Institute, the New York Tarot School, and the World Tarot Congress. He has also appeared on Discovery and the Learning Channel. Robert is currently working on *The Saints' Tarot*, to be published in 2001. He can be reached through his website at: www.crosswinds.net/~alchemicalegg/.

ROSLYN REID is a Discordian Druid and a member of the Richard P. Feynman Memorial Cabal in Princeton, New Jersey. She lives on a former farm, where she grows a variety of fruit, raises Great Pyrenees dogs, and teaches yoga and tarot. She is a long-time contributor of art and articles to Llewellyn, as well as to publications such as *SageWoman* and *Dalriada* (a Scottish magazine of Celtic heritage and spirituality). Her work has also appeared in consumer magazines like *Tightwad Living* and *Thrifty Times*, and in Susun Weed's book, *Breast Cancer? Breast Health!*

K. D. SPITZER has loved herbs all her life. In the years before they became readily available, she wildcrafted plants from the woods and abandoned cellar holes, and relied on her French mother-in-law to send seeds from Europe. She is a master weaver, and one corner of her herb garden is devoted to dye herbs. She teaches in New Hampshire, where she also reads tarot.

CARLY WALL, C. A. is the author of *Naturally Healing Herbs, Setting the Mood with Aromatherapy*, and *The Little Giant Encyclopedia of Home Remedies*, all published by Sterling Publications, as well as *Flower Secrets Revealed*, published by A.R.E. Press. She is a member of the National Association for Holistic Aromatherapy, and holds a certificate in aromatherapy.

Editor's Note

The contents of this book are not meant to diagnose, treat, prescribe, or substitute for consultation with a licensed heath care professional. Herbs, whether used internally or externally, should be introduced in small amounts to allow the body to adjust and to detect possible allergies. Please consult a standard reference source, or an expert herbalist, to learn more about the possible effects of certain herbs. Llewellyn Worldwide does not participate in, endorse, or have any authority or responsibility concerning private business transactions between its authors and the public.